Third Party Policing

Third party policing represents a major shift in contemporary crime control practices. As the lines blur between criminal and civil law, responsibility for crime control no longer rests with state agencies but is shared with a wide range of organizations, institutions or individuals. The first comprehensive book of its kind, *Third Party Policing* examines this growing phenomenon, arguing that it is the legal basis of third party policing that defines it as a unique strategy. Opening up the debate surrounding this controversial topic, the authors examine civil and regulatory controls necessary to this strategy and explore the historical, legal, political and organizational environment that shape its adoption. This innovative book combines original research with a theoretical framework that reaches far beyond criminology into politics and economics. It offers an important addition to the world-wide debate about the nature and future of policing and will prove invaluable to scholars and policy makers.

LORRAINE MAZEROLLE is an Associate Professor in the School of Criminology and Criminal Justice at Griffith University. She is the author of *Policing Places with Drug Problems* (1999) and co-editor, with Jan Roehl, of *Civil Remedies and Crime Prevention* (1998).

JANET RANSLEY is a senior lecturer in the School of Criminology and Criminal Justice, Griffith University. She has worked extensively in legal practice, and in providing research and policy advice for parliamentary and government agencies in Australia. Dr. Ransley is the co-editor, with Tim Prenzler, of *Police Reform: Building Integrity* (2003).

Cambridge Studies in Criminology

Edited by
Alfred Blumstein, *H. John Heinz School of Public Policy and Management, Carnegie Mellon University*
and David P. Farrington, *Institute of Criminology, University of Cambridge*

The Cambridge Studies in Criminology series aims to publish the highest quality research on criminology and criminal justice topics. Typical volumes report major quantitative, qualitative, and ethnographic research, or make a substantial theoretical contribution. There is a particular emphasis on research monographs, but edited collections may also be published if they make an unusually distinctive offering to the literature. All relevant areas of criminology and criminal justice are included; for example, the causes of offending, juvenile justice, the development of offenders, measurement and analysis of crime, victimization research, policing, crime prevention, sentencing, imprisonment, probation, and parole. The series is global in outlook, with an emphasis on work that is comparative or holds significant implications for theory or policy.

Other Books in the Series:

Third Party Policing

Lorraine Mazerolle
and
Janet Ransley

CAMBRIDGE
UNIVERSITY PRESS

CAMBRIDGE UNIVERSITY PRESS
Cambridge, New York, Melbourne, Madrid, Cape Town, Singapore, São Paulo

Cambridge University Press
The Edinburgh Building, Cambridge CB2 2RU, UK

Published in the United States of America by Cambridge University Press, New York

www.cambridge.org
Information on this title: www.cambridge.org/9780521535076

© Lorraine Mazerolle and Janet Ransley 2005

This book is in copyright. Subject to statutory exception
and to the provisions of relevant collective licensing agreements,
no reproduction of any part may take place without
the written permission of Cambridge University Press.

First published 2005

Printed in the United Kingdom at the University Press, Cambridge

A catalogue record for this book is available from the British Library

ISBN-13 978-0-521-82783-6 hardback
ISBN-10 0-521-82783-3 hardback
ISBN-13 978-0-521-53507-6 paperback
ISBN-10 0-521-53507-7 paperback

Cambridge University Press has no responsibility for the persistence or accuracy of
URLs for external or third-party internet websites referred to in this book, and
does not guarantee that any content on such websites is, or will remain, accurate or
appropriate.

For Matthew and Jacob, LM
For Nigel, David and Rachel, JR

Contents

Tables

Acknowledgments

Our thanks to colleagues David Weisburd and Peter Grabosky for their insightful comments on earlier drafts; to Ross Homel and the Key Centre for Ethics, Law, Justice and Governance for financial assistance towards completing the manuscript; to those at Cambridge University Press, particularly David Farrington and Sarah Caro for their patience in waiting for the final manuscript; to our research assistants Brigitte Bouhours, David Soole, Rebecca Wickes and Georgie Gardner; and to our colleagues at the School of Criminology and Criminal Justice at Griffith University.

CHAPTER 1

Governance, risk and crime control

A police officer recently told us a story about a "rogue" caravan park. The caravan park was a known problem site with an average of twenty calls being received each month by the police department about disturbances, domestic disputes, drug dealing, car breaks and malicious damage at the park. Police had power under state laws to enter caravans and issue directions to prevent serious nuisances, including a provision that allowed them to exclude offenders from the park for up to twenty-four hours (*Police Powers and Responsibilities Act 2000* (Qld) ss368–371), but this was not preventing the problems from recurring. After many frustrating attempts to deal with the problem, the police learned that the manager was in violation of capacity conditions set in a permit from the local council (issued under the Brisbane City Council Local Law *Caravan Parks and Relocatable Home Parks 2000*), slotting more residents into the park than was allowed. The police created a crime control partnership with the local council as well as with the company that held the caravan park insurance policy. The local council instigated action (for failure to comply with the conditions of the permit, an offence attracting a maximum penalty of up to 50 penalty units or $3750 under s13 of the Local Law, and also leading to possible revocation of the permit, under s19). The insurance company investigated the caravan park and cancelled their insurance because of breach of policy conditions. The caravan park manager was thus compelled to adhere to the capacity rules: he reduced the caravan capacity by twenty vans and evicted seventy-two people from the park. His goal was to avoid council fines and re-invoke his insurance policy. The caravan park owner was thus inducted as one of the third party partners. He was unwilling, yet nonetheless a third party partner and made responsible for reducing the problems associated with the park. The calls for police service were reduced from twenty to three calls per month and the gains continue to be maintained.

We refer to this type of policing as "third party policing" where a multiple of regulatory "nodes" (including both willing and unwilling partners) come together to solve a crime problem. As the example above illustrates, third party policing occurs within a legal framework that establishes the authority for police to partner with or coerce third parties, the contexts in which they can do that, and the types of intervention this may produce. Indeed, we argue that it is this legal basis of third party policing that both defines it as a unique strategy and distinguishes it from other policing interventions, most notably problem-oriented policing.

Third party policing is a growing phenomenon in policing. Indeed, our analysis of applications to the Goldstein problem-oriented policing awards (1993–2003) shows that about 50 percent of problem-oriented policing (POP) projects have utilized at least one third-party policing tactic. What is interesting, however, is that our systematic reviews of third party policing evaluations (see Chapters 5 and 6) show that less than one third of third party policing interventions occur as part of a problem-oriented or situational crime prevention initiative. Indeed, most third-party policing initiatives operate outside of the SARA (Scanning, Analysis, Response and Assessment) four-step approach to problem-solving. Third party policing initiatives are typically ad-hoc, episodic and many have been implemented in response to "external pressures" operating on the police. We argue that these "external pressures" are increasing not by accident, but rather as a result of societal transformations that have shifted the responsibility and interest in crime control across a range of regulatory "nodes." Thus, third party policing is further distinguished from other models of policing through its intrinsic links with societal trends in regulation. Indeed, we argue that the recent proliferation of third party policing has not occurred in a vacuum or as an idea born at the grassroots of policing. Rather, we argue that the pace, context and prominence of third party policing initiatives has escalated in recent years for two reasons: first, in response to the "blurring" of civil and criminal laws (see Chapter 4) and second, as one of many consequences in the move from centralized state control to a system of de-centered networks of governance and crime control agents. The development of third party policing is, we suggest, part of a general transformation of government and governance taking place in contemporary society.

Third party policing is defined as police efforts to persuade or coerce organizations or non-offending persons, such as public housing agencies, property owners, parents, health and building inspectors, and business owners to take some responsibility for preventing crime or reducing crime problems (Buerger and Mazerolle, 1998: 301). In third party policing, the police *create* or *enhance* crime control guardians in locations or situations where crime control guardianship was previously absent or non-effective. Sometimes the police use cooperative consultation with community members, parents, inspectors and regulators to encourage and convince third parties to take on more crime control or prevention responsibility. Central, however, to third party policing is the use of a range of civil, criminal and regulatory rules and laws, to engage (or force) third parties into taking some crime control responsibility.

What do we know about this police strategy? Is it effective? Is it fair? How is third party policing distinct from (or a part of) problem-oriented policing and community policing? What is the legal basis for third party policing? What is the coercive basis for third party policing? What has propelled third party policing to prominence? What is the future for third party policing? These, among others, are some of the questions we shall seek to answer in our book. In short, our book provides a critical analysis of the use of legal levers and third parties in crime control activities.

What's to follow?

Our first chapter introduces readers to the global context in which third party policing operates and provides a thumbnail sketch of some themes that we will return to in various chapters in the book. In Chapter 2 we delve into the role of the public police in the new regulatory state and we discuss the challenges of police-regulator partnerships within the context of third party policing. In Chapter 3 we provide a detailed analysis of the dimensions of third party policing. We discuss the types of problems that third party policing addresses, the types of ultimate and proximate targets and the nature of civil levers used to control and prevent crime problems. Chapter 4 surveys the types of law likely to be useful in third party policing, and the types of sanctions available under those laws in Australian, United States, Canadian and British jurisdictions. We examine the consequences for the law arising from police cooption for criminal justice purposes and ask several questions: what are the unintended consequences of co-opted law? Will third party policing have an impact on the law it uses, perhaps through the imposition of further judicial or administrative controls to counter any abuses by police? We also explore the prospect of challenges against the application of civil processes and standards of proof for criminal law purposes.

Chapters 5 and 6 provide the results of a systematic review of third party policing evaluations. We review the extant literature on third party policing and discuss the evidence that has been gathered so far on its effectiveness as a crime control/crime prevention strategy. In Chapter 7 we discuss the equity issues surrounding third party policing initiatives. In this chapter, we discuss some of the potential and actual side effects of third party policing. For example, we will discuss potentially negative side-effects of third party policing such as the impact of eviction, retaliation from domestic violence perpetrators, retaliation from displaced or arrested drug dealers, and strained relations with service providers and local regulators (e.g. building inspectors, local council code enforcers etc). Chapter 7 also unpacks the variety of ethical issues that the practice of third party policing poses and suggests some strategies that would ensure greater accountability across the range of third party policing activities. In this chapter we examine whether and how use of persuasion and influence by third parties, at the request of or on behalf of police, can be made ethical and accountable. We examine the problematic nature of decisions *not* to become involved in controlling or preventing crime: that is, to under-police – to focus on one housing estate or shopping center and at the expense of another – can be even more significant than the decision to over-police. In this chapter we also examine incentive-based systems of compliance that exist in regulatory networks outside of the criminal justice system and we explore ways that third party policing could likewise adopt incentive-based systems of control.

Our final chapter, Chapter 8, points to the future of third party policing both in terms of future research as well as our ideas for where third party policing might take us into the twenty-first century. We discuss the assumptions underlying third party policing and offer insights as to what factors inhibit or enhance adoption of third party policing in democratic countries. In this chapter, we provide some likely answers to the following types of questions: Why are some officers more likely to use third party policing tactics than others? Why are there spatial (by country, jurisdiction and neighborhood) variations in the distribution of third party policing activities? What organizational characteristics of police departments are more likely to support the adoption of third party policing? Under what circumstances or conditions does third party policing use the most coercive of tactics to insure compliance? In this chapter we also explore the challenges of mobilizing the police as well as third parties to engage in third party policing practices. We discuss the challenges that police managers face in mobilizing their subordinate officers to engage third parties in their crime control or crime prevention activities. We also review the issues that confront the police in their efforts to motivate and mobilize third parties. In particular, we ask to what extent are police making use of formal law, and to what extent do they rely on persuasion or threats?

The transformation thesis

In this introductory chapter, we argue that the development of third party policing is part of a pattern of major change, indeed a transformation, of government and governance taking place in contemporary society. This political, legal, economic and social transformation has affected not only the institutions of government and civil society, but is also transforming how we think about and research problems like crime, its prevention, and its control. Old disciplines and divisions are giving way to new networks of knowledge. John Braithwaite (2000: 222) illustrates this with his analogy of the new biological science themes (DNA, evolutionary biology, ecology) that now dominate the discrete disciplines (zoology, botany) of thirty years ago. His point is that new globalizing forces are also affecting the social sciences, and we need to think outside the old boxes, incorporating insights and methods from criminology, sociology, law, politics, regulatory studies, psychology, policing studies and whatever else helps in understanding the problem at hand.

The new knowledge affecting crime control and policing is arising around big organizing themes like governance, risk and plurality, and this chapter explores these themes as they affect and shape our topic of third party policing. We begin by surveying the notion of transformation that has dominated recent theoretical debate in the separate fields of sociology, politics, economics, regulation and criminology. Despite their separate disciplinary origins, we demonstrate how these debates all cluster around our big themes of governance, risk and plurality. We go on to examine the specific application of these themes to police and policing, and show how third party policing is a logical extension of the transformation that has been taking place in government and the provision of its services. The themes from the various theoretical debates both inform our understanding of third party policing and point to some of its problems and pitfalls. The object of this chapter then, is to place the rise of third party policing in the context of broader trends in governance and crime control.

An increasing body of recent literature places "the late modern state," or developed western economies at any rate, in a condition of change, upheaval, transformation or even catastrophe. O'Malley (2000: 153) categorizes three main themes from the most notable of this "transformation" literature – the replacement of penal modernism by postmodern criminal justice (see Simon, 1995; Reiner, 1992, 1994; and also Garland, 1996, 1997, 2001); the rise of risk as a dominant social structure (see Feeley and Simon, 1992, 1994; Ericson and Haggerty, 1997; Kemshall, 2003); and the "death of the social" and the displacement of the modernist welfare state by neo-liberal governance (Rose, 1996; O'Malley, 1994; Cohen, 1995; Haggerty, 2004). O'Malley's focus is on the criminological and sociological literature, but related debates have been occurring in other social sciences. Social theorists (Giddens, 1990; Beck, 1992; Rose and Miller, 1992) developed the transformation notion about social and economic structures in general. The politics and public policy literature has been focused on changes in governance structures and the rise of policy networks (Rhodes, 1997; Bevir, Rhodes and Weller, 2003; Loughlin, 2004), while economists and regulation scholars predate all of these debates with their concern from the 1970s onwards with changes in regulatory structures (see Clarke, 2000; Baldwin, 2004). Finally, it is impossible to ignore the contribution of Michel Foucault (1991) and the body of governmentality literature developing around his later writings on the nature of government and its ability to control and be controlled by those it governs (see for example Dean and Hindess, 1998; Rose, 2000).

While some of these debates may seem far removed from police and what they do, writers like David Bayley and Clifford Shearing (1996) have applied the transformation thesis specifically to policing, saying "future generations will look back on our era as a time when one system of policing ended and another took its place" (p. 585). Loader (2000) suggests this transformation to be one from "the police" as the guardians of order and security, to policing by a plural and fragmented selection of providers and technologies:

> We are living in the midst of a potentially far-reaching transformation in the means by which order and security are maintained in liberal democratic societies, one that is giving rise to the fragmentation and diversification of policing provision, and ushering in a plethora of agencies and agents, each with particular kinds of responsibility for the delivery of policing and security services and technologies. What we might call a shift from police to policing has seen the sovereign state – hitherto considered focal to both provision and accountability in this field – reconfigured as but one node of a broader, more diverse "network of power".
> (p. 323)

Dupont, Grabosky and Shearing (2003) suggest the contemporary debate to be about the "governance of security," by which they mean that public security from both external and internal threats is now provided by a "constellation of institutions, whether formal or informal, governmental or private, commercial or voluntary, that provide for social control and conflict resolution" (p. 331).

Given this broad and disparate literature, how can we make sense of the transformation thesis, and assess its relevance to third party policing? While many approaches are possible, we choose to tackle this task in broadly chronological and thematical sections, examining in turn the rise of neo-liberalism and the death of the Keynesian welfare state, the impact on civil society or the "death of the social", the alternative explanations of the governmentality school, the role of risk and the rise of the postmodern new penality. This discussion will then lead into an examination of the current state of police and policing.

Liberalism, the welfare state and neo-liberalism

A common concern runs through much of the literature we are examining – how does government work, how does it relate to society, how are its decisions and policies put into effect? While Foucault (1979) described government broadly as "the conduct of conduct", it is generally taken to mean the exercise of state sovereignty in some formal institutional way (Burchell, 1996). In modern western societies, this occurs through some form of democratically elected, political government exercising power through a public service framework. This model developed from the sixteenth century onwards, driven by complementary forces. One force was what Foucault (1979) described as the movement from sovereignty to governmentality. By this he meant that the sovereign state was one focused on the maintenance of the ruler's territorial power against both external and internal threats. This was replaced by the governmental state, less reliant on force and domination, and more on the development of technologies for governance, both of the state and of the self, where the object of exercising power is generally to increase the well-being of the governed (Burchell, 1996; Rose, 1996; Hindess, 1998). This move then, was one from despotism to natural rights, from sovereignty to solidarity, where the goal of governance becomes the integration of society (Boyne, 2000). The process of governmentalization incorporates and explains the development and extension of democratic forms of governance, and liberal notions of individual rights and autonomy.

While governmentalization was a political force driving the development of western models of government, another force was the emergence of new ways of governing economic life (Hindess, 1998). Adam Smith's account of a liberal economy saw the free market as the most efficient mechanism for maintaining an effective society, with a minimal role for government intervention and regulation (Fitzgibbons, 1995). These notions under-pinned liberal conceptions of independent, responsible and autonomous citizens engaged in a minimally regulated public sphere, left to get on with their lives without interference, but also suffering the consequences of their own choices. The role of government was to maintain the free market, and to protect the integrity and security of the state, both from external threats, and from the internal threat of crime and disorder. The classically liberal state then, was limited to being a "nightwatchman" (Nozick, 1974), with functions simply to protect "its citizens from violence, theft, fraud" and to promote a stable marketplace by maintaining a law of contract that could govern market transactions (Braithwaite, 2000: 223). The real business of society took place outside government, in the market.

Liberalism ruled, in its various manifestations, until confronted by the catastrophic financial events of the late 1920s and 1930s, but also by the growth of unionism and labour parties at the start of the 1900s. They believed that strong government control was necessary both to contain the excesses of capitalism, and to increase the range of services available to working people, such as education, health services and occupational safety laws. The markets would not do these things, and it was the proper role of governments to step in and shape society.

From around World War II to the 1960s then, the dominant western framework was a Keynesian one, where the welfarist state operated through government to control and regulate the economy, society and the provision of services to the community. In this conception of the state, government is everything and all social, economic, regulatory and political action occurs within its framework. The emphatic shift to a Keynesian framework occurred with the New Deal in the United States (Braithwaite, 2000), where govern-ment sought to recover from the depression of the early 1930s through a program of controlled economic stimulation, accompanied by detailed, central regulation of economic activity. Within subsequent Keynesian sys-tems there was considerable variation, permitting both the British welfare state, with its national health system and government-owned industries, and the United States system of free enterprise subject to a detailed system of regulation, but the uniting theme was that governments were in control, regulating markets, structuring society, ensuring the provision of services (Loughlin, 2004). Some of the tightest controls were reserved for the econ-omy, where financial policies, practices and trading were strictly regulated so as to maintain a strong and stable marketplace: "trade controls, particu-larly quotas and tariffs, were major instruments of government intervention (Gow, 1997: 116)."

The 1960s challengers to Keynesian government argued for a return to liberalism, and hence their identification as neo-liberals, advocates of a new, modernized form of liberalism. Neo-liberals based their conception of government on several precepts, including a minimal role for the state, the need for a free market, the idea of individual responsibility, freedom of choice and the need to accept the consequences of that choice (Ericson, Barry and Doyle, 2000). Hayek (1949) argued that economies had become too large and complex for central states to govern effectively, and that control had to be returned to the local – constituted by the market. The most immediate need was a massive reduction in the role of the state – government was, big, bloated, and getting in the way of an efficient marketplace. The mantra for reform became deregulation, privatization, tax cuts and reductions in the size and power of the public sector (Mitchell, 2001). This agenda was followed later by a plan that promoted internationalization, globalization and free world trade. Particularly with the economic crises of the early 1970s, including the oil crisis and the overtaking of western manufacturing industries by second world competitors, the welfare state became the villain, with its excesses responsible for these economic ills. The result has been described as "a genuine political revolt, a growing demand for fewer public programs and reductions in taxes" leading to California's Proposition 13 in 1978, freezing taxes, followed by the election of the governments of Ronald Reagan and Margaret Thatcher (Feeley, 2003: 123). The political attack on welfarism was sustained by economic and cultural critiques – increasing taxes in the 1970s had not stopped unemployment from increasing and service levels from declining (Pratt, 1999, 2002).

So the last decades of the twentieth century saw major economic and social change as the reformers sought to return the Keynesian state to something like what had preceded it. In fact, what they created was something quite different, not a deregulated state but a new regulatory state, as discussed in the next chapter. But despite this, there was change, and that change did amount to a transformation of the role of governments in western developed economies. The contrast between Keynesian welfare states and neo liberal states is between centrally controlled, closed, essentially redistributive economies, and open, global, competition-based economies:

> The distinctive policy objectives of Keynesian welfare states were the promotion of full employment in relatively closed, national, "autocentric" economies through demand-side management and the provision of redistributive welfare rights enabling new forms of mass and collective consumption. Conversely, the objectives of Schumpterian welfare states are to strengthen the structural competitiveness of national economies, through the promotion of

(organisational, product, labour process and market) innovation in relatively open, "globalised," economies, and to subordinate social policy to the needs of flexible labour markets and/or the constraints of international competition.
(Stenson and Edwards, 2001: 73)

The mechanics of the transformation to neo-liberalism are familiar. They include (see Davis and Rhodes, 2000; Mitchell, 2001; Ericson, Barry and Doyle, 2000):

- deregulation of key industries, especially banking and financial services, and a new focus on the outputs of regulation, such as quality assurance, rather than detailed oversight of inputs and activities;
- privatization of commercial activities previously operated by governments, particularly in key industries such as aviation, banking and telecommunications, and in some places, in the provision of basic infrastructure and services (e.g. water, gas and electricity in the UK and in Victoria in Australia);
- leading to a reduced role for the state and increased responsibility by individuals for themselves;
- reduction of barriers to free trade and competition, both within states and globally;
- marketization of non-privatized government services, to make public services operate on private sector terms (e.g. contracting out, intra-agency purchaser-provider splits);
- imposition of corporate management, or new public management, on public sector agencies (including performance standards and evaluation);
- decentralization of decision-making and implementation, including to the local level;
- tax incentives for businesses and enterprising individuals.

In Australia for example, a relatively late entrant to the field and therefore able to follow the models established in the United States, United Kingdom and elsewhere, the federal government deregulated banking and the financial markets, gave up its control over the dollar and interest rates, reduced taxation and eventually introduced a transaction tariff to lessen the reliance on income tax, reduced the size and functions of the public service, privatized previously government run businesses in banking, aviation, shipping telecommunications and many other industries, and developed new models for welfare provision (see Goldstein and Hart, 2003, for a discussion of economic reforms in the 1980s). It mandated competition policy for services provided by state government entities, to replace the previous emphasis on service provision. No area of economic or social life had an automatic immunity to being exposed to the marketplace, including internal and external security (aspects of the armed services, such as catering and recruitment, have been privatized, along with the same development of private policing and corrections seen in other western countries).

The death of the social

The rise of neo-liberalism was based on numerous assumptions, including economic arguments that interference with the market had stifled innovation and enterprise and led to inefficiencies, and that government had become bloated, inefficient and over-bureaucratized. If government's role was reduced and constrained then the market could perform its proper role and provide services efficiently. But another group of assumptions was morally based (Pratt, 1999) – that the welfare state had led to a culture of dependency, bludging and lack of incentive for individuals to take responsibility for improving their lot. Liberal notions of autonomy and responsibility required the replacement of welfarism with enterprise and incentives. This was particularly so given that welfarism seemed to have failed in its most basic roles – for example, the growth in unemployment and related social problems throughout the 1970s despite increased high levels of taxation and government intervention (Pratt, 1999).

Garland (2001: 92–94) describes the welfare system as being engaged in a "self-negating" attack. This was three-pronged – first, welfare agencies had a self-interest in finding more and more unmet needs, and bigger budgets, leading both to high political visibility and to a shifting of dependency from families or selves, to the state. Second, increasing prosperity in the postwar years led to increased expectations of the welfare state and what it could provide, which could not be fulfilled when the economy turned in the 1970s. And Garland's third self-negating aspect of the welfare state was the unwieldy and unresponsive bureaucracy it created, which did not compare well to client-focused private sector firms. Garland concludes:

> The welfare state's success tended to undermine its credibility. As collective memories of depression, mass unemployment and destitution began to fade, the state appeared to many to be the problem rather than the solution.   (2001: 194)

Welfare policies had rested on technologies of the social, in that government was to be achieved through society and its components, and by integrating individuals within social frameworks. Government through the social required technologies such as "social engineering, social security, social work, social benefits" (O'Malley, 2000). Neo-liberalism sees these as destructive of individual autonomy, and seeks to govern:

> without governing *society*, that is to say, to govern through the regulated and accountable choices of autonomous agents – citizens, consumers, parents, employees, managers, investors – and to govern through intensifying and acting upon their allegiance to particular "communities". As an autonomizing and pluralizing form of rule, it is dependent upon the proliferation of little regulatory instances across a territory and their multiplication, at a "molecular" level, through the interstices of our present experience.   (Rose, 1996: 61)

Thus the social is replaced by a system of loose networks, or communities. The technologies for achieving this rely heavily on the language of economics (marketization, deregulation, privatization) but this should not disguise their other, moral purpose, the reinvention of the autonomous active citizen, no longer dependent on the apparatus of social protection. As Pratt (1999) says, "neo-liberalism claimed to offer a new sense of freedom – freedom from the supposed constraints and debilitating consequences of welfare – and an altogether new set of possibilities designed to maximise the potential of human existence" (p. 143). According to Garland:

> The framework of Keynesian social democracy ceased to be a catch-all solution and became, instead, the key problem to be attacked by government policy. Its faulty economic assumptions and permissive styles of thought lay at the root of all the new social and economic ills – low productivity, high taxes and inflation, the culture of dependency, declining respect for authority, the crisis of the family.   (2001: 98)

Hence it was the social, that apparatus of state intervention in the lives of individuals, that was one of the main objects of neo-liberal reforms, along with the bureaucracy of state intervention in the marketplace that is more commonly identified in the literature. This is not to suggest that neo-liberalism has succeeded in completely obliterating the social apparatus of the welfare state – parts remain, in varying degrees of strength and viability, in the forms of public health systems (in Australia and Britain at least), state education, social security benefits and the like. O'Malley (2000) suggests that even in areas where we expect welfare intervention to have been abandoned or discredited, it is reviving, albeit under different labels. He gives the example of the old social welfare interventions on the 1960s medical model being reborn as developmental psychology approaches to crime prevention, which target family support, parenting skills, poor social attachment, poor social skills and the like. The consequence of neo-liberalism may be less the death of the social and more its re-badging under a different guise. Even so, the re-badging requires service provision to be cast in the new mould of communities, networks and partnerships, in place of the old social interventions.

Governmentality

We have already dealt with Foucault's account of the transformation of the sovereign state into the governmentalized, liberal state. But Foucault and subsequent writers in the governmentality school have more to contribute to the analysis of neo-liberalism. They have described how in the governmentalized state, power and control become more diffuse and spread over institutions both of the state and of civil society. In addition, the subjects of power are active, making choices and aligning themselves with the objectives of governments. Power comes not through discipline and conformity, but through the development of technologies of the self, adopted by active individuals (Garland, 1997). In particular, Foucault breaks down barriers between governmental authorities and those of civil society, seeing authority and control as also exercised in such locations as the family, churches and the professions. The state is a "nodal point" (Garland, 1997: 175) for authority, but not the only mechanism for its exercise. This notion provides the rationale and justification for new forms of intervention, including into the family, education and health, in pursuit of a well-integrated society (Boyne, 2000).

Building on the work of Foucault, later governmentality scholars have developed further understandings of how power and authority flow through networks of agencies, professions, locations and individuals – or a system of "the social" constructed in welfare societies and reliant on private powers and voluntary alliances (Garland, 1997: 179). Power is then seen as arising from networks and alliances, with government-at-a-distance occurring via these means (Rose, 1996). Rose suggests an advanced liberal form of government with four significant features: first, a government which seeks to know its population, by collecting statistics, using experts, developing theories, holding inquiries, publishing reports and numerous other means. The second feature is that governments produce strategies resulting in individuals governing themselves, through education, the family, and if all else fails corrections. Third, advanced liberal systems afford respect and authority to experts, in order to enhance government at a distance. Fourth, advanced liberalism is constantly reflexive, seeking better ways of governing.

The key technologies assisting the governmentalized state have been the development of statistics and risk. Statistics have become the central method by which the state knows about its population, and identifies social problems:

> Censuses and statistical enumerations helped create a conception of the population as an entity with its own regularities, and . . . ideas such as probability, the law of large numbers, normal distributions, and deviation from the mean developed as ways of understanding the social dynamics and aggregate patterns that characterised this new entity. (Garland, 1997: 180)

Statistics pave the way for the formulation of social risks, by identifying patterns, hotspots and deviations from the norm in large and complex societies where judgments can no longer be made on an individual basis. And it is risk that has become the predominant strategy of neo-liberal society, underpinning its approach to social problems.

Risk

If neo-liberalism is now the dominant political, economic and regulatory paradigm, then risk is its key technology. The literature about risk began emerging in the early 1990s (Beck, 1992). It argues that increasingly government works through frameworks of risk, so that risk now describes how we are governed. Late modernity is seen as an age full of ecological, economic and social risks, and it is argued, these risks now shape institutional and governmental practices, along with individual decision-making (Chan and Rigakos, 2002; Ericson and Haggerty, 1997; Beck, 1992). Actuarial justice (Feeley and Simon, 1994) and risk profiling are the new crime control surveillance, the new panopticon (Boyne, 2000). The rise of risk is theorized as being a consequence of neo-liberalism, and the declining activity of the state, but as O'Malley points out, risk has always been a part of government, although it now has a new pervasiveness:

> For well over two hundred years, then, risk has been a rationality of government incorporating diverse technical and moral configurations. Many of these configurations are statistical in nature, but many are not. Thus, insurance, which we often take for granted to be actuarial, has a history including forms of lottery in which the last member alive sweeps the pool, in which speculative policies were taken out on the lives of the famous, and today, which link the benefits of life and retirement insurance policies to the uncertain performance of the share market. The human and social professions, whose judgement was once thought to have been displaced by technologies of risk (Feeley and Simon, 1992), have been required to adapt their expertise to the estimation of risks posed by released offenders, psychiatric patients or even different types of drug legislation. Further away still from the familiar technologies of actualiarism, extreme sports have

become a currently fashionable technology of the self in which risk is mobilised in such highly individualised ways as the estimation of a rock climber's, hang-glider's or base-jumper's personal capacity to control their environment . . . As this suggests, while risk long has been an identifiable and variable technology, in the last thirty years or so it has seemingly become even more diverse than before. It is now a term employed in a multitude of contexts, referring to an apparently ever-expanding range of rationalities, programmes, activities, commodities and so on.   (2000: 458)

Risk underpins governmental explanations of neo-liberal government, because it is risk that provides Foucault's apparatus of security. Ericson and Haggerty (1997) explain that "in risk society, governance is directed at the provision of security" (p. 85). Institutional goals and strategies become focused on identifying, ordering and responding to risks, and providing insurance, or assurances that the risks are under control. For individuals, the focus shifts from achieving the good, to preventing the bad, ideas of which are formulated in response to fear and anxiety. Risks are identified through scientific measurement and statistical analyses and categories. These categories in turn shape individuals' conceptions of risk, and their own identities, place or habitus, in the terminology of Bourdieu (1984). Deviation from the norm means not only identification as part of a risky group, but also self-identification of the same thing. Miller and Rose (1990) demonstrate how risk management enables management at a distance of various groups and populations.

Garland (1996, 1997) argues that risk and insurance promote a form of "responsibilized autonomy." That is, the burden of managing risk has been shifted from governments to individuals, who must become responsible for the outcomes of their own decisions on risk. Prudent individuals will obtain insurances, identify and minimize risk, and manage their own security.

Feeley and Simon (1994) apply the concepts of risk to criminal justice, to develop the notion of actuarial justice. They describe an old and a new penology – the old marked by "concern for individuals, and preoccupied with such concepts as guilt, responsibility and obligation, as well as diagnosis, intervention and treatment of an individual offender" (Feeley and Simon, 1994: 173). Crime then is a deviant act for which an individual must be found responsible and held accountable. The new penology, however, is "concerned with techniques for identifying, classifying and managing groups assorted by levels of dangerousness. It takes crime for granted. It accepts deviance as normal" (Feeley and Simon, 1994: 173). Interventions are not directed at determining responsibility or ensuring accountability, but managing and regulating risky groups. Feeley and Simon's elements of actuarial justice include what they call the new practices of incapacitation (by redistributing groups in society based on their risk profiles, for example, in prison); preventive detention, of arrestees based again on "selective stereotypes" (for example, by denying bail); the development of offender profiles (they give the example of drug courier profiles). What sets these actuarial elements apart is that they are targeted on the population rather than individuals, aimed at prevention and risk minimization rather than detection and punishment of wrongdoers, and rest on their own rationality, a pseudo-scientific system of statistical indicators.

In the ten or so years since the term was first used, more and more actuarial approaches have been noted. Rates of imprisonment have continued rising, with increased focus on the incapacitation of the dangerous, rather than the objectives of rehabilitation or even punishment (Pratt, 1999). Mandatory sentencing is directed at keeping "dangerous" recidivists incapacitated. Preventive detention has become a new key strategy, seen particularly clearly in statutes aimed at indefinite sentences, and at prolonged detention, after the completion of a sentence, of repeat sexual offenders, and individuals with dangerous anti-social personality disorders. The mentally disordered, released from institutions in the 1970s and 1980s, are increasingly detained in prison as both an incapacitation and prevention mechanism. And terrorists have become the new object of profiling, with everyone from airline baggage handlers to aviation schools on the lookout for terrorist types. Added to these elements has been the growth in electronic monitoring, with CCTV commonplace in all types of public and private locations. Surveillance of risky populations is just another method of containing their threat.

The overall impact of these forms of actuarial justice, say Feeley and Simon (1994), is the rediscovery of an "underclass." But this is not the underclass of Dickensian London, largely unregulated and left to their own devices. This underclass is a segment of society increasingly excluded and marginalized, and treated by actuarial justice as a high risk group, to be managed and controlled. For these authors, writing of the United States, the underclass is easily identified in urban ghettos, by race, lack of employment and social exclusion.

Some commentators have critiqued the new reliance on risk (see Kemshall 2003, for a summary of these critiques). O'Malley (2000) argues that the thesis may be over-stated – that while the discourses of risk are prevalent, actual practice remains little changed. He gives the example of social work risk assessments, which in fact are based on clinical rather than actuarial judgments. This may be at least partly due to the lack of real scientific evidence on which to base many such risk assessments. For example,

Wortley (2003) argues that psychological and psychiatric assessments of the risk that sexual offenders are likely to re-offend are just as likely to prove wrong as right, in the few evaluations that have taken place. But it is on the basis of these assessments, confidently offered by experts, that preventive detention laws rest.

O'Malley (2002) also argues that risk has been over-stated in its supposed universality – that a "governmental consciousness" (p. 206) of risk has been to globalize, and that parallel forms of neo-liberal governance based on risk operate in diverse western nations. He suggests that the neo-liberalism of the USA is quite different to that of countries such as Britain and Australia, which have vestiges of the welfare state relatively intact. Risk, he argues, may be restorative and inclusive through strategies such as insurance and drug harm minimization. What sets these categories of risk apart is the political role, and he goes on to suggest that actuarial justice has taken less of a hold in Australia than elsewhere because of its effective lack of an excluded underclass and its social-democratic tradition.

Neo-liberalism, risk and postmodern penality

What has been the impact on crime control and the criminal justice system of the transformations just described, from welfarist to neo-liberal forms of government, from sovereign to governmentalized state, from state security apparatuses to risk society? Garland (1997) suggests that the governance of crime is now problematized in different ways, leading to new rationalities for the governance of crime and criminal justice. Rather than being a social and legal problem, crime, its control and criminal justice, he suggests, are now seen in economic terms, such as "risk and rewards, rationality, choice, probability, targeting and the demand and supply of opportunities" (p. 185). Criminals have become opportunistic risk-takers, and victims supply the risk opportunities. Crime is controlled through limiting risks and opportunities, rather than the correction and rehabilitation of offenders favored by the welfare state. Liberalism can be seen in the imputation of autonomy, both on the part of the criminal who chooses to offend, and the victims who are responsible for reducing their own risk of being targets. This responsibilization strategy extends beyond individuals, who are responsible for making safer choices, to communities and groups, who become responsible for their own safety, through strategies such as neighborhood watch. The responsible individual, homo prudens (Adams, 1995; O'Malley, 1996) has transferred from insurance contracts to crime prevention literature.

Garland argues elsewhere (1996) that increasingly western criminal justice has become marked by a retreat of the sovereign state, not just in terms of governmentality, but also in its ability to control crime. What he calls the "myth of crime control" (1996: 448), that states could control and correct criminal behavior, has been replaced by a tacit acknowledgment that the state could do little to affect the escalating crime rates of the 1970s onwards. This acknowledgment is seen in the development of new strategies directed not at stopping crime and rehabilitating offenders, but at limiting the effects and reach of crime. Garland calls these strategies adaptations, and bases them on criminologies of the self, the notion that crime is normal and commonplace, rather than committed by a pathological other.

The adaptive strategies include the notion of responsibilization already discussed, by which the burden of crime control shifts from the state to individuals (to change their own behavior or circumstances e.g. by installing locks), or groups, such as neighborhood watch, manufacturers (such as car makers installing immobilization devices) or multi-agency partnerships (responsible for community services). Hence, "property owners, residents, retailers, manufacturers, town planners, school authorities, transport managers, employers, parents and individual citizens" (Garland, 1996: 453) become responsible for reducing criminal opportunities. But the state does retain a role too, as coordinator, funder, and manager at a distance. This system bears the hallmarks of the governmentality literature's focus on risk, de-centered government and diffuse communities.

Garland (1996) also argues that postmodern criminal justice systems have adapted to failure, in that the normality of high crime rates has now been accepted, along with high rates of imprisonment and heavy caseloads in criminal justice systems. The result, he suggests, is increased systemization, case management, reliance on statistical models and performance indicators. Thus the technologies of science and statistics increasingly shape government.

Some key concepts about crime control and criminal justice emerge from this chapter's discussion so far. The first is that with the shift from welfare to neo-liberal state, and from sovereign to governmental state, the role of government and its relationship to the governed, has changed. While it has not withered away, government no longer does everything. In classic public administration terms, it may steer rather than row (Osborne and Gaebler, 1993), although in fact what it does is a complex mixture of steering and rowing, depending on the job at hand. It relies on communities, networks, or partnerships comprising business, local governments, community and family organizations to identify needs and deliver services. And the identification and management of risk has become a key framework for government service provision in all areas.

For the criminal justice system, this means that government monopolies of policing, justice and corrections have been replaced by shared models, of public and private policing and corrections, of community and restorative justice along with the state-based model. And the predominance of risk re-casts government agencies in new roles. The next section examines the re-casting of the police role.

From police to policing: transformation and pluralization

Our notion of policing as a state centered activity is fixed in time, in the middle part of the twentieth century. Both earlier and later models depart significantly from this picture, which still dominates popular perceptions. Braithwaite describes the early modern idea of police as multi-faceted and all-embracing:

> Police until the 18th and early 19th century in Europe continued to mean institutions for the creation of an orderly environment, especially for trade and commerce. Police certainly included the regulation of theft and violence, but also of weights and measures and other forms of consumer protection, liquor licensing, health and safety, building, road and traffic regulation and early forms of environmental protection. The institution was rather privatized, subject to considerable local control, heavily orientated to self-regulation and infrequent (if somewhat draconian) in its recourse to punishment.   (2003: 9)

The nineteenth-century model changed not just in its organization, but also in its focus, to become increasingly more focused on crime, and also on its after the event punishment, rather than prevention, and increasingly targeted on the poor, to the virtual exclusion of commerce (Braithwaite, 2003: 8). A new regulatory apparatus began to be established to deal with commerce, operating on a quite different basis, as described in Chapter Two. The policing of crime, by contrast became more centralized, paramilitary and hierarchical, developing into the familiar model of reactive, public policing.

But policing has never been performed just by the public police. Reiner (1997) identifies organizations and individuals who carry out policing functions to include: professional specialist police, hybrid policing agencies (e.g. transport police), private specialist police, in-house security, volunteer citizens in a state organization (special constables), volunteers sponsored by police (neighborhood watch), independent volunteers (Guardian Angels), other state security bodies (military or security organizations), employees (shop assistants guarding against theft). He adds policing by technology, such as CCTV (pp. 1005–1006). We can add to Reiner's list, to include the crime commissions now established in Australia on US lines, cash transaction reporting authorities designed to detect organized crime, and regulatory agencies with criminal functions, such as taxation and corporations commissions, and environmental protection and occupational safety agencies.

The police, like other government agencies, were profoundly affected by the transformation from the Keynesian welfare state to neo-liberalism. According to O'Malley and Palmer (1996), the welfarist model deployed imageries of public dependency on police expertise, whereas the neo-liberal imagery stresses networks of "agentive, expert and independent actors who enter *partnerships* with police" (p. 138). This should come as no surprise after this chapter's earlier identification of key elements emerging from the transformation of governance and government – namely, networks of de-centered service providers, dominated by technologies of risk. The move from centralized hierarchies to risk-based networks also happened to the police.

While elements of network approaches had been developing with the move to community policing from the 1970s, O'Malley and Palmer (1996) differentiate their focus on "expert-driven, state-centered social" (p. 140) interventions in the welfarist mode, from the neo-liberal decentering of the state, with its focus on customers and localized responses to risk. Loader (2000) calls this a shift from police to policing, with the state as one node in broad networks of power. He describes this transformation by listing a myriad of policing forms, of which only one is traditional policing by government, through police, hybrid agencies and local government provided services such as CCTV surveillance in city centers, city patrols and guards, and crime reduction strategies mandated under the *Crime and Disorder Act* (UK) 1998. Loader's second form of policing is through government, where governments purchase policing services and CCTV and other technology from private providers. Third is policing above government, comprising transnational, globalized policing services. Policing beyond government refers to the private policing market, in-house security and protective technology. Finally, policing below government is the local, sponsored (neighborhood watch) or unsponsored (vigilantism) form of action. These multiple modes of policing are in effect multiple sites of power, many of which are beyond the reach or even interest of government regulation.

Bayley and Shearing (1996) note two key developments in the transformation of policing, the end of the monopoly of policing by public police because of the rise of private, community and citizen policing, and the search for identity by public police, fed by doubts about their effectiveness in preventing crime. They conclude "policing now belongs to everybody – in activity, in responsibility, and in oversight" (1996: 591).

Some writers dispute aspects of this thesis. Jones and Newburn (2002) argue that there never was a public monopoly over policing, and that other forms of social control, along with regulatory policing, have existed for a long time. They describe the withdrawal of police from regulatory activities such as licensing bars and parking regulations as part of a long-term functional shift of responsibilities between agencies, welcomed by police, rather than as a loss of monopoly. Their main argument is that "current trends in policing can be related to the decline of more indirect (and arguably more effective) forms of social control" particularly the decline in custodian occupations such as "bus conductors, railway station masters, train guards, ticket inspectors, park-keepers etc" (pp. 140–141).

Kempa, Stenning and Wood (2004) link the development of the new "nodal policing" (performed by a mixture of public/private/voluntary agencies) with the rise of "mass private property" – the shopping malls, amusement parks and gated communities that have fed the growth in private policing. In their view, the decline of other forms of social control, the rise of mass private property and neo-liberal governance combine to cause the new policing environment.

What is the role of the public police in this new, multi-modal environment? This has been an issue of some concern, not just to scholars, but also to governments and police services and justice agencies themselves. A report recently commissioned by the United States National Institute of Justice, and written by Bayley and Shearing (2001: vii) has as its first finding:

> Policing is being reconstructed worldwide. Its distinguishing features are (a) the separation of those who authorise policing from those who do it and (b) the transference of both functions away from government.

A later finding is that:

> In response to the restructuring of policing, the role of the public police may be changing significantly. In particular, its agenda is becoming increasingly that of government rather than individuals; it is specialising in criminal investigation and undercover surveillance; its operations are undertaken in groups; and it is increasingly militarised in equipment and outlook.

In a discussion paper (2002), the Law Commission of Canada addressed many similar issues, saying "policing in Canada is in the process of transformation" (p. 2). Again it is concerned with the regulatory environment for both public and private police, and the relationships between them, and also with policing in a risk environment.

Ericson and Haggerty (1997) offer an answer to these dilemmas, by painting a new role for public police as central to networks of risk communication. In this role, public police coordinate the activities of all agents within the network to provide a basis for risk management and security. Increasingly, this role is one of police brokering of information obtained through surveillance. The information is brokered to a range of government and non-government agents with an interest in maintaining social control (Gimenez-Salinas, 2004). However, this role depends on police being prepared to share the social control function, to share information and to understand the functions and limits of the other nodes in the system. As Johnston (2003) notes, police ownership of these forms of policing is likely to be an increasingly contested area as new forms of nodal governance prevail. We return to these challenges for police in later chapters.

CHAPTER 2

Policing and the new regulatory state

In the previous chapter we described how in the neo-liberal, governed-at-a-distance, risk-managing state, police form communities of interest with other actors for crime control and crime prevention purposes. We defined third party policing as police efforts to persuade or coerce other non-offending parties such as health and building inspectors, housing agencies, property and business owners, parents and schools to take responsibility for preventing or reducing crime problems. We showed how third party policing is part of a transformation of governance generally, a shift from welfarism to neo-liberalism, directed at making individuals and groups within society more responsible for their own governance. In the transformed world of crime control, risk assessment and management has become the new primary goal of governance networks. These new networks require police to form partnerships with potential guardians to prevent or respond to criminal activity. As governments accept that crime is a problem to be curtailed and contained, rather than corrected, the police role moves increasingly from front-line patroller to facilitator, or information hub and risk assessor (Ericson and Haggerty, 1997) within the third party policing network.

In the following chapters we go on to describe these partnerships in detail, to evaluate how they work, and to examine their impact on both levels of criminal activity and police. But to examine only the role of police in third party policing is to examine only one side of the third party policing equation – the other parties to the partnerships and networks and their goals and motivations should also be considered. There are many potential partners in third party policing (discussed further in Chapters 3, 5 and 6), including insurance companies who require the installation of anti-theft devices in motor vehicles they insure, education authorities who prosecute the parents of truants, social workers who notify police of suspected drug houses visited on child protection call-outs, bar owners who work with police to reduce street drunkenness and shopping mall security workers who monitor CCTV tapes for possible criminal activity.

However, a predominant group involved with police in third party policing networks comprises regulatory authorities. We will define this term in detail below, but in brief we use it to mean government agencies or officials with a function of regulating and maintaining standards in some legal activity, such as housing, building, business or industry. Typical regulatory officials who might become involved in third party policing include building, health and safety inspectors and environmental protection officers. These officials are attractive to police because their functions are often accompanied by coercive powers, to enter properties, inspect and search, issue closure orders, or take other retaliatory action against people in breach of the regulatory scheme. For police, partnering with such officials can act as a de facto extension of their own powers, as well as increasing their potential weapons and sanctions against people they suspect of involvement in criminal activity.

But it is important to remember that crime control and prevention is not the primary aim of regulators, who instead have specific statutory functions to fulfill. In addition, just as policing has undergone the major transformation discussed in Chapter 1, so too has regulation evolved and transformed in recent decades. This chapter explores how regulation has changed, and the extent to which we now live in a "new regulatory state" (Braithwaite, 2000). We examine what the changing nature of regulation means for third party policing – what impact does the new regulatory state and its changed emphasis, away from command and control towards compliance structures and incentives, have on police seeking to network with these regulators? Do third party policing and the new regulatory structures have common aims and goals, or could networking with police be counter-productive for regulators? This chapter starts by discussing the nature of regulation and how and why it has been transformed in western democracies. It describes the rise of the new regulatory state and the consequences of that development for regulators. Finally, it analyzes the relationship between modern regulation and the crime control and prevention objectives of police, to tease out the implications of third party policing from the regulator's perspective.

Regulation

What is meant by regulation and how do we identify a regulatory authority or regulator? How does regulation relate to the legal system, and especially the criminal law and the criminal justice system? This task of definition is not as simple as it sounds. There is no single, accepted meaning for regulation (Friedrichs, 2004; Gow, 1997; Tombs, 2002), and the term is often used in quite different ways. Ogus (1994: 1), for example, surveys previous scholars and suggests three separate ways they use the term. The first meaning of regulation he finds in the literature is "any form of behavioral control"; the second, "a sustained and focused control exercised by a public agency over activities that are valued by a community"; and the third, and his preferred definition, is "regulation is fundamentally a political-economic concept and, as such, can best be understood by reference to different systems of economic organization and the legal forms which maintain them."

Baldwin, Scott and Hood (1998: 2–4) also suggest three meanings of regulation which are quite similar to those of Ogus, the simplest of which is a set of rules accompanied by a mechanism to monitor and promote compliance with them. Their second meaning is broader, encompassing "all the efforts of state agencies to steer the economy" (p. 3), including not just enforcement systems but also those promoting economic and political goals, such as taxation and even methods of government organization such as contracting out. Their third and broadest definition focuses on all forms of social control, which can include non-state processes such as the development of social norms (p. 4).

The most common approach of those studying regulation has been to focus on the first two meanings identified by Baldwin and his colleagues (1998), to examine public agencies charged with monitoring compliance with some set of rules applying to a social, political or economic activity. This focus explains why much of the literature dealing with regulation can be found in the disciplines of law, economics and political science, rather than criminology or criminal justice – regulation has been seen as a way of structuring economic and political activities, rather than as another type of law enforcement. Hence the study of regulation has developed relatively independently of the study of criminal law, and the approaches of regulators have also developed differently to those of police, prosecutors and the criminal justice system.

But the recent developments in regulation that are discussed later in this chapter, together with the trends in governance covered in the previous chapter, are changing this situation. New forms of regulation increasingly rely on a wide range of methods to achieve compliance, including using non-state agencies and voluntariness as well as the traditional public agencies. Additionally, even the nature of rule-making is changing, from detailed bureaucratic regulation to monitored, self-written and imposed codes. The spreading focus of regulation away from the agencies of the state to include corporate, social and economic aspects of civil society closely mirrors the spread of responsibility for crime control and prevention from purely public police to many aspects of society, as discussed in Chapter 1. These trends make the study of modern regulation much more focused on the third definition offered by Baldwin et al. (1998), namely as involving all forms of social control, state and non-state, rule-based and based on the development of social norms. This new focus on social control and behavior suggests that some of the traditional differences between regulation and criminal justice are weakening, and that it is timely to take a new look at the commonalities and differences between on the one hand, the criminal law and its enforcement, and on the other, regulation and its compliance mechanisms. The next sections do this by looking first at the development of regulation, then its relationship historically with policing, followed by analysis of the types of regulation, regulatory structures and tools currently in use.

Development of regulation

If law comprises a system of order that is sanctioned, enforceable and largely enforced (Cotterrell, 1992), then the criminal law is only a small and relatively minor part of this system. For most people, their primary contact with law comes through its regulatory arm. Here the goal is not to prohibit behavior outright, as the criminal law prohibits murder, assault and burglary, but to regulate activities that are primarily legal. When we build homes, get married, run businesses, sell products or services, rent out houses, or employ staff, laws regulate the way in which we do these things. These laws are made by governments or their delegates, and compliance with the laws is monitored and enforced by government regulatory agencies or officials. Prominent examples of regulatory agencies common to most western democracies include occupational health and safety inspectorates and food safety agencies; environmental and consumer protection organizations; corporations, taxation and competition commissions; anti-discrimination bodies; health, building and sanitation inspectors; and manufacturing standards agencies. The primary goal of these types of agencies is to secure compliance with laws directed at achieving the orderly, safe or efficient conduct of desirable and legal activities, and the study of regulation has been concerned with how effective they are in this role. The regulation of economic and social activity is as old as the criminal law:

> Market regulation by local officials is no new phenomenon. It was considered to be a basic function of the state . . . in eighteenth-century "police science". Even before that, markets were subject to detailed common law rules in medieval

England to ensure produce was only sold on market-day at the appointed place, and that middlemen did not buy and resell in the market for profit. Additionally, statutory schemes were developed to prevent the dilution of staples such as bread and beer with cheaper impurities and universal standards to be enforced locally were developed for regulating weights and measures. Today analogous functions are exercised through legislative standard setting for consumer protection . . . Recently the membership of the United Kingdom in the European Union has been an important new source of regulatory norms in relation to domains such as consumer protection, occupational health and safety, equality regulation, and environmental protection.   (Baldwin, Scott and Hood, 1999: 5)

Ogus (1994) also discusses the antecedents to modern regulation, showing its mass expansion in the Tudor and Stuart periods, when highly elaborate and detailed controls were established on a national basis. This pattern re-emerged with increased strength as a response to the industrialization and urbanization of the nineteenth century, and the ensuing economic and social problems. Ogus points out that the key development of this period was of a system of administrative structures to take charge of the body of regulation (1994: 7). The legal system developed in Britain and transported to its former colonies then, was a highly specialized one, with "many different kinds of sanctions, enforcement processes and enforcement agencies focused on different parts of a legal order . . . In these legal systems a variety of highly developed enforcement agencies exists. They include, particularly, police, with responsibility for the general enforcement of criminal law, and many different regulatory bodies, inspectorates and commissions charged with the enforcement and overseeing of particular areas of legislation" (Cotterrell, 1992: 245).

Within this system, the nature of regulation has been described in many different ways. Baldwin and Cave (1999) note that while regulation is primarily considered as restrictions placed on behavior to prevent undesirable practices, regulation can also be enabling or facilitative. They describe these as "red light" and "green light" approaches respectively, so that red light regulation, for example, seeks to stop anti-competitive or unsafe business practices, while green light regulation promotes orderly conduct in an area which, unregulated, could be chaotic, for example broadcasting and the allocation of airwave space.

Much of the legal and economic literature has focused on explaining why regulation has developed in certain areas. These rationales fall into several categories, the first of which is often referred to as the market failure thesis – government intervention in the economy is justified when one of the conditions for market failure is present or potentially present (Baldwin, Scott and Hood, 1999; Gow, 1997; Tombs, 2002). These conditions typically include anti-competitive behavior and monopolies, negative externalities as when factory emissions adversely affect the environment or community, information inadequacies and unequal bargaining power leading to consumers being unable to properly exercise choice, the need for public goods such as sanitation and defense, a scarcity of goods or the need to coordinate their production and sale, or to achieve some social end such as public health or maintaining the environment (ALRC, 2003; Baldwin and Cave, 1999; Breyer, 1998; Gow, 1997). Because the market fails, governments intervene to protect the public interest (Baldwin, Scott and Hood, 1999; Ogus, 1994). This theory assumes regulation to be the result of the state acting to correct market imperfections, to protect the public interest where the market is incapable of doing so. Regulatory authorities and officials become agents for achieving the public good (Posner, 1984).

The notion of government regulation of the market being justified as in the public interest has been criticized on several grounds. First, what is the public interest, and how can it be translated into rules and guidelines? How can it be distinguished from what politicians and other rule-makers perceive to be in their own interests, to secure re-election or retain power and authority (see Gow, 1997)?

These criticisms led to notions that regulation exists as a result of private interest groups grappling for power and advantage, with the most powerful able to exert influence over the law and regulation making processes to secure their own advantage (Gow, 1997). The private interest approach sees regulation not in the public interest, but for the benefit of either powerful groups involved in the activity being regulated, or regulators themselves seeking to retain and expand their own powerbase. Additionally, there are well-developed notions, particularly in the United States, of regulatory capture, which hold that however it begins, regulation ultimately becomes captured by powerful interests subverting it to their own ends (Cotterrell, 1992; Makkai and Braithwaite, 1998). The notion of capture is reinforced by the revolving door syndrome, where regulators look for their staff from among people employed in the industry being regulated, and in turn the industry poaches senior regulators for its own managerial positions. Capture theorists argue this process leads to a sympathetic approach to the industry (Gow, 1997). The capture theory has itself been criticized, for its assumption that regulation begins to protect a public interest and is subverted by capture, with the reality suggested to be a far more sophisticated blend of situational factors and powerful interests (Makkai and Braithwaite, 1998; Gow, 1997).

Apart from this brief survey, arguments about *why* regulation exists are not our main focus. For our purposes, it is enough that a vast body of regulation now structures economic, social and political life in western nations. The scope of regulatory activity is such that it has "become a central form of state intervention in the economy" (Baldwin, Scott and Hood, 1999: 1), all pervasive in its reach. Malcolm Sparrow (2000) reflects on the enormous power of regulators:

> Society entrusts regulatory and enforcement agencies with awesome powers. They can impose economic penalties, place liens upon or seize property, limit business practices, suspend professional licences, destroy livelihoods. They can restrict liberty, use force, and even kill – either in the heat of some dangerous moment on the street or through the cold calculation of the execution room. They use these powers not against foreigners in war but against citizens in peacetime. How regulatory and enforcement agencies use these powers fundamentally affects the nature and quality of life in a democracy.   (p. 2)

These coercive and aggressive powers are similar to those vested in the police, and in many areas the powers of regulators are much greater than those of the police (for example, to enter property, to search and seize without a warrant and to confiscate). The study of police organizations and their use of power therefore seems to be a logical starting point for considering how regulators work, and the next section examines the links between the study of regulation and policing.

Policing and regulation

Analyses of regulation have traditionally seen it as similar to but separate from the criminal law and its policing. Cotterrell (1992) for example, describes police and regulatory inspectorates and commissions as being jointly engaged in law enforcement, but with different structures, kinds of commitment, internal organizations and resources (pp. 246–247). He distinguishes police from regulatory agencies by the agencies' level of local control, and discretion in how they enforce the law. Baldwin et al. (1998) say that the "traditional criminal law is generally excluded from the definition [of regulation] on the basis that it seeks to punish anti-social conduct rather than encourage particular forms of purposive activity" (p. 3). Cotterrell (1992) concludes that while police work focuses on the criminal acts of ordinary citizens, regulatory agencies are concerned with "the control of business firms" behavior (p. 259). He adds that although policing and regulation share common pressures, they fundamentally differ as a result of the differing environments in which they enforce the law.

Robert Kagan (1984) notes that while regulatory enforcement staff are not called police, but inspectors, safety consultants, equal opportunity specialists, auditors, compliance agents and nursing home surveyors, "they are in fact special police forces for industry" (p. 37). Despite this, he goes on to explore the basic commonalities and differences between police and regulators, concluding that the differences are substantial. His list of commonalities include that police and regulators each face the problem of preventing the unpreventable (rule-breaking), thus making measurement of their effectiveness and efficiency difficult. The reactive form of law enforcement is also shared by many police and regulators, that is a focus on after-the-event infringement citations or prosecutions, the forming of investigative judgments, and the tendency towards legalistic strictness in applying rules (although as discussed below, this style of regulation is more likely to be found in the United States, of which Kagan (1994) was writing, than in most other jurisdictions).

Kagan (1994) also highlights differences between police and regulators. Whereas the social function of police historically has been to preserve the status quo in the distribution of property, many regulators have a redistributive function, to ensure that business assumes the costs of social goods such as health and safety, care of the environment and the like. He also differentiates the focus of action – police are focused primarily on individuals, regulators on corporations, with the individuals often being viewed as primarily "bad" offenders, with corporations seen as "largely good" providers of wealth and employment and other socially useful activities. Their misconduct, then, is more often seen as an unintended by-product of essentially valuable activities. Kagan's (1994) final category of difference between police and regulators is the types of offense they focus on, with police responding to *transient*, separate activities committed by individual suspects, and regulators on *patterns* of behavior – compliance records, standards and conditions, emission levels. These patterns are the responsibility of the organization, with breaches not easily connected to identifiable individuals, even where the breaches themselves are immediately obvious, as in the discharge in a creek, or broken sanitation equipment. Of course, Kagan (1994) notes throughout his analysis that these are generalizations only, and that there are some regulators who act very like police, but his final point of difference is clearer. The criminal law, he argues, has a function to denote socially and morally repugnant activities – the culprit who commits murder, child abuse or assault is morally culpable. Regulatory rules, he argues, are more morally ambiguous, unless they have resulted in a clear identifiable harm, such as a workplace death or injury (and even then, the harm is often perceived as less morally culpable – see Haines (1997) for an example). Many regulatory offenses only raise the possibility of, rather than result in actual, harm. The requirement to fix a toilet, or a factory, or change a business activity, is not accompanied by the same degree of culpability as most criminal offenses (although he notes not all criminal offenses are so morally clear e.g. minor drug possession, prostitution, gambling offenses). Hawkins and Thomas (1984) refer to this as the moral ambivalence of regulation.

Kagan's (1994) argument is that these differences and particularly the moral ambiguity or ambivalence of much regulation has led to the difference in approach between regulators and the criminal justice system. Regulators can be more flexible in exercising their discretion, more focused on sanctions other than prosecution, more inclusive in the setting of standards, because of these differences.

Contrary to this view, de Lint (2000) argues that "beat" policing has traditionally been concerned with maintaining legitimate commerce, and involved observation, negotiation and discretion rather than the legalistic application of rules. Drawing on Foucault, he examines the role of police as part of the apparatus of security of the state, maintaining surveillance over citizens. He notes that "German and French police regulations of the sixteenth and seventeenth centuries concerned all aspects of social relations, from health to commerce and from education to social welfare. They dealt with the 'moral quality' of life in much the same way that present-day community police organization is justified by reference to 'quality of life' indicators" (p. 58). Much of the contemporary literature on policing draws attention to the predominance of the order maintenance role, compared to the detection and prosecution of crime (e.g. Kelling and Coles, 1996; Waddington, 1999). In this conception of policing, law enforcement is of lesser importance than facilitating orderly social, business and economic activities. The focus here, just like in much of regulation, is on the application of discretion to achieve a stable environment, rather than the pursuit of individual transgressors. Braithwaite (2003) makes a similar point when he talks of the early modern idea of police as quite different to current notions of police as crime fighters. He describes the early police as regulators of trade and commerce, health, safety and the environment, as well as of theft and violence. The police organizations he describes were localized, and "heavily orientated to self-regulation and infrequent (even if sometimes draconian) in its recourse to punishment" (p. 9). These organizations bear many of the hallmarks Kagan (1994) ascribes to contemporary regulators.

Gill (2002) takes up this argument, rejecting what he says is the implication from the policing and regulation literatures that there is an essential difference between the two activities. He argues that policing should be considered properly as "broadly analogous to economic and social regulation" (p. 524), saying that:

> Prosecution is no more the "normal" outcome of policing than it is of regulation: in 1997 28 percent of recorded crime was cleared up by police, less than half of that (13 percent) was prosecuted. It is generally accepted, that where there is a clash, law enforcement will be subordinated to order-maintenance goals and many police now seek to implement variations of "problem-orientated" policing that involve multi-agency attempts to regulate communities.   (p. 526)

According to Braithwaite (2003), business regulation and policing should be regarded as two branches of the same genealogy (p. 12). The branching occurred when the nineteenth-century shift to para-military models of policing led to a focus on crime and its punishment, while new agencies were created to deal with regulation:

> Unlike police forces, these regulatory institutions mostly started out rather punitive, making heavy use of criminal punishment as a regulatory tool, but mostly became less punitive over the next 150 years . . . The business regulatory agencies grew to be more significant law enforcers than the police because the corporatisation of the world in the 20th century changed the world to a place where most of the important things done for good or ill in the world were done by corporate rather than individual actors.   (Braithwaite, 2003: 10–11)

As Braithwaite (2003) notes, regulatory agencies, while individually smaller than police organizations, now collectively comprise a much larger law enforcement sector than police. He argues that many of the features of the transformed criminal justice system (the audit society, actuarialism, responsibilization risk and partnership, as discussed in Chapter 1) are not new, but simply transposed from the regulatory state. In Braithwaite's view, regulatory models will increasingly translate across the fractured branches of social control to shape new forms of policing and punishment.

We develop this theme later in this chapter, when examining the implications for third party policing of changes in governance and regulation, arguing that the transformation in these areas is forcing the policing and regulation functions to become more alike. Now though, having examined the nature of regulation and its relationship to policing, we move on to consider regulatory tools, typologies and structures.

Tools, typologies and structures

The primary tools of regulation comprise the rules and sanctions overseen by the regulatory agencies. The nature and range of rules and the ways they can be used are discussed more fully in Chapter 4, but in summary they generally comprise primary legislation, delegated legislation (including regulations, by-laws, ordinances and quasi-legislation), informal policies and guidelines, codes of conduct and self-regulated schemes. These tools can impose penalties and sanctions including criminal penalties such as imprisonment, fines and property forfeiture. Civil penalties can include fines, injunctions, banning orders, license revocations and orders for reparation and compensation. Administrative penalties can also include fines and charges, infringement notices, negotiated penalties and adverse publicity (ALRC, 2003).

Within the literature, one of the main discussions about regulatory tools looks at the extent to which they should involve the criminal law and sanctions, as opposed to civil and administrative systems. While regulatory law has typically been regarded as separate from criminal law, the trend to criminalization has seen this distinction blurred, with many agencies now supervising some aspects of criminal law (Cheh, 1991, 1998; Cotterrell, 1992), such as corporate misconduct, market-related offenses, pollution and other environmental offences, racial or cultural vilification, and consumer offenses to name just a few examples. Some writers have suggested that criminalization has been over-used, to the extent that the notion of criminality has been debased (Bagaric, 2001), and that the association between moral opprobrium and the criminal law has been weakened (ALRC, 2003). Baldwin and Cave (1999) suggest that regulators may be reluctant to prosecute if there is a prospect of severe criminal penalties, while the requirement to meet a criminal rather than civil standard of proof may also make regulators' prosecutory and evidence gathering tasks more difficult and expensive.

Governments, on the other hand, in the wake of regulatory failures leading to corporate scandals and collapses, health risks such as Britain's mad cow and foot and mouth disease outbreaks, and environmental degradation, see criminalization both as a real deterrent and an indication that they are taking the problems seriously. Some writers see this approach as justified in the case of regulation dealing with health and safety and environmental protection, but less justifiable for the protection of economic interests (Yeung, 1999). Regulators do not always agree with this distinction, with the Australian Competition and Consumer Commission, for example, campaigning in recent years for criminal penalties for cartel price-fixing offences on the basis of the severe impact of such activities on the nation's economy as a whole. Ultimately, as the ALRC (2003) suggests, the choice between criminal and civil penalties is a matter for governments, with ramifications for regulators, such as different evidentiary standards and a different onus of proof, compellability of witnesses, and flow-on effects to staffing, budgets and the development of regulatory strategies.

More recently, Baldwin (2004) suggests a shift to punitive criminal sanctions in areas of regulation including competition, financial services and information regulation. Writing of the UK, he argues this trend to have been led by recent crises, government responses and media focus on white-collar crimes.

Within the legislative frameworks imposed by governments, various typologies have been attempted to help describe the range of regulation and the activities of regulators. Gow (1997) for example, refers to three main types of regulation. Economic regulation structures particular industries or markets (e.g. telecommunications or banking and finance). Social regulation sets community-wide standards, in health, safety or to protect the environment. Functional regulation indirectly affects business by imposing rules on discrete activities, such as land use or transport regulations. Friedrichs (2004) contrasts economic regulation as addressing market relations and stability, and social regulation as protective of workers, consumers and citizens, with social regulation having expanded enormously since the early 1970s (p. 247).

Within this broad categorization, the range of regulators is very large. One review of Australian regulators (ALRC, 2003) for example, found within the federal system alone, separate bodies in the following functional areas:

- Marketplace – competition and consumer protection, market conduct in the financial sector, prudential behavior in the financial sector, cash transaction reporting;
- Revenue – taxation;
- Border control – customs, immigration, quarantine, fisheries management;
- Environment – environment protection, maritime safety;
- Social security;
- Communications – communications, broadcasting, competition and consumer protection, civil aviation authority, maritime safety authority;
- Health and aged care – aged care standards and accreditation, food standards, therapeutic goods;
- Gene technology – registration of agricultural and veterinary chemicals, therapeutic goods, food standards, gene technology;
- Privacy;
- Discrimination and human rights – human rights and equal opportunity commission, equal opportunity for women in the workplace.

Considering that in Australia more regulation takes place at state and local authority level then federally the range of regulators is clearly enormous. As well as possessing complementary jurisdiction to several areas of federal regulation, such as consumer protection, human rights, food safety, the environment and financial services, the states regulate in areas such as occupational health and safety, mine and road safety, child protection, agriculture and primary production, education, weights and measures, building codes, property rentals and dangerous activities (e.g. those producing radiation or hazardous products). Local authorities develop standards for building, sanitation and safety, commercial services, transport, animals, noise and other nuisances.

Across these different regulatory agencies and activities, there is a wide range of regulatory styles and techniques. Jurisdictional differences help shape regulatory style, so that Baldwin, Scott and Hood (1997) for example, attribute to United States agencies a "formalized and legalistic style of regulation, administered by powerful agencies having rule-making, enforcement, and sanctioning powers. Processes are formal, relatively transparent, and often involve lengthy decision cycles" (p. 22). They contrast this with the United Kingdom approach to regulation, which they characterize as less formal, less transparent and subject to less accountability. Hawkins (1984) also describes British government-business relations as consensual and cooperative. The regulatory systems of other countries are seen as even more informal, with Japanese authorities exercising wide discretion in giving guidance but compliance being largely voluntary (Baldwin, Scott and Hood, 1997; Grabosky, 1993). Thus the United States system represents one end of a spectrum of approaches, being formal and legalistic, and Britain tends towards the other end, relying more on consensual relations between government and regulated industry.

In Australia, Peter Grabosky (1993) assessed where Australia stood in relation to international approaches to regulation. Based on his earlier research with John Braithwaite (1986), he describes a general rejection by Australian regulators of the adversarial, prosecution-based approach of the United States, in favor of a focus on cooperation. But he notes a slightly increased tendency towards adversarialism along United States lines among some of the more powerful regulators.

The landmark study by Grabosky and Braithwaite (1986) of Australian regulators developed a typology of agencies. Their analysis of ninety-six regulators revealed the following types:

- *Conciliators*, who were characterized by a rejection of the law enforcement model in favor of attempts at conciliating conflicting groups. Nine examples included anti-discrimination and some consumer affairs agencies.
- *Benign big guns*, had extensive powers that were rarely used, but could not be ignored. The seventeen members of this group included the

Reserve Bank and Australian Broadcasting Tribunal and some environmental agencies.

- *Diagnostic inspectorates*, were mainly directed at providing technical assistance to regulated industries. The eleven agencies were mainly mining and radiation safety authorities.
- *Detached token enforcers* and *detached modest enforcers* (groups of nine and seven respectively) were not focused on cooperation and self-regulation, but likely to undertake occasional prosecutions.
- *Token enforcers* (group of twenty-five) were the predominant style of Australian regulator, and rulebook rather than diagnostic orientated. They initiate prosecutions that largely result in derisory average penalties.
- *Modest enforcers* (group of eighteen) also relied on prosecutions and other punitive sanctions, with more significant penalties.

A similar approach by a United States author developed a typology comprising four regulatory styles – service, watchman, legalistic and free agent (Frank, 1984). The service and watchman styles favor persuasion, with the service style focusing on proactive technical assistance, and the watchman approach being more reactive. The legalistic style is mechanistically prosecutorial, and the free agent style more informal and autonomous (Friedrichs, 2004).

In the British context, Cotterrell (1992) concludes that advice-giving is a primary activity of regulators including consumer agencies, anti-pollution authorities and environmental health officers, with prosecutions being a relatively rare occurrence (pp. 260–261). This was because prosecution was not seen as useful for deterrence in these agencies. He suggests factors contributing to the policies of accommodation revealed by most studies of regulatory agencies. These include the inadequacy of agency resources to perform their task, inadequate sanctions, the insecure basis of agency authority leading them to adopt policies protecting them from political and business attack, the lack of support from courts for regulatory functions and processes, a lack of clear and unequivocal public support for the work of regulatory agencies, and the complexity of the regulatory and business environment leading to difficulties in establishing culpability, causation and responsibility for breaches. Friedrichs (2004) refers to similar factors, but also includes features of the regulatory task environment, such as the visibility of violations and the size and sophistication of the regulated businesses.

What then, is the best method to secure compliance with the law? Traditional theory ranges across approaches including punishment, condemnation, deterrence and reparation, but the debate in regulation has been specifically focused on prosecutorial enforcement versus less punitive means of achieving compliance, including cooperation, education and self-regulation. As the preceding discussion points out, no single approach is possible, and regulatory style has varied across time, jurisdiction, industry, regulatory scheme and individual philosophy. Regulatory style and practice has also been subject to external pressures and forces for change, and the next section discusses the impact of these pressures and forces, and how they have molded a "new regulatory state."

The new regulatory state

Historically, regulation has been characterized by cyclical development, from its medieval origins through more recent developments. Friedrichs (2004) describes major cycles of regulation affecting the United States, starting with the progressive era in the early 1900s, when public opinion against the abuses of big business supported the development of anti-trust and other economic regulation. Another cycle occurred with the depression-era New Deal, when the excesses of financiers and corporations seen as responsible for the crisis provided the impetus for extensive corporate and financial regulation. In the *Great Society* era of the 1960s and early 1970s social regulation began to grow, as the benefits of economic prosperity were extended to provide occupational safety, consumer and environmental protection. Until the late 1970s, there was "a reasonably high level of consensus on the desirability of government regulation" (Friedrichs, 2004). As Ogus (1994) points out, it was not just the growth in regulation that was important, but also developments in the methods and forms of control exercised by regulators, including what he calls the most interventionist of all methods, the requirement for prior approval (p. 9).

This support for new forms of regulation and control transcended jurisdiction and industry, resulting in a high level of state intervention in most western countries (Gow, 1997). Gow describes the high water mark of economic regulation in Australia in the late 1960s when tariff protections equated to a 40 percent consumption tax (p. 117). Moran (2001), writing of Britain, describes a high point of regulation in about 1950, when nationalization had led to state ownership of many key industries (steel, coal), public utilities (electricity, water, gas) and services (transport). Tight administrative controls, introduced during the war, still governed production and consumption, in the form of rationing, industry stabilization and controls over raw materials. Public administration was a unified, hierarchical bureaucracy. Despite the extent of control, some key areas remained beyond the reach of regulation, including occupational health and safety and food standards, with these areas, the activities of professionals, education and other key areas of social activity remaining largely self-regulated, until the major expansion of social regulation that occurred in the 1960s and early 1970s.

In the mid-1970s the tide of opinion on regulation turned, and the rhetoric of regulatory reform, privatization and deregulation emerged, strongly championed by the governments of Margaret Thatcher in Britain (elected in 1979) and Ronald Reagan in the United States (elected in 1981). They articulated arguments against regulation, drawing on emerging neo-liberal thought to justify their position. This involved criticism of regulatory regimes as bloated, bureaucratic and an unnecessary hindrance on the operation of the free market. The economic critique of regulation was that the interference with free market mechanisms led to inefficiencies and distortions, restricted competition and reduced technological progress and diversity (Gow, 1997). These criticisms were given more weight by the apparent failure of regulation, as economic downturns reduced productivity and competitiveness (Friedrichs, 2004).

As a result, deregulation and privatization were pursued in most western jurisdictions. The United States deregulated inter-state commerce, transportation and airlines (Gow, 1997), while Britain sold off its state-owned industries and services. Australia deregulated its financial system and sold off key public institutions. Along with the deregulation and privatization agenda was another push for regulatory reform. Even in areas where regulation was still seen as necessary, governments focused on reducing the level of intervention, streamlining processes and reducing restrictions. In Australia, governments set up regulation reform agencies (Gow, 1997) specifically charged with reducing the red tape burdens seen as holding back business and industry competitiveness. The focus on regulatory reform was global, with the Organization for Economic Development (OECD) strongly advancing its agenda, based on notions that market liberalization and deregulation would provide economic growth in both developed and developing nations (OECD, 2000).

With the emphasis on regulatory reform, deregulation, liberalized trade and competitive markets (OECD, 2000), also came notions of the need to refocus government institutions and structures. Led by influential works such as Osborne and Gaebler's (1992) *Reinventing Government*, states were urged to abandon the "rowing" activities of government, such as service provision and ownership, and adopt a "steering" position, coordinating and overseeing the activities of other agencies and private organizations in service provision, including the development of partnerships if necessary. The end result was a remarkable western consensus for the need for less government intervention in the market, particularly by way of direct ownership or involvement in service provision, and less intrusive regulation.

The hollowing out of the state or the new regulatory state?

These trends to deregulation, privatization and the retraction of state activities led some writers to talk of a "hollowed out state." Rhodes (1994) argues that four factors contributed to this occurring in Britain: privatization and the limiting of the scope and forms of public intervention; the diversion of functions from central government to alternate agencies and service-providers; the loss of functions by British government to European Union institutions; and the introduction of new forms of public management focused on accountability and clearer political control. The results of these factors, Rhodes (1994) argues, include fragmentation, reduced accountability, and loss of regulatory effectiveness and government capability. Moran (2001) also defines what he calls components of change, including a change in focus of state responsibilities to focus just on market failures rather than the whole economy; the decline of the centralized bureaucracy in favor of loosely coordinated agencies; the displacement of public ownership by regulated privatized industries; the increase in social regulation; and the transformation of self-regulation in the professions and other areas to become subject to statutory regulatory schemes.

Key outcomes of this process have been: reduced reliance on public ownership as a form of regulation, and its replacement by sophisticated regulatory schemes; the growth of social regulation; and the injection of competition into previously monopolistic industries (Ogus, 1994). The new regulatory schemes are less reliant on the classical model of command and control typically associated with United States progressive-era regulation (Baldwin, Scott and Hood, 1998), where legalistic rules are applied with little discretion or cooperation. The new regulatory styles favor less prescriptive rules, incentives rather than sanctions, and the adoption of self-regulatory codes and instruments. Power (1997) identifies three overlapping programs of reform, including new methods of public management, shifts in regulatory style, and the development of new markets for assurances and services.

Rather than the hollowing out of the state then, the shift towards deregulation and the rhetoric of market solutions has in fact led to a new form of regulation or a new regulatory state (Braithwaite, 1999, 2000). But the new regulators differ from the old, state-centered models. They recognize a plurality of regulatory methods, departing from reliance on command and control as the only way of securing compliance, towards theories of responsive regulation (Ayres and Braithwaite, 1992). Here, regulation becomes a layered web, with strands contributed by public agencies, professional and community organizations and individuals, and increasingly international organizations as part of globalized regulatory networks (Braithwaite and Drahos, 2000). The new regulatory state then is based on neo-liberal combinations of market competition, privatized institutions, and de-centered, at-a-distance forms of state regulation (Braithwaite, 2000). The new forms of governance require strong central state control of the direction of regulation and risk management, with many of the operational regulatory and compliance functions shifted to the market, community and other social institutions.

The impact of these changes on regulatory agencies is to transform them from reactive, hierarchical command structures to problem oriented, team-based units focused on risk management (Sparrow, 1994). The emphasis moves from after the event use of formal legal sanctions, to cooperation, persuasion and the creation of incentives for compliance. The attraction for the regulated is the comfort that the "big stick" of coercive sanctions will only be used as a last resort, and also that those who are regulated will have some input into the rule-making and compliance processes. The attraction for governments is also twofold – first, persuasion and the other techniques are cheaper and give quicker results than formal legal process, but more importantly, they help build an image of government as supportive of business, rather than focused on bureaucracy and red tape.

Responsive regulation

Despite these developments, criticisms and pressures on regulators have continued, with Sparrow (2000) identifying major themes beginning with the volume and complexity of regulations. He points out that the cost reductions achieved by reduced economic regulation have been outweighed by increases in social regulation (p. 19) and cites Australia's regulatory reform agenda as an example of the world-wide concern with this issue. This is reinforced by the OECD's strong focus on regulatory reform, and its setting of goals for member nations in these areas (OECD, 2000). While traditional command and control style regulation has focused on the development and enforcement of rules, the new focus is efficiency and effectiveness, and the identification of key outcomes.

The second critical theme Sparrow (2000) identifies is that the costs of regulation are seen as outweighing the benefits. Here again the focus is on regulatory outcomes and their measurement. This task has traditionally been difficult for agencies where the best outcome might be that nothing happens – no pollutants are dumped in the ocean, no occupational deaths occur. Measuring costs is difficult too, where they may be incurred not just by government agencies but by industry or business groups (see Chapter Eight for further discussion on this issue).

Sparrow's (2000) third critical theme is that regulatory attention is seen as irrationally distributed, particularly in areas where risks are scientifically difficult to quantify. How can agencies justify their requirements of industry in some areas but not others? The fourth critical theme on regulation focuses on its inflexibility and one-size-fits-all approach, particularly within a rigid, command and control style system, where little discretion is applied. Finally, many regulatory schemes are seen as outdated, particularly in light of technological innovations and industry change. This is particularly problematic when the same innovation and change produce new risks, not yet regulated.

The swings between regulation and deregulation, and between adversarialism and cooperative approaches have been described by Sparrow (2000) as the regulatory pendulum, with the swing of the pendulum determined by social and historical contexts. Ayres and Braithwaite (1992) developed a pioneering alternative to the pendulum in their notion of responsive regulation, a new approach to mixing both gentle persuasion with big sticks. They say that:

> Good policy analysis is not about choosing between the free market and government regulation. Nor is it about simply deciding what the law should proscribe. If we accept that sound policy analysis is about understanding private regulation – by industry associations, by firms, by peers, and by individual consciences – and how it is interdependent with state regulation, then interesting possibilities open up to steer the mix of private and public regulation. It is this mix, this interplay, that works to assist or impede solution of the policy problem.
>
> (Ayres and Braithwaite, 1992: 3)

In other words, responsive regulation is directed at getting the best of both worlds, both negotiated compliance and the threat of tough sanctions. But the important aspect of responsive regulation is that the mix between sanctions and negotiation, state and private regulation, changes to suit the regulatory context – the industry, jurisdiction, environment and problem of the day. Sparrow (2000) raises interesting questions about how this can work in practice – do officials within individual regulatory agencies get to determine their own regulatory mix from occasion to occasion, or must there be an agency style? Who authorizes variations? Should agencies try to blend conciliatory and tough approaches, or should they maintain functional divisions between educators, and as he puts it, bulldogs (p. 38)?

While there are no absolute answers to these questions, the system of graduated sanctions, or enforcement pyramid, developed by Ayres and Braithwaite (1992), shows how it is possible for an agency to progress through a ranked system of sanctions in a systematic and increasingly punitive way, depending on the conduct of the subject of regulation. Under the pyramid, regulatory breaches are dealt with by sanctions of increasing severity, with the ultimate sanctions at the tip of the pyramid ever present as a threat or big stick. Most regulatory activity occurs at the base of the pyramid, where transgressors are educated and coaxed into compliance. Continued transgression invokes a warning letter, followed by civil penalties, criminal penalties, license suspension and license revocation. Regulatory agencies using such a model would fit the previously described benign big gun model, possessing serious sanctions but reserving their use for the most serious of breaches and first trying to achieve compliance through other means. Other proactive approaches to regulation have also been advocated. Gunningham and Grabosky's (1998) "smart regulation" uses non-state as well as state agencies and measures to regulate, while Christine Parker's (2002) "meta-regulation" seeks to link internal capacity for self-regulation within corporations and commitment to self-regulate, with external regulatory goals.

Sparrow (2000) suggests three core elements of reform leading to more proactive regulation: a clear focus on results rather than traditional productivity measures, the adoption of a problem-solving approach tailor-made to each identified non-compliance or risk, and an investment in collaborative partnerships with industry groups, unions, employees and other government agencies. These three regulatory strategies correlate to key policing strategies. Community policing focuses on police partnerships, problem-solving policing focuses on proactive identification of both problems and solutions, and incorporates a results orientation. Sparrow's (2000) linking of regulatory reform back into key reforms of policing bring us back to considering the links between the two areas, and particularly how police partnerships with regulators can best be structured.

Malcolm Sparrow (2000) has provided one model for assessing the partnerships that we know about, focusing on how they are driven. He compares partnerships driven by the desire to provide a customer service focus, with those driven by a compliance focus. The first category largely aims to demonstrate the responsiveness of government to segments of the regulated community, while compliance driven partnerships are focused on a specific hazard or risk area, and focus on actors central to that problem. He comments on this second category of partnerships:

> These programs show the value of partnerships in achieving the central purposes of the agency . . . the partnerships are not driven by a customer service motivation, nor by a politically inspired desire to please, to make government popular, or to transform regulatory agencies from enforcers into service providers. Rather, they are driven by a clearly articulated goal and the realization that close engagements with other parties, some good and some bad, can produce more effective, resource-efficient resolutions.   (Sparrow, 2000: 106)

We revisit these issues later in this book, but for now it is enough to note that this categorization of partnership, between those produced according to plan, to be seen as responsive and popular (i.e. customer service partnerships), and those created by need around a specific problem (i.e. compliance-driven partnerships), also characterize some of the third party policing partnerships. In third party policing, however, we argue that many of the partnerships that are forged and used to gain a crime control benefit are largely episodic in nature and centered around the desire to gain compliance and solve immediate problems. Indeed, we suggest that third party policing tactics as manifest in compliance-oriented problem-solving are leading the way in the transformation of contemporary policing away from the traditional mode of the police as enforcers towards a more regulatory-like model of public policing. Braithwaite's (2003) prediction that regulatory models will increasingly translate across the fractured branches of social control to shape new forms of policing and punishment is evident in the emergence of third party policing as an increasingly common form of solving local-level crime problems.

Summing up

The earlier sections of this chapter paint an historical picture of the relationship between police and regulators, beginning with their shared origins in medieval European police, through their separate branching in the nineteenth century, and ending with the dissolution of many differences – between criminal and regulatory law, and prosecutorial and conciliatory functions and strategies. We finished with Malcolm Sparrow's (2000) emphasis on problem-solving partnerships, which is strikingly similar to the emphasis on community partnerships in much of the governance literature discussed in Chapter 1 and the problem-oriented policing literature. Risk, problem identification and solving and partnerships are the new primary focus for regulatory practice, as well as policing (see Goldstein, 1990; Scott, 2000). From this focus emerges the importance of our subject, third party policing, as the mechanism for bringing together police and regulators so that both can practice these new ways of doing business, helping each other achieve efficiencies and improve effectiveness along the way.

In later chapters we examine in detail how effective these strategies have proved to be (Chapters 5 and 6), and examine ways of improving this effectiveness as well as accountability (Chapter 7). As we will show, the literature on these issues is still very thin.

CHAPTER 3

Dimensions of third party policing

A central part of contemporary police work is forging partnerships with individuals, groups and organizations in an effort to regulate, control and prevent crime (Sparrow, 2000). Police team up with property owners, building inspectors, environmental regulators, education department representatives, community groups, insurance companies, business leaders, local government personnel and anyone else who is motivated and able to work with police. But what happens when police co-opt and coerce organizations and/or individuals to help the police pursue their crime control and crime prevention functions? What happens when organizations and/or individuals are unmotivated or unwilling to go outside of their routine activities to take on a crime control or crime prevention responsibility? In our caravan park example described in Chapter 1, the park manager was unmotivated to deal with the multitude of problems stemming from his caravan park. It was not until the police found a "lever" (in this case the "lever" was a local council regulation and an insurance policy) – to "motivate" the park manager (a "third party") into altering his practices. This process of using legal levers to regulate, co-opt and coerce third parties is central to what we describe as "third party policing" (see also Buerger and Mazerolle, 1998: 301).

Third party policing exists in many forms. In about 30 percent of all third party policing initiatives, the police use coercion or persuasion of third parties to solve ongoing problems within the context of their problem-oriented policing program. In some police agencies third party policing exists as an especially designed, stand-alone-policing program using a one-size-fits-all third party solution (e.g. Oakland's Beat Health Program). In some jurisdictions, forms of third party policing are now being mandated by governments, such as the crime and disorder reduction partnerships established under Britain's *Crime and Disorder Act 1998* (Section 5). This part of the act requires police and local authorities to work together to formulate and implement strategies for the reduction of crime and disorder in their local areas (Loader, 2000).

In most police agencies, however, the police implement third party policing in very episodic ways either as part of a crackdown or during routine patrol work. In third party policing laws and legal mechanisms are used to co-opt willing or unwilling non-offending third parties, with the object of facilitating or coercing them into helping to control the behavior of offending ultimate targets. For example, the police might "drop-in" on a local shop owner whom they know has problems with people hanging out in front of their business selling drugs. During this visit the police discuss the Health and Safety Code violations they notice in the store, and suggest crime control options the store-owner might want to "consider." The police might stop at a bar that they know has been recently targeted by the local liquor licensing authority and ask the bar manager about the approaches they have introduced to reduce underage drinking and the fights occurring outside the bar at closing hour. The police might phone a city fire code inspector, whom they have come to know during years of working in a particular neighborhood, and ask him or her to "check out" a property the police have received an inordinate number of calls about in recent months. These are all examples of what we consider to be ad hoc, episodic implementation of third party policing practices. We suggest this trend in policing is part of two general societal trends: first, third party policing is part of the general blurring of the criminal and civil laws and second, third party policing is the manifestation of societal trends towards the regulatory state. The result is that the police are becoming more like regulators than enforcers especially in their use of proactive compliance measures (see Braithwaite, 2003).

The impact of third party policing is quite striking. On the one hand, our systematic reviews (see Chapters 5 and 6) reveal that third party policing is effective at reducing crime problems. On the other hand, there are many negative side effects of third party policing (see Chapter 7). For example, the impact on recipients of third party policing action might be enormous. The property owner who receives a surprise, "informal" visit from a city inspector begrudgingly makes costly repairs to their property; the shop keeper who feels pressured by the police, yet fears retaliation from the people selling drugs outside his store, further retreats from the threatening people outside the store; and the bar owner visited earlier in the week by the police feels manipulated by the police and fearful of future harassment if he does not act swiftly to curb the underage drinking at the bar.

Many third party policing activities involve actions that occur outside of any programmatic intervention and involves coercive and ad hoc actions taken against third parties – such as bar owners, parents and property owners – that the police at least believe to have some responsibility for creating or controlling the conditions that encourage or aggravate lawless behavior. We argue that ad hoc, third party policing activities occur frequently and with little regard to the ethical dilemmas raised by the third party policing actions. In Foucault's language these third party policing practices are disciplinary, insidious and generally invisible (Foucault, 1979; 1991), but it is also the most efficient kind of social control (see Grabosky, 1996; Simon, 1988). As such, it is this ad hoc, episodic category of third party policing on which we focus much of our attention in this book.

In this chapter, we delve into the range of components that define and distinguish third party policing from other police tactics and crime control strategies. We begin the chapter by identifying some key dimensions of third party policing. We differentiate and define third party policing within the context of other crime prevention and policing practices and we scope out the range of legal levers used in third party policing.

What is third party policing?

Purpose of action

We identify two primary purposes of third party policing activities: crime prevention and crime control. In crime prevention, the police seek to anticipate crime problems and reduce or alter the underlying criminogenic conditions that may cause crime problems to develop or escalate. Third party policing that has crime prevention as its purpose of action operates to control those underlying criminogenic influences that may (or may not) lead to future crime problems. When third party policing is preventive in its orientation, police actions tend to be directed towards fostering good relations with local business owners, cultivating partnerships with government employees (e.g. school teachers, building inspectors, probation officers and family welfare workers) and gathering knowledge about local community conditions from people living and working in their patrol target area. Obviously, the more work that the police can do to cultivate good working relationships with potential third parties before crime problems develop or escalate, the less likely that the police will mobilize legal provisions to threaten or coerce a third party into taking some crime prevention responsibility.

By contrast, third party policing that seeks to control existing crime problems explicitly aims to alter the routine behaviors of those parties that the police believe might have some influence over the existing crime problem. The Oakland Police Department's Beat Health Program is a prime example of third party policing with a crime control purpose (see Green, 1996). Beat Health Officers in Oakland organize what they call "SMART" (Specialized Multi-Agency Response Team) inspections of properties with drug dealing problems. The aim of SMART inspections is to cite the property owner for building, housing, vector control, fire code violations (as well as any other violation that might be found on the property) and thus compel the property owner to alter their routine behavior and initiate actions to control the drug problems on their property.

The threat of, or actual initiation of, legal action to coerce third parties into complying with the wishes of the police is more likely when the police engage in crime control, as opposed to crime prevention, actions. We also observe third party policing practices aimed to control crime (as opposed to prevent crime) to be clustered in poor, socially disorganized communities. There are a variety of reasons why we observe spatial variation in third party policing and greater use of third party policing practices for crime control as opposed to crime prevention. For instance, the police generally have not established working relationships with people whom they pressure into taking some crime control responsibility using legal threats. The police variously define these co-opted third parties as obstructionist, duplicitous, unhelpful and anti-police. As such, they become easy targets for police initiating legal action against them. The police do not have an inter-personal relationship with these third parties and thus the police objectify the utility of these people as agents of crime control.

We note that the spatial variation in formal, third party proceedings offers important parallels with broader, theoretical arguments put forth by many contemporary social theorists. Both Coleman (1988) and Putnam (1995), for example, argue that in neighborhoods where social capital is high, there is generally little crime and little need for formal police action. By contrast, places with low levels of trust and few social norms are believed to be places where community members will only cooperate in joint action under a system of formal rules and regulations. Fukuyama (1995) suggests that these rules and regulations have to be negotiated, agreed to, litigated, and enforced, sometimes by coercive means, leading to expensive legal costs.

Robert Sampson and his colleagues (1997, 2001, 2002) extend the social capital arguments about the spatial variation in crime and community-based action in their Chicago-based research. They argue that spatial variations in crime are not so much dictated by levels of "social capital" but rather by variations in what they call "collective efficacy." Collective efficacy is a *task-specific* construct that describes community-based mechanisms that facilitate social control without necessarily requiring strong ties or associations amongst community members. We argue that third party policing is very much a practical application or outcome of the theory of collective efficacy. We agree that there could be a variety of ways that efficacious collective action could be engendered within a community. We suggest that one way to create collective action is for the police to coerce third parties, using legal levers, to become task-oriented into solving a local problem. We discuss further the linkages of third party policing to contemporary theories on crime and place in Chapter 8.

In short, we acknowledge the variation in third party policing across different communities and recognize that this variation is, in part, due to the spatial distribution of collective efficacy, crime and the accompanying crime control versus crime prevention goals of police action. We note, however, that in practice the relationship between crime control and crime prevention is not a zero-one dichotomy. While crime control and crime prevention may have different objectives, they often share similar tactics. Despite these semantic differences and similarities, we find it a useful exercise to distinguish crime control from crime prevention at various times in our book for explanatory purposes, thus enabling us to illustrate different forms of third party policing.

Types of problems

Third party policing can be directed against many types of crime or quality of life problems (see Finn and Hylton, 1994; National Crime Prevention Council, 1996). In our systematic reviews described in Chapters 5 and 6 we identify a range of third party policing approaches to controlling drug problems, violent crime problems, property crime problems, problems with juveniles and problems in public space. We chose to review these categories of problems because of biases in the evaluation literature favoring these types of issues. But we recognize that third party policing can be directed against white-collar offenders including tax evaders, environmental polluters, fraudsters, sexual crime offenders and even terrorists. For example, the police often partner with taxation department investigators to work with companies and reduce tax fraud problems (see Grabosky, 1995). To deal with terrorism problems, police throughout the world have used asset forfeiture legislation to target those people whom they believe have harbored or in some way facilitated terrorist activities (*Canberra Times*, 2003; DeYoung and Eggen, 2001).

Most research appearing in academic journals as well as anecdotal accounts of third party policing appearing in newspapers, bulletins, in-house policing publications, magazines and television reports, however, describe police efforts to control low level, local problems such as drug problems (see Eck and Wartell, 1998; Green, 1996; Mazerolle, Kadleck and Roehl, 1998), violent crime (see Braga et al., 1999; Hauritz et al., 1998) disorderly behaviour (see Katz et al., 2001) and youth offending (Baker and Wolfer, 2003; Penrod, 2001).

There are several reasons why we concentrate in our book on third party policing efforts that seek to control low-level, street-level types of crime activity: first, third party policing is not an articulated or developed doctrine (but see Buerger and Mazerolle, 1998; Roach Anleu, Mazerolle and Presser, 2000). As such, very little discourse surrounds third party policing activities and there exists very little systematic assessment of third party policing practices (see Chapters 5 and 6). Having said that, for what evidence is available, the preponderance of research focuses on street-level problems. As such, we have more systematic knowledge about the processes and legal levers that are utilized to target street crimes than those used to target other categories of crime. Second, we suspect that a large percentage of third party policing practices, as we define it, occur at the grassroots of policing and in episodic, ad hoc ways. Our trawling of the literature and clippings of newspaper and magazine articles has certainly uncovered a bias towards street-crime problems. This is possibly an indicator of a general bias in practice towards street level implementation of third party policing. This is, of course, just a hypothesis, open to be tested empirically (see Chapter 8). Third, the ad hoc nature of much of this "grassroots" third party policing means that the police are not generally retrospective in their implementation of third party policing, linkages are not made between various third-party policing practices, and best practices are not openly discussed, developed and distributed. We thus use this book as a vehicle to begin the process of creating a preliminary evidence base of what works in third party policing. We recognize, however, the need for further research into the use and prevalence of third party policing in other areas of regulation.

Initiators of third party policing

A variety of collectivities and individuals can (and do) initiate third party policing activities. Prosecutors, policy makers, government agencies, regulatory agencies, citizens, victims of crime, community groups, businesses (Felson and Clarke, 1997), multi-agency partners (Walters, 1996) and individual regulatory agents are all potential initiators of third party policing practices. For example, in an attempt to identify and deter money laundering, legislation exists that compels financial institutions to report large transactions (see Roach Anleu, 1998). Taxation laws regulate business practices and give taxation agents the authority to compel businesses to adopt accounting methods and procedures that reduce risks and the likelihood of business fraud (Braithwaite, 2003; Grabosky, 1996). Aviation regulators compel airport management corporations to adopt standard screening practices that are thought to reduce illegal importation, immigration and terrorism (Seidenstat, 2004). Governments also place an onus on many other professionals (such as medical practitioners, tax advisors, auditors, lawyers, psychologists) to report suspected law infractions with legal action possible for failure to take action (see Grabosky, 1996; Roach Anleu, 1998). In these examples, legislation or government policy compels a third party to engage in practices that are potentially outside of their routine activities in an effort to prevent or control crime problems. This multiplicity of regulatory "nodes" creates unprecedented opportunities for the police to forge partnerships to control and prevent crime.

In our book, we are principally interested in the way that the public police intersect with willing, mandated and/or unwilling partners (including regulatory "nodes") to control and prevent crime problems. Indeed, the widespread, global adoption of regulation through third parties is of great interest to our analysis of third party policing. Throughout our book we pay particular attention to the processes and practices of the police as the initiators of third party policing. Third party policing, as we define and describe it, involves the police knowing (or being informed of) some general legal levers, identifying a problem that could be alleviated with a legal lever and co-opting non-offending persons or organizations to take on a crime control role. In order to insure compliance, the police motivate third parties to cooperate by drawing on some type of "lever" that, in our definition, includes a range of criminal, civil and regulatory laws and provisions (see Chapter 4).

But there are many unanswered questions in our analysis of the processes of third party policing (see Chapter 8). Of central interest to us is to explore and understand the intrinsic motivations that the public police have for initiating third party policing activities. Why are the police using third party policing as a way to control and prevent crime? Is it because of the global "success" (but see Goldstein, 2003) of problem-oriented policing? We suggest that proliferation of third party policing is not driven by the police. It is not tied to the marketing of problem-oriented policing. It is not an articulated doctrine. It is not something the police have set out to institutionalize. Rather, we argue that external forces, driven by the societal transformation toward responsive regulation and the blurring of criminal and civil laws, have compelled the police to initiate third party policing activities. The push towards partnership policing is not so much the result of successful marketing of problem-oriented policing, but rather as a consequence of the external pressures on the police to forge partnerships to control crime problems. The police are not being "proactive" about forging partnerships, initiating third party policing activities and solving problems. Rather, we argue that third party policing is the manifestation of a reaction to external demands. Some of these external demands include the shift to neo-liberalism and notions of responsibilitization (see Chapter 1) starving the police of resources and channeling public monies into law and order policies where correctional options predominate (see Hinds, 2002: 132); creating new, regulatory agencies and agents that foist working relationships upon the police; a general "blurring" of the civil and criminal codes, that creates legitimate avenues for utilization of a wider range of legal levers (see Chapter 4). With these types of external demands, the police have little choice but to initiate third party policing, co-opt crime control partners and use as many legal levers as possible to control crime problems.

Focal point

The focal point of third party policing can be people (individuals or groups of people), places or "scenes," situations, crime targets (victims), accomplices, and props (instrumentalities) (see Cornish, 1994; Mazerolle and Roehl, 1998; Smith, 1998). Cornish's (1994) procedural analysis of offending (referred to as "scripts") is instructive in dissecting the range of focal points that third party policing can (and does) use to reduce crime opportunities (see also Smith, 1998). We use this model to describe the range of third party policing foci.

An example of third party policing with an individual person as the focus of attention is when the police coerce a property owner (proximate target) to evict a specific and troublesome tenant (ultimate target) from their rental accommodation. Alternatively, sometimes a crime target (victims or potential victims) may be the focal point of third party policing activities. For example, the police often convince domestic violence victims to take out restraining orders (injunctions) against their batterers. At other times, third party policing actions are geared to specifically target categories of people such as young people (White, 1998), gang members (Cheh, 1998) or drug dealers (National Crime Prevention Council, 1992). Third party policing efforts against people can also be further categorized as being targeted towards suspected or categories of potential offenders. We further discuss the variety of third party "targets" in the next section.

Whilst the behavior of people is always in the background of third party policing activities, alternative focal points of third party policing might be directed against criminogenic situations, props, or specific places or "scenes." More often than not targeted *places* are those locations that have been defined by the police as hot spots of crime (see Sherman et al., 1989). Drug dealing corners (Weisburd and Green, 1995), parks where gangs hang-out (Grogger, 2002; Maxson et al., 2003), and public malls (Delta Police Department, 1997) are typically the focal point of third party policing activities that address specific places as opposed to certain categories of people. In these instances, third party policing activities strive to control the activities of people frequenting public places with ongoing crime problems. For example, in San Fernando, California the city council passed an "urgency" ordinance where a $250 fine could be imposed if a known gang member entered Las Palmas Park. The ordinance provided for a two-step approach toward eliminating the gang problem in the park. Known gang members were given written notice not to re-enter the park and were fined $250 if they were subsequently found in the park (see National Crime Prevention Council, 1996: 43).

Another focal point of third-party policing activities includes situations that give rise to criminogenic activity. Examples of criminogenic situations include bus stop placements that facilitate strong-arm robberies (Braga et al., 1999) as well as serving and pricing practices for licensed premises that lead to bar room violence (Homel and Clark, 1994). In third party policing, the police utilize the techniques of situational crime prevention (see Clarke, 1992) to coerce third parties (government agencies, liquor licensing authorities etc) to change the locations of bus stops or alter the serving and pricing practices of problematic bars. In the background of third party initiatives to engage government agencies (including statutory authorities and local governments) to cooperate with the police are threats of "duty of care" civil suits and other legal initiatives that rest on the liability of those who create "unsafe environments" (see Sherman et al., 1989). Third party policing is thus defined and further differentiated from situational crime prevention because third party policing relies exclusively on the coercion (or implicit threat of coercion) used by the police to recruit place managers or their crime prevention partners.

The final focal point of third party policing activities includes what Cornish (1994) and Smith (1998) have described as "props controllers" or those who have some control over the instrumentalities of crime. Props can include spray paint cans, cars, bogus identification cards, mobile phones or any other "prop" that might be used in the commission of a crime. This construct is analogous to Clarke's (1992) situational crime prevention technique referred to as controlling facilitators. In third party policing, the police co-opt the "props controller" – or the person who controls the instrumentalities of the crime – as the third party and draw upon legal regulations and statutes to insure their compliance with the police in dealing with the crime problem.

Ultimate targets

The ultimate targets of third party policing efforts are people involved in deviant behavior. The ultimate targets of third party policing could include those persons engaged in any type of criminal behavior including domestic violence, white-collar offending, street crime or drug dealing. The preponderance of ultimate targets of third party policing (at least in our review) are typically those offenders who are vulnerable, disadvantaged and/or marginalized. Young people (see White, 1998), gang members (Grogger, 2002), drug users and dealers (Green, 1996), truants (Gregory, 2003), vandals (Smith, 1996), and petty criminals (National Crime Prevention Council, 1992) typically feature as the ultimate targets of third party policing.

In a review of newspapers, journals, reports and web sites (see Chapters 5 and 6), we note that much of third party policing is geared towards controlling low level criminal offending (ultimate targets). For example, in Australia, young people graduating from high school celebrate the end of school with what is known as "Schoolies Week" (not unlike "Spring Break" in the United States and the United Kingdom). High school students from around Australia flock to coastal cities such as the Gold Coast in South-East Queensland. The usual problems of underage drinking, public drunkenness, violent behavior and sexual violations occur. The police on the Gold Coast have engaged in third party policing practices by proactively seeking out high-risk apartment managers and "suggesting" to them that they include "lease conditions" for the high school graduates when they rent apartments for a week during "Schoolies Week." The lease conditions have been known to include rules that prohibit visitors to the apartment after 10 pm at night, prohibition on alcohol on the premises, and single sex apartment rentals.

Third party policing has also targeted street level drug market activity that is more likely to involve younger people than upper level drug trafficking (Reuter, MacCoun and Murphy, 1990) and injunctions that prohibit known gang members from associating with one another are more likely than not to target young people (Cheh, 1998). While we note the proliferation of third party policing activities that target young people, we also note that third party policing can be directed against any suspected or potential offender.

Proximate targets, burden bearers and third parties

On November 7, 2002 the Brisbane *Courier Mail* carried a front page story stating "Parents charged over truants" (*Courier Mail*, 2002b). Education reporter, Matthew Fynes-Clinton reports "parents of children who wag school are being prosecuted as part of a crackdown on truancy." The Education Department spokeswoman, however, informs readers that the prosecutions were launched as a "last resort" after an inter-agency team was formed comprising school principals, representatives from police juvenile aid and the Department of Families to visit homes and counsel parents and offenders. More recently, the *Courier Mail* reports that "two far north Queensland mothers have been placed on probation after a State Government blitz on truancy" (Gregory, 2003).

Holding parents accountable for the delinquent actions of their children and using the threat of prosecution (or actually instigating a prosecution) against a parent is an example of how third party policing co-opts proximate targets (the parents) to control the behavior of the ultimate targets (the truants). Indeed, any person or entity that is engaged by the police to take on some type of role in controlling or preventing crime could potentially be identified as a third party or what Buerger and Mazerolle (1998) refer to as "proximate targets," what Mazerolle and Roehl (1998) have referred to as "burden-bearers" and what Goldstein (1990) refers to as entities of social control. These are the people or entities that are co-opted (or coerced) by the police and who carry the burden for initiating some type of action that is expected to alter the conditions that allow crime activity to grow or exist. Scott (2000: 156) provides the following examples: parents over children, teachers over children, landlords over tenants, employers over employees, contractors over sub-contractors, universities over fraternities, friends over one another, neighbors over one another, youth over one another, banks over account holders, bar owners over patrons, motel/hotel owners over guests, businesses over private security companies, military commanders over soldiers. A defining feature of third party policing is the presence of some type of third person (or third collectivity) that is utilized by the police in an effort to prevent or control crime.

Proximate targets of third party policing are generally stakeholders, guardians (Cohen and Felson, 1979), intimate handlers (Felson, 1994) or place managers (Eck, 1994) who are identified by the police as being useful conduits for controlling crime problems. Nonetheless, the roles in third party policing can change rapidly, they can be varied depending on the situation, are sometimes reciprocal in nature and idiosyncratic to the problem at hand. Indeed, the proximate targets of a third party policing activity in one context may become the ultimate targets of third party policing in another context. Moreover, cooperative police partners in one context might become hostile "partners" in another context. We suggest that the dynamic nature of third party policing is testament to the fluidity and chaotic nature of crime prevention and crime control more generally.

Nonetheless, variations on the third party policing theme are important. In its simplest form (and the most common), the police identify a "third party" (e.g. a property owner) and use some type of "lever" (i.e. a legal provision) to coerce the third party to bring about a change in the routine activities of the offending parties. In some instances, the police might partner with a multiplicity of third party nodes such as another regulatory agency (e.g. local council inspector, insurance company) to coerce the third party (property owner) to change the criminogenic conditions of their property. The police might even contract out the crime control responsibility to a regulatory authority (e.g. local council inspector) and use the regulatory authority to take the lead in convincing and coercing the property owner to change the conditions.

Legal levers

Another defining feature of third party policing is that there must be some sort of legal basis – or what we would call a "legal lever" – to shape police coercive efforts to engage third parties to take on crime prevention or crime control roles (see Chapter 4 for a more detailed exposition of the legal basis to Third Party Policing). We argue that legal provisions shape and define third party policing processes. We suggest (see Chapter 4) that third party policing is distinguished from problem-oriented policing insofar that third party policing generally begins with a legal lever (e.g. police knowledge of a legal provision) that is matched to a problem (or similar problems). In contrast, problem-oriented policing begins with the problem and then subsequently matches a response (or responses) that is expected to solve the problem.

The most common legal mechanisms used in third party policing include local, state and federal statutes (including municipal ordinances and town bylaws), health and safety codes, uniform building standards, and, liquor licensing and a wide variety of statutory and common law programs using injunctive remedies (e.g. domestic violence restraining orders, gang injunctions, drug nuisance abatement). We point out that the legal basis does not necessarily need to be directly related to crime prevention or crime control. Indeed, many third party policing practices utilize laws and regulations that were not designed with crime control or crime prevention in mind (e.g. Health and Safety codes, Uniform Building Standards). For many third party policing activities, the legal basis that provides the coercive power for police to gain the "cooperation" of third parties derives from delegated legislation and obscure, non-criminal sources.

The legal basis for third party policing is what Herman Goldstein (1990) refers to as the pinnacle of the problem response triangle. Indeed, in our ten-year review of problem-oriented policing submissions to the Goldstein Awards from 1993 to 2003, we calculated that slightly less than 50 percent of problem-solving responses involve what we would define as a third party policing initiative.

Types of sanctions and penalties

The types of sanctions and penalties that result from third party policing activities vary greatly depending on the legal lever activated. Some common third party policing penalties include court-ordered repairs of properties, fines, forfeiture of property (see Cheh, 1998) or forced sales to meet fines and penalties, eviction, padlocking or temporary closure (typically up to a year) of a rented residential or commercial property, license restrictions and/or suspensions, movement restrictions, lost income from restricted hours and ultimately arrest and incarceration (see Mazerolle and Roehl, 1998). Oftentimes, several civil remedies and sanctions may be initiated simultaneously to solve one problem.

One reason why third party policing activities occur more at the street-level of enforcement rather than being aimed at corporations and businesses is that the sanctions chosen and used by the police generally carry relatively low levels of penalties. For example, in Queensland, parents of truants can be fined $375 for a first offence and $750 for subsequent offences. The police, in accessing these low-level civil remedies, can use volume of sanctions over quality to gain the crime control edge that they seek.

The use of property forfeiture is one of the more likely penalties that can be utilized against both lower level as well as upper level criminal activity. Cheh (1998) describes several cases where civil asset forfeiture statutes have been used against third parties (e.g. parents, boat owners) to control the low level illegal activity of their children or clients. For example, in United States v. 1978 Chrysler LeBaron Station Wagon, 1986 inattentive parents lost the family car because their teenager smoked marijuana in the vehicle. In

United States v 141st St Corp., 1990 a parent's home was seized because their son was selling cocaine from the premises. And in Calera-Toledo v Pearson Yacht Leasing Co., 1974 a boat rental business forfeited a yacht because a rental party on board used marijuana. In this case, the Supreme Court of the United States held that ". . . forfeiture laws do not violate due process simply because they apply to the property of innocent owners" (Cheh, 1998: 57).

The low-level "volume" approach of many third party policing activities applies the principles of zero tolerance (see Cordner, 1998; Katz, Webb and Schaefer, 2001) to gain control over growing crime problems. For example, the police in New York City, under the reign of Commissioner Bratton, brushed the dust from long-shelved laws to co-opt third parties and "crack-down" on misdemeanor offenses (see Kelling and Coles, 1996). Earlier in New York, the Padlock Law Enforcement Program enforced an ancient law that authorized the police commissioner to padlock premises that were "deemed a public nuisance" due to involvement in a variety of illegal activities, including drug sales (Ward, 1987). The program evolved from an initiative started by the Westside Crime Prevention Association, a group of neighbors in New York City, who in 1986 had exhausted all traditional avenues to eliminate drug activity at a local crack house. A private attorney, working pro bono on the association's behalf, filed a lawsuit against the property owner based on a 125-year-old state statute originally enacted to control "bawdy houses" (i.e., prostitution establishments). The statute defined a nuisance property as any real property used for "illegal trade, business, or manufacture," and outlined civil sanctions (up to a $5000 penalty) that a property owner could face if the owner "does not in good faith diligently" move to evict the tenant (Real Property Actions and Proceedings Law, Section 715). The neighborhood association won its case: the tenant was evicted, the house was sold, and the legal costs of the association were paid from the proceeds (see Mazerolle and Roehl, 1998).

Real estate is often targeted in third party policing activities. In Miami, Florida, for example, the police department organized a task force designed to control crack houses by seizing the real estate if owners did not cooperate by evicting drug selling tenants and reclaiming the buildings. After publicizing the program through the successful forfeiture of an apartment building notorious for freebasing activities, the city of Miami offered low-interest loans to owners of similar buildings to reclaim the buildings from drug dealers (Dickson, 1988).

Similarly, police in Seattle, Washington have used the civil law as a means of controlling crack houses. Following passage of two laws in 1988 designed to assist in drug enforcement (one an abatement law, the other an eviction law), the department designated two detectives and support personnel working with one city attorney to investigate and control crack houses. In its first two years, the program resulted in over 625 actions against crack houses; over 90 percent were resolved through owner action. That is, rather than risk their property, owners evict tenants involved in the drug market (Ferguson and Fitzsimons, 1990). We discuss the range and debates of the legal basis of third party policing further in Chapter 4.

Tools and techniques of coercion

Dozens of examples can be provided to illustrate the processes by which third parties are recruited and used by the police. Against the backdrop of a legal foundation to force a third party to cooperate (see Chapter 4), the police operate on a continuum to engage third parties in their crime prevention or crime control activities. At the more benign end of the spectrum, the police can approach third parties and politely ask them to cooperate. The police might consult with members of the community as well as local property owners and ask them about ways that they see fit to control an existing crime problem or help them to alter underlying conditions that the police believe might lead to future crime problems. At this low-key, benign end of the spectrum, the ultimate sanctions that might be unleashed on third parties most likely go unnoticed. The police may, themselves consciously utilize their persuasive powers, yet not be conscious of the alternative methods of coercion that they may resort to if the third party target proves to be an unwilling participant.

At the more potent end of the spectrum the police coerce third parties to participate in their crime control activities by threatening or actually initiating actions that compel the third party to cooperate. We point out that there are several stages in the forcible initiation of third parties in taking a crime control role: the first stage may involve a building services agency issuing citations to a property owner following building inspections of their property (see Green, 1996). The latter stages of this most coercive practice involve the initiation of prosecutions against the non-compliant land-owner and ultimately court-forced compliance by the third party (see Green, 1996).

The apparent influence of "third parties" in creating or supporting crim-inogenic conditions might be conscious or unconscious, it might be explicit or implicit, and it might be planned or unplanned. The police might be wholly indifferent to the relationship that a third party has with the crime problem. On the other hand, the police may in fact be sensitive to the vulnerable situation a third party may be placed in whilst contributing to a crime problem. The non-English speaking, ethnic storeowner who fears retaliation from local drug dealers is a case in point. The storeowner might be recalcitrant in communicating with the police, he may lie to the police about the problem to avoid conflict and he may actively obstruct police efforts to clean up the drug dealing outside his store. If the police are indifferent to the storeowner's vulnerability, the police may unleash civil remedies to force the storeowner to cooperate with the police. For example, the police might organize health and building inspectors to cite the storeowner for health violations (e.g. the temperature of the refrigerator may not be up to code) or building code violations (e.g. the stairs leading to the store are not regulation height and length). Alternatively, the police may engage the help from an Ethnic Task Force to help sort through the vulnerabilities felt by the storeowner and gently convince the storeowner to cooperate with the police in taking a stand against the local drug dealers. The carrot or the sledge-hammer approach to co-opting third parties is generally the two ends of the spectrum that characterize the tools and techniques used by the police to engage a third party.

Types of implementation

There are many different ways that the police implement third party policing practices including episodic, ad hoc use of the principles of third party policing. Alternatively, the police can utilize the principles of third party policing within the context of problem-oriented policing or situational crime prevention programs. Problem-oriented policing provides a management infrastructure (see Goldstein, 1990) and step-wise approach to solving a crime problem (Eck and Spelman, 1987) of which third party policing might be just one of the responses used by the police to solve a problem (see also Goldstein, 2003; Scott, 2000). Situational crime prevention offers the police with a range of ideas and techniques for reducing crime opportunities (Clarke, 1992; 1995). Indeed, third party policing can be conceived within any one of the twenty-five techniques of crime prevention suggested by Cornish and Clarke (2003).

When third party policing is implemented as part of police problem solving or crime prevention efforts, the legal provisions of the third party "tool" dictates the procedural and strategic foundation for how opportunities might get blocked and problems solved. The procedures that underpin the legal provisions used in third party policing specify the form of third party policing interventions. This stands in contrast to problem-oriented policing and situational crime prevention where the nature of the problem specifies the choice and form of the implemented responses. While third party policing is merely one of many categories of problem-solving responses or situational techniques, it is defined and differentiated from other crime prevention tactics or problem solving responses through the sources of its coercive power (see Buerger and Mazerolle, 1998) and, more generally, through the intrinsic links that third party policing has with global transformations towards responsive regulation. In third party policing, the police convince, coerce, manipulate and draw upon laws and civil remedies to engage third parties to take on crime control or crime prevention respon-sibilities that they had not previously initiated of their own free will. A key defining feature of third party policing is that there must be some sort of "legal lever" that shapes police coercive efforts to engage a third party to take on a crime prevention or crime control role. That does not mean to say that problem-oriented policing or situational crime prevention cannot be coercive in nature. They can and they are depending on the problem or situation (see Goldstein, 2003; Scott, 2000). What we highlight in our book are the links of third party policing to the global trends in regulation. We suggest that third party policing has not proliferated by accident or through grassroots efforts to institutionalize problem-oriented policing. Rather, we believe the proliferation of third party policing with its concomitant com-plexities, dilemmas and wide-reaching scope parallels trends in regulation and also the blurring of criminal and civil laws.

Third party policing is often initiated within the management infrastruc-ture (see Goldstein, 1990) and step-wise approach of problem-oriented policing to solve crime problems (Eck and Spelman, 1987). Importantly, however, third party policing can, and often does, operate entirely outside of any problem-solving activity or program. Indeed, in many instances of third party policing, the police do not engage in any type of analysis of a crime problem, but rather react to the crime problem using a civil remedy solution that works through a third party to reduce a crime problem. In our systematic review of the evaluation literature, we calculated that less than 50 percent of problem-oriented policing projects used a third party tactic and that less than one third of all third party interventions we identify in Chapters 5 and 6 were part of a problem-oriented policing project.

As with problem-oriented policing, some third party policing activities overlap with situational crime prevention and aim to alter the situational contributors to a crime problem. Situational responses to crime opportuni-ties provide an important framework for identifying and implementing third party policing initiatives. Situational crime prevention theory (see Clarke, 1992), however, is silent on the sources and targets of coercion and abstains from identifying the *processes* for achieving situational controls. Our evolving theory of third party policing (see Chapter 8) fills this void and illuminates the various dimensions and processes of third party policing practices.

Policing through what we call "third parties" also shares common ground with Routine Activity Theory concepts of capable guardians, intimate handlers and place management (Eck, 1994; Felson, 1995). Routine Activity Theory posits that direct-contact predatory crimes occur when motivated offenders and suitable targets (or victims) converge in space and time in the absence of capable guardians. The original presentation of routine activities theory suggests that targets are not equally distributed in space and time, that victimization is not the function of random events, and that broad social transformations have implications for creating criminal opportunities (Cohen and Felson, 1979).

Recognizing the importance of place attributes in explaining criminal events, Eck (1994) extended routine activities theory to address the significance of amenable places and the role of "place managers" who discourage criminal events at specific locations. A "place manager" refers to those individuals such as building managers, security guards, and homeowners who discourage crimes and reduce opportunities for criminal events through their presence and daily activities at specific places (Eck, 1994; Felson, 1995). This extension of routine activities theory suggests that opportunities for crime are not simply created by motivated offenders (who have ineffective handlers) but rather emerge when locations are not well managed and controlled by place managers. Eck's (1994) extension of routine activities theory suggests, therefore, that crime events (like drug dealing) occur when motivated offenders, who have ineffective handlers, choose amenable places that do not have effective place managers.

The goal of third party policing could thus be defined as using legal levers to create place managers, effective handlers, and capable guardians in places and situations with criminal opportunities or where crime problems already exist. In using third party policing the police might recruit place managers voluntarily using their persuasive powers, but make no overt threat to the potential place manager. Alternatively, the police might identify a reluctant potential place manager and then foist upon this third party the responsibility for place management with the threat of legal action should the person refuse to cooperate. Again, we argue that it is external forces (as opposed to internal police policies) that have driven the police to co-opt place managers, recruit effective handlers and engage capable guardians to control and prevent crime.

Third-party policing is mandated by governments now in some jurisdictions. For example, the crime and disorder reduction partnerships established under Britain's *Crime and Disorder Act 1998* require police and local authorities to work together to formulate and implement strategies for the reduction of crime and disorder in their local areas (Loader, 2000). This form of implementation has the potential to entrench third party tactics and thus requires a good deal of thought about the potential side effects (see Chapter 7).

Another way that the police might implement third party policing is through "contracting out" crime control. In this situation, the police might recruit a multitude of third party "nodes" (e.g. city inspectorate, an insurance company) and initiate early efforts to control crime. At some stage in the crime control process, the police might contract with this third party to take over the job of controlling crime and step to one side. In this situation, the police abdicate their crime control responsibility to this "third party" contractor and leave the crime control arena for the third party to manage.

The most common manifestation of third party policing, however, is the ad hoc utilization of third party principles initiated in an unconscious manner by patrol officers who are being pushed (more than likely from the media, community members and external stakeholders) to find a way to solve a problem. These police are simply "flying by the seats of their pants," there is no script for them to follow, no police department policy that they are working within, and generally very little accountability for their actions. The police are working within the law, but using the non-criminal laws to control crime with little regard to the possible negative side effects (see Chapter 7). It is this ad hoc category of third party policing implementation that most interests us in this book.

Summing up

This chapter has sought to elucidate the various dimensions of third party policing and identify a number of key themes that are expanded upon in later chapters. We identify essentially two necessary conditions that must be satisfied in order for a police tactic to be defined as "third party policing." First, there must be a third person or entity that works with the police to control or prevent crime either willingly or subsequent to some pressure from the police. The second necessary condition is that some type of legal lever must either be in the background or overtly used to induce the third party to take some crime control responsibility. Sometimes these legal levers are used by regulators (e.g. building inspectors, local councils) and sometimes the legal levers are used directly by the police to co-opt private citizens (e.g. parental responsibility laws, restraining orders) to gain control over an ultimate target. The most important message that we sought to deliver with this chapter is that whilst we identify some basic criteria and conditions that characterize third party policing, we understand third party policing to operate on a continuum. For example, sometimes the coercion of a third party is undertaken in a cooperative, conciliatory manner. At other times, cooperation from a third party is made only after legal action is taken. Sometimes the penalties attached to legal provisions are quite small, and at other times, the financial implications of policing through a third party might be financially devastating (e.g. asset forfeiture, business closure etc).

The spectrum of third party policing activities is broad and is likely to become more diverse in the future. As Braithwaite (2003) observes: ". . . regulatory models will increasingly translate across the fractured branches of social control to shape new forms of policing and punishment" (p. 23). Third party policing, as a form of regulatory-based police activity, is thus likely to become a dominant mode of police action into the twenty-first century.

CHAPTER 4

In the shadow of the law

In previous chapters we have shown how, from the second half of the twentieth century, there have been significant trends in the governance, regulation and policing of contemporary society. These trends rely on risk identification to achieve social, economic and political goals. In criminal justice, this has meant less focus on the identification, prosecution and rehabilitation of guilty individuals, and more on identifying, preventing or reducing potential crime risks. Also, the broadening scope of governance has involved non-traditional agencies and individuals in the process of crime control and prevention, and placed traditional agents such as police in a new role. Police now partner with other state and non-state agencies in crime control and prevention networks. Third party policing occurs when police strategies to control or prevent crime involve partnerships or networks, voluntary or coerced, police-initiated or directed by government, with non-offending third parties (such as regulators, business owners, landlords, community groups, schools and parents).

Third party policing occurs within a legal framework that establishes the authority for police to partner with or coerce third parties, the contexts in which they can do that, and the types of intervention this may produce. Indeed, we argue that it is the legal basis of third party policing that both defines it as a unique strategy and distinguishes it from other policing interventions, most notably problem-oriented policing. This chapter begins with an overview of the types of legal frameworks in which third party policing can occur. Here we describe the range of statutes, delegated or subordinate legislation or regulations, contractual relationships and tort laws that have been used to facilitate third party policing. The distinction between the types of laws discussed in this chapter and the normal criminal law is that criminal law is typically directed at *participants* in wrongdoing – whether as principals, accessories or conspirators. In this chapter we discuss laws and legal mechanisms or levers directed at willing or unwilling *non-offending third parties*, to facilitate or coerce them into helping control the behavior of offending ultimate targets.

The chapter makes sense of these frameworks by looking at the use of legal levers in a range of contexts in which third party policing has arisen. The types of legal levers used can be criminal or civil, and indeed as discussed below, the distinction between these categories is becoming increasingly blurred (see also Cheh, 1991, 1998). The legal levers may be established specifically for the particular crime control purpose, or may be directed at some other issue but co-opted by police to achieve crime control or prevention goals. The ultimate targets sought to be controlled also vary widely, but as discussed previously, certain categories are common, including drug houses, public housing estates, young people, street prostitutes, bars, beggars and panhandlers. All of these categories involve what police typically see as *criminogenic individuals* (such as drug users, young people, prostitutes, racial minorities, homeless or mentally ill people), or *criminogenic places* (for example, public housing estates, bars, malls). While the law provides a facilitative framework for third party policing, it can also impose barriers, and we also review the range of legal barriers to third party policing.

This analysis is illustrative only, to show the relationship between law and third party policing. There are many other laws and contexts in which third party policing is possible. Our goal is not to be exhaustive, but to point out the potential range of third party policing, drawing broadly on examples from Australasia, Britain, the United States and Canada, and also noting any significant differences in practice between these jurisdictions.

Legal frameworks for third party policing

Various legal frameworks provide the authority for third party policing and set out the types of interventions, or levers, that can be used, the necessary preconditions for their use, and whom they can be directed against. These interventions have different outcomes, ranging from criminal prosecution through civil and regulatory penalties, damages or compensation, restitution orders or injunctions. The type of outcome is determined by the categories of law from which the interventions are derived, including criminal law, regulatory law and private civil law. Before describing in detail the legal frameworks of third party policing, the next section briefly examines the changing nature of these traditional broad categories of law and their impact on third party policing.

The converging nature of law

As referred to in Chapter 2, there were once strong distinctions between the criminal law, directed at wrongdoers who commit morally repugnant offences, and regulatory law, directed at maintaining the orderly conduct of legal activities (Cotterrell, 1992). A third category was private law. While both criminal and regulatory law were used by the state to regulate public life, individuals used private law to resolve private and domestic disputes. This historical distinction in rationale saw the evolution of different methods and actors to achieve the different goals of each system. For example, the criminal law involved detection and prosecution; regulatory law tended to use negotiation, inspection and administrative sanctions; and private law focused on civil court actions to resolve disputes.

The differences between the traditional categories of law are summarized in the first part of Table 4.1. These differences lead to contrasting styles of justice (Roach Anleu, 1998), also shown in Table 4.1. The criminal justice system's style focuses on the violation of laws and the guilt and punishment of individual offenders. The regulatory law system focuses on the consequences of conduct – the creation of business obligations enforced by the payment of fines or limits on the right to continue in business. Private law focuses on the creation and enforcement of domestic and private obligations. But with the trends in governance and regulation discussed in earlier chapters, these distinctions are being eroded, as shown in the second part of Table 4.1.

Increasingly, the criminal law makes use of civil processes and remedies, while in both regulatory and private law serious misbehaviors are criminalized. For example, as discussed in detail later in this chapter, schemes for the forfeiture of assets gained through suspected criminal activities use civil law processes to prevent and control criminal behavior. Similarly, private law remedies such as injunctions are used to control the criminal activities of gangs, and building or health regulations are used to shut down drug houses. On the other hand, criminal sanctions are now imposed for serious regulatory breaches – for example, in Australia, the *Environmental Protection Act 1994* (Qld) and *Workplace Health and Safety Act 1995* (Qld) authorize imprisonment for five years and three years respectively for offences against their regulatory schemes (see also Baldwin, 2004, on the trend to punitive measures and criminalization in regulation). And areas formerly regarded as purely private are now also increasingly subject to regulation or criminalization. For example, in Australia criminal sanctions apply to

Table 4.1 *Changes in categories of law*

Focus	Criminal	Regulatory	Private
Traditional			
Goal	Detection, prosecution, punishment, rehabilitation of offenders	Orderly conduct of economically desirable activities	Dispute resolution in private financial and family activities
Activities	Morally repugnant offences	Business activities	Commercial and domestic interactions
Targets	Individual offenders	Businesses	Private individuals and groups in dispute
Methods	Investigation, arrest, criminal trial	Conciliation, negotiation, self-regulation, inspection, limited prosecution	Private court action to enforce rights under contracts and tort
Outcomes	Fines, incarceration	Penalties, rectification orders, licence revocation	Damages, injunctions, specific performance
Actors	Police, prosecutors, courts, correctional staff	Regulatory agencies, local governments, industry associations	Individuals in private relationships, civil courts
Style	Guilt and punishment for individual offences	Creation of business obligations, consequences enforced by sanctions	Creation of private obligations, consequences enforced by sanctions
Current			
Goal	Identification and prevention of potential crime risks, detection and prosecution of offenders	Identification and prevention of potential regulatory risks	Prevention and resolution of private disputes
Activities	Morally repugnant offences	Business activities	Commercial and domestic interactions
Targets	Groups and places with high risk of crime, offenders	Businesses and industries at risk of non-compliance	Individuals and groups at risk of or in dispute

Table 4.1 (*cont.*)

Focus	Criminal	Regulatory	Private
Methods	Investigation, arrest, trial, surveillance, statistics, profiling, incapacitation, responsibilization	Codes of practice, reporting, statistics, audit, enforcement pyramids, responsive regulation, criminalization	Private court action to enforce contract and tort rights, statutory remedies, criminalization
Outcomes	Fines, incarceration, forfeiture, injunctions, preventive detention, behavior contracts	Penalties, rectification orders, license revocation fines, incarceration, damages, injunctions	Damages, injunctions, specific performance, fines, incarceration
Actors	Police, prosecutors, courts, correctional staff, local governments, health and housing agencies, community groups, forensic specialists	Regulatory agencies, local governments, industry associations, consumer groups, international regulators	Individuals in private relationships, government and community agencies, police, prosecutors, courts, tribunals, welfare agencies
Style	Guilt and punishment, consequences enforced by sanctions, therapeutic, restorative	Guilt and punishment, consequences enforced by sanctions	Guilt and punishment, consequences enforced by sanctions, therapeutic

some breaches of child custody arrangements under the *Family Law Act 1975* (Cth), and most employment contracts and sporting associations are liable for anti-discrimination remedies under federal and state laws. And in the traditionally private area of family relationships, there has been a movement in many jurisdictions to provide civil remedies, such as non-contact or domestic violence orders, and to increased criminalization, through pro-prosecution policing policies, and specialized domestic violence courts and tribunals.

We argue that Table 4.1 shows the dynamic convergence of types of law and legal methods that is occurring, so that it has become increasingly difficult to describe neat categories of criminal, regulatory and private law. As well as converging categories of law, the style of social control embedded in laws is also changing. Roach Anleu (1998) suggests that boundaries are becoming less distinct because increasingly a compensatory approach is becoming dominant, including in the area of criminal justice, with judicial institutions gradually being incorporated into a continuum of mostly regulatory apparatuses. Our analysis is slightly different, as shown in Table 4.1. While criminal law makes increasing use of regulatory approaches, it is also experimenting with restorative and therapeutic approaches, seen in community conferencing systems and drug courts and mental health courts respectively, where there is an attempt to restore disturbed social relationships, or deal with underlying problems. Also, as discussed, regulatory systems now adopt a criminal justice style for some breaches, and private law makes use of therapeutic approaches, in domestic violence courts for instance. Rather than regulation and compensation becoming the primary approach of law, our thesis is one of general convergence, where categories have become blurred and methods borrowed and shared.

The implication of this convergence for criminal justice is that it is no longer limited to the sanctions and processes of the criminal law, but increasingly can draw on regulatory actions and private law mechanisms to achieve its goals. There are several reasons why regulatory and private law have become attractive for police and other criminal justice operatives. First, there has been a growing social and governmental realization that criminal law has not been particularly effective at controlling difficult social problems (Cheh, 1998). Removing individual offenders, who are easily replaced by others, does not solve entrenched crime problems. But civil and private mechanisms can target the support and incentive systems for crime, rather than just individual criminal offences. For example, civil forfeiture laws can remove the economic infrastructures supporting criminal enterprises, as well as the financial incentives for the crime activity.

Second, these alternative methods suit the criminal justice system's increasing focus on prevention and problem-solving approaches. Instead of just reactive investigations and prosecutions, criminal justice systems can become more proactive and monitor criminogenic individuals and situations, possibly intervening before crime actually occurs. For example, the monitoring of large cash transactions, the distribution of methadone or agricultural and veterinary chemicals capable of being used in bombs, can indicate the risk of organized and drug crime, or terrorism. Unsupervised children can be removed from malls and other criminogenic situations using truancy laws, or special closing times or procedures instituted in nightclubs to prevent late-night violence and disorder. New schemes instituted in some Australian jurisdictions take a multi-pronged approach to preventing crime by children under the influence of inhalants. Retailers in problem areas voluntarily agree not to sell spray cans or glue to juveniles, and police are empowered to seize these products, and to remove children affected by inhalants from public places to a place of safety, such as a hospital, shelter or home (for example, see ss371A-C of the *Police Powers and Responsibilities Act 2000* (Qld)). The objective is to limit the precursor to criminal activity, and not just respond to the activity itself. Retailers avoid disorder caused by affected children, and also the threat of more punitive regulation if voluntary schemes fail, while children are not prosecuted for their substance abuse, but directed to treatment or care facilities. Similarly, curfews directed at keeping young people out of public areas at night, or the use of regulatory schemes to shut down brothels or gambling dens (Cheh, 1998), are aimed at prevention.

As well as improving effectiveness and prevention, the third attraction of civil law for criminal justice purposes is that the involvement of regulatory and community partners has fitted with the movement to networks and partnerships (Mazerolle and Roehl, 1998), by involving a much larger range of state, business and community actors in the process of crime prevention and control. Networks spread the responsibility for crime to a whole range of government and non-government actors, as well as enabling police to draw on the special expertise, skills, procedures and powers of these other agencies and groups. The emphasis on whole-of-government approaches means that these networks are increasingly imposed on police and other government agencies.

The fourth advantage of civil mechanisms and penalties is procedural: they provide an expanded range of sanctions and incentives, lower standard of proof, and less rights-based constraints (such as due cause and process requirements, especially in the United States). It is this factor that is most problematic for the cooption of civil law for criminal justice purposes, with courts having to determine the appropriate boundaries for the operation of the protections of the criminal law. In addition, as Michael Buerger (1998: 96–97) points out, there is a further problem of the legitimacy of the use of civil law to achieve criminal justice targets, particularly when it is achieved by police cooption. He suggests that police intervention in private or business situations may lack the authority created when they respond to a traditional call for service. The result is that police involved in new forms of intervention have to develop new forms of authority, or risk resistance. These issues are taken up again in the discussion of accountability in Chapter 7. In the next section, we analyze more precisely the type of legal frameworks that can support third party policing.

Legal frameworks

Despite the general convergence of categories of law we have just described, the source of law used in third party policing interventions remains important. While criminal justice can look to regulatory and private law to borrow different levers for intervention, those levers come with conditions on their use which can only be understood by reference to their origins. For example, to understand the extent to which injunctions can be used for criminal justice purposes, it is necessary to understand the legal framework from which that tool is borrowed as well as the criminal justice situation in which it is to be used.

Table 4.2 presents a summary of frameworks identified in our analysis. The frameworks have been categorized first by the source of legal authority for the third party policing activity, that is whether it is statute-based, arises under subordinate legislation (or delegated legislation, regulations, by-laws, ordinances etc), from a contract, or under tort law. In each category of framework we analyze the source of authority, because this determines the legal basis and limits of any third party policing arrangement. The second column of the table looks at the extent of application of the framework, because this determines who the third parties can be; that is either anyone in the community, those in a specified community, or those in a special relationship (contractual or involving a duty of care) with the ultimate targets of the third party policing action. The third column describes the potential range of outcomes of each category of action. The fourth column suggests how each legal framework produces potential levers for third party policing interventions, and the types of intervention this might lead to. The final column lists potential third parties capable of being targeted by police for each intervention.

Our analysis in Table 4.2 is crucial to unpacking the processes and legal levers used in third party policing, because it describes the scope, usages and possible sanctions for the types of lever most frequently used. Any additional levers can be analyzed in the same way, but our analysis is a critical foundation for understanding third party policing and ensuring that appropriate levers are used in appropriate situations. One problem in trying to classify these levers is that there is a great deal of jurisdictional difference in what types of legal frameworks are directed at specific criminal problems, so that curfews and truancy laws are generally imposed by state legislation in Australia, but local government ordinance in the United States. The source of authority is important in understanding third party policing processes, for determining the proximate and ultimate targets, and for examining the type of outcome that may be used against these targets. But on the issue of determining whether third party policing interventions are possible and potentially useful, the type of framework is relatively unimportant – what matters is that *some* legal authority exists. It is the scope and targeting of the intervention that will be affected by the lever's place within the framework. So Table 4.2 gives a general indication of the types of intervention, which are then discussed further in the following section, by placing them in various contexts in which third party policing interventions are commonly used, and giving examples of the relevant legal instruments.

Legal levers used in third party policing interventions

Having summarized in Table 4.2 the types of legal levers used in third party policing, we now move on to discuss some of the more common applications of these levers. This is not an exhaustive discussion, but indicates the range of possible interventions. Because of the differences between the frameworks used in different jurisdictions, the discussion is structured around types of crime problems, rather than types of legal instrument (legislation, ordinance, contract or tort). Third party policing responses in any situation will depend on the problem being addressed, but also on the actual legal instruments available (or known) in the particular circumstances. The nature of the available legal levers will to a very large extent determine the type of third party policing possible in each situation. For consistency, we have broken the following discussion down into levers used in controlling drug problems, and other forms of crime, to be consistent with the evaluations considered in Chapters 5 and 6.

Drug houses, hot-spots and illegal laboratories

Federal, state and local authority laws or ordinances can be directed at shutting down premises repeatedly used for drug dealing or misuse. The third party policing focus here is on making property owners, landlords and tenants proximate targets responsible for the drug activities occurring at their premises. The ultimate targets of the intervention are producers and sellers of drugs. In the United States for example, federal statute 21 USC s.856 makes it unlawful for the owner, lessee, agent, employee or mortgagee of any building or room to knowingly and intentionally make it available for the manufacturing, storing, distributing or use of a controlled substance. Therefore, a landlord or tenant who otherwise takes no part in illegal activity commits an offence simply by knowingly making premises available, with penalties of up to twenty years' jail or significant fines.

Table 4.2 *Legal frameworks for third party policing*

Source of authority	Extent of application	Legal outcomes	Types of TPP levers and interventions	Third parties targeted by the intervention
Statute	General, or a specified population e.g. liquor retailers, parents, gangs.	Criminal or civil action leading to criminal or civil penalties, or administrative measures.	*Orders to control the behavior of offenders* e.g. anti-social behavior orders; truancy and gang orders; child welfare and domestic violence orders; mental health and vagrancy laws.	Parents, schools, non-offending gang members, institutions and shelters, housing authorities.
			Movement and association limits e.g. curfews; traffic, move-on and crowd control powers; probation and community corrections conditions limiting criminal contacts.	Parents, local councils, probations/corrections staff.
			Conduct licensing e.g. alcohol, firearms and prostitution licensing; pawn/second hand shops and dealers.	Retailers, service providers.
			Formalized surveillance e.g. offender notification; probation and community corrections reporting conditions.	Probations/corrections staff.
			Property controls e.g. drug house and rave site limits.	Property owners, local councils.
			Mandatory reporting e.g. methadone prescribing, cash transactions, chemical sales, child and spousal abuse.	Doctors, pharmacists, health funds, banks, retailers, schools.
			Civil forfeiture e.g. assets gained through crime, "hoon" cars.	Banks, vehicle licensers.

Subordinate legislation	General, within a specified area e.g. local council or housing authority area.	Criminal or civil action leading to criminal or civil penalties, refusal of consent, eviction, rectification orders, property forfeiture or confiscation.	*Orders under regulatory codes* e.g. building, fire, health, safety, noise, animals, liquor licensing, environmental, public housing, parking, venue by-laws and codes requiring closure, rectification, removal of hazards or restrictions on use.	Property and business owners, local councils, housing authorities, regulatory agencies.
			Product and service standards e.g. requiring vehicle immobilizers.	Manufacturers and service providers, standards associations.
			Controlled zones e.g. begging, busking, drug and alcohol free areas, limits on street prostitution.	Local councils, retailers and business owners, prostitutes.
Contract	Specific – parties to a contract.	Civil action for specific performance, damages or injunction, non-renewal of contract, eviction, loss of bond.	*Enforcement of conditions* e.g. property use and maintenance in private housing and commercial leases; crime reduction measures in service provision contracts e.g. lighting and security standards in commercial car parks.	Property and business owners and associations, housing authorities.
			Incentives e.g. insurance bonuses and rebates for crime prevention measures.	Landlords, insurers.
Tort	Specific – duty of care owed.	Civil action for damages or injunction.	*Actions for nuisance, trespass or negligence* e.g. against noise, physical disorder, pets, physical access, breach of duty of care, misfeasance.	Landlords, local councils, housing authorities, liquor retailers, licensed venues.

State laws may go even further. In California for example, the *Health and Safety Code* (s.11570) creates a specific statutory nuisance of using a building for drug purposes. This creates both public and private rights of action, available to city prosecutors and attorneys, and any state resident. Prior to filing an action, notice must be given to property owners requiring them to take action to remove the problem tenant. Failure to do so within the specified time can lead to a court awarding damages, costs, temporary restraining orders and partial eviction orders, as well as requiring improvements to security at the property, the owner's membership of an association, and property maintenance training. These actions may be taken against property owners without any requirement to prove their knowledge of the relevant drug activity occurring at the property (unlike the federal law discussed above, where prosecutors must prove knowledge).

Factors associated with or supportive of drug activity may also be targeted. For example, in the Oakland policing initiative discussed in more detail in Chapter 5, police and city council inspectors teamed to inspect and issue breach notices for derelict buildings suspected of being used as drug houses (Green, 1995). The breaches were of city building codes and ordinances to do with noise, rubbish and safety. Owners were required to secure their buildings, clean up litter, improve the physical environment, and evict tenants suspected by police of drug involvement. These actions could be taken without any requirement to prove the actual occurrence of illegal activity at the premises, or that the property owners had any knowledge of any such activity. So here, there is no requirement to prove knowledge of illegal activity, or even the fact that illegal activity has occurred.

Similarly, some cities have designed "nuisance abatement programs" formalizing multi-agency partnerships to combat drug crime. The Los Angeles Citywide Nuisance Abatement Program created in 1997, coordinated by the City Attorney, targets abandoned and nuisance properties via five core agencies: the police, City Attorney, building and safety department, housing department and planning department (Molidor, 2003). When police become aware that a specific place is a nuisance, for example through repeated calls for service, the property is inspected and breach notices issued. Enforcement sanctions include fines, boarding up of the property, seizure and forfeiture. In another instance in Vancouver, Canada, in cooperation with police, local dog pound officers strictly enforced a park ordinance against unleashed dogs in parks where drug dealers had allowed dogs to roam free to intimidate people from using the park (Vancouver Police Department, 2000).

In other examples, civil ordinances in the United States city of Buena Park require landlords to evict tenants convicted of certain crimes committed on the premises (Simpson, 1999; Weisel, 1990). In Joliet, a city ordinance requires landlords to cooperate with police requests to reduce criminal activity at their property, or face loss of a rental inspection certificate (Joliet Police Department, 2000).

Apart from removing the requirement to prove illegal activity or the property owner's knowledge, another approach is to reduce or remove procedural barriers to effective policing of drug houses. In New South Wales, Australia, state legislation combats drug houses (the *Police Powers (Drug Premises) Act 2001*). The Act creates offences to do with drug premises, and entitles police to apply for search warrants of premises on the basis of factors such as the presence of syringes, fortified doors and persons appearing to be affected by drugs. For the offences of being found on or near, or organizing such premises, or of an owner knowingly allowing the property to be used as drug premises, the onus of proof is reversed, requiring suspects to prove they were not involved in illegal activity (ss12-14). Hence landlords must satisfy a court that they did not know and could not reasonably have been expected to know their premises were used for drugs purposes. Second or subsequent convictions activate confiscation provisions for the property. In Britain, similar powers exist under the *Anti-Social Behaviour Act 2003* (discussed further below).

In summary, third party policing interventions directed at drug houses typically involve police partnering with city inspectors and property owners. They use federal, state and local laws, some created specifically for the purpose of dealing with drug houses, and some directed more generally at building and health standards, to require owners to become involved in the prevention of crime on their premises. Use of this lever may result in criminal penalties (as in the US federal code and NSW provisions), regulatory sanctions (as in breach notices or the loss of rental certificates) or civil penalties (as in nuisance actions). The advantages of these actions include the coerced involvement of property owners to police conduct on their premises, the broader range of sanctions, and the relaxation of criminal procedural requirements such as the need to prove complicity in or knowledge of criminal conduct, the reversal of the onus of proof, and the use of a civil rather than criminal standard of proof.

As we showed previously in Table 4.2, the actual lever available for use by police will dictate the type of intervention adopted in each situation. Where governments of any level have introduced specific drug house laws, the types of possible usage will be found in the terms of the law itself. In those places lacking specific drug house laws, the best option for third party policing will involve police forming alliances with city inspectors and enforcement agencies, either in formal teams (as in Oakland) or more ad hoc arrangements. In these cases, the sanctions for non-cooperation by landlords and property owners are co-opted from other regulatory schemes. The motivation for involvement by inspectors and regulators is less clear, but likely to be wanting to maintain good relationships with police, and seeing some benefits for their own regulatory objectives in a joint approach.

Other interventions directed at drug crimes involve increasing the supply of surveillance information to police, so that they can locate suspected illegal activity. For example, child welfare agencies may report to police cases of children in suspected drug abuse environments, such as living in a house used as an illegal laboratory for producing amphetamines (McEwen and Uchida, n.d.). Similarly, suppliers and pharmacies may be required to report unusual sales of chemicals and materials used in manufacturing illegal drugs, or medical practitioners may be required to report prescriptions for methadone (see discussion in Chapter 6). The government of South Australia has announced its intention to regulate the sale and use of hydroponic equipment, to control its use in growing cannabis (Brokenshire, 2001). The regulation would restrict who could sell the equipment, and require them to ascertain customers' proposed use of the equipment, with reporting requirements to police. These third parties (welfare agencies, manufacturers, retailers) become partners in the policing of drug crime.

For police, the challenge in these schemes may be accessing the information in usable forms, to sufficiently identify particular problems suitable for intervention. Motivating compliance by the third parties is less of a problem, because in these cases the lever generally arises under statutory authority which carries with it specific sanctions (for example, possible de-registration or other sanctions for medical practitioners not complying with the reporting of methadone prescriptions, or loss of a license to sell dangerous or restricted products).

Anti-social behavior – the UK scheme

Anti-social behavior includes a broad spectrum of activity ranging from the clearly criminal (drug, property and violence offences), through harassment (beggars and pan-handlers), nuisance (loud noise and uncontrolled pets), and non-compliance (truancy, run-down properties). The common link is that these activities affect the quality of life of the non-offending population, especially in crowded urban areas, as well as possibly leading to more serious forms of crime. In the United Kingdom an ambitious scheme under the *Crime and Disorder Act 1998* and *Anti-Social Behaviour Act 2003* is intended to

Table 4.3 *Orders under the Crime and Disorder Act 1998 (UK)*

- *Anti-social behaviour orders* (s1), directed at any person aged 10 or over acting in a way likely to cause harassment, alarm or distress to one or more other people.
- *Sex offender orders* (s2) directed at people convicted of or cautioned for defined sexual offences, where an order is necessary to protect the public from serious harm.
- *Anti-social contracts* are a quicker and less formal alternative to orders, entered into voluntarily and not enforceable, although breach may lead to an order.
- *Parenting orders* (s8) made for children subject to child safety, sex offender or anti-social behavior orders, or truancy offences, requiring the child's parent to comply with conditions including counseling or guidance sessions.
- *Child safety orders* (s11) for children aged under 10, who commit acts which, but for their age, would be offences, or who breach curfews, or act in an anti-social way.
- *Child curfew schemes* (s14) enable local authorities to ban children under 10 from specified public areas in specified hours unless under the control of a responsible adult. Police may inform the local authority of contraventions, and remove the child.
- *Truancy powers* (s16) enable police who believe a child found in a public place is of school age but absent without lawful authority, to remove the child to the school or to premises designated for this purpose by the local authority.

prevent and respond to anti-social behavior, described by the then British Home Secretary as:

> noisy neighbours who ruin the lives of those around them, "crack houses" run by drug dealers, drunken "yobs" taking over town centres' people begging by cash points [automatic teller machines], abandoned cars, litter and graffiti, young people using airguns to threaten and intimidate or people using fireworks as weapons. . . . Anti-social behavior creates an environment in which more serious crime takes hold. It can occur anywhere – in people's homes and gardens, on estates, in town centres or shopping parades and in urban and rural areas. It blights people's lives, undermines the fabric of society and holds back regeneration. (Home Office, 2003a: 6)

The *Crime and Disorder Act* makes local governments specifically responsible for formulating and implementing strategies to reduce crime and disorder in their area. They must review crime statistics, prepare and publish analyses of crime and disorder patterns, and act in cooperation with police, probation, health and other relevant authorities. They must consider the effect on crime and disorder in the pursuit of all of their functions. Their strategies must set objectives and long and short term performance targets (sections 5–7, 17). These requirements constitute government-mandated third party policing, under the joint leadership of local authorities and police. The Act also provides a suite of tools (see Table 4.3 below) for crime prevention and control, which while civil in nature, can incur both civil and criminal penalties for breaches (for example, eviction from public housing, fines or imprisonment).

These tools have been operationalized through providing more police and support staff, including up to 4000 Community Support Officers to conduct street patrols, enhanced neighborhood warden schemes operating on deprived housing estates, a new system of fixed penalty notices for disorder offences, delivered administratively, and targeted policing of street crimes such as robbery and vehicle theft (Home Office, 2003a). This operationalization has been assisted by budgetary and administrative measures, such as providing specific allocations of funds for Crime and Disorder Partnerships, a training academy, telephone and web-based help-lines and resource centers, sentencing guidelines for magistrates, specially trained anti-social behavior prosecutors, funds and awards to recognize innovative programs and reporting requirements for police agencies, requiring them to specify progress towards crime and anti-social behavior reduction targets. Specific interventions have been targeted at nuisance neighbors, begging, and environmental crimes such as abandoned cars, graffiti and street disorder (Home Office, 2003b). The types of third party interventions produced by these measures include:

Third party	Intervention
Parents	Parenting classes, contracts and orders
Owners of licensed premises	Limits on opening hours and sales
Retailers	Limits on sale of spray paints
Local authorities	Crack house closures
Public and private housing providers	Injunctions against anti-social tenants
Residents and community groups	Neighborhood watch and other problem-solving schemes
Courts	Must consider the impact of anti-social behavior on housing estates in eviction cases
Victim support services	Support for witnesses testifying about anti-social behavior

(adapted from Home Office, 2003a)

New powers under the *Anti-Social Behaviour Act* also enable police to give orders for crowd dispersal, where groups of people are engaging in anti-social behavior and to move on trespassers from common lands, and local authorities to close noisy premises and deal with graffiti and waste. Further proposed expansions would enable individual citizens to seek anti-social behavior orders, rather than police or local authorities, and establish a network of street wardens with the power to make orders in their areas (*Observer*, 2004).

In each of these cases, the legal lever is provided under the two key Acts (*Crime and Disorder Act, Anti-Social Behaviour Act*), and the range of specific orders they provide for, as discussed above. The application of each order is as specified in the Act (for example, parenting orders apply to parents of offending children, sex offender orders to people convicted of sex offences etc). The third parties, as identified above, are motivated into assisting police crime control objectives through fear of the sanctions also set out in the legislation. Other agencies, including local authorities, schools, and public and private housing providers, cooperate either because this too is mandated under the legislation (as it is for local authorities and public housing providers), or because of a desire to maintain good relationships with police. Police have a key role in these interventions, in providing the information that identifies problem areas and individuals, and coordinating with other agencies to select appropriate interventions.

In summary, the British statutory scheme provides a comprehensive, integrated approach to common problems of crime control and prevention, directed at typical criminogenic people and places. It is especially relevant to third party policing because of the way it mandates partnerships and team approaches, particularly targeted at police and local authorities working together to reduce crime and disorder. The whole scheme is yet to be evaluated, but one evaluation just of anti-social behavior contracts found that participants tended to engage in less anti-social and criminal behavior (Bullock and Jones, 2004). Of the study's 104 young people on contracts, four were involved in serious breaches leading to eviction. On the other hand, researchers found that the young people often had little input into their contracts, parents received little feedback, and while contracts were supposed to be monitored by housing and welfare agencies and police, in reality police were primarily responsible. Other objections to the scheme include: that it impinges on freedom in a draconian way while not addressing the causes of anti-social behavior; only results in the displacement of problems; and produces in two-tier policing where hot spots focus police attention on areas with large ethnic minority populations (*South Wales Evening Post*, 2003; *Cohen*, 2004). A preliminary evaluation of on-the-spot fixed penalty notices under the scheme found they had a net-widening effect, in that only between a quarter and a half of the notices in the study went to offenders who would otherwise have been cautioned or prosecuted.

Of notice recipients, fewer than 2 percent requested a court hearing rather than incurring the fixed penalty (for offences such as causing harassment, alarm or distress, or disorderly behavior while drunk) (Halligan-Davis and Spicer, 2004). Adverse side effects from third party policing such as the targeting of minorities, net-widening and lack of fairness, are discussed in detail in Chapter 7.

An unsuccessful legal challenge to the UK scheme argued that parts of it contravene the European Convention on Human Rights because of the possibility of anti-social behavior orders being made without notice to the subject (*Independent* 25 March 2004). Other critiques have noted the lack of apparent barriers to what constitutes anti-social behavior. One case involved Westminster City Council taking action to prevent the presence of screaming teenage girl fans outside entertainment venues where celebrities appeared (Milmo, 2004). Other critiques note the differential use of orders, their punitive rather than rehabilitative nature and the adverse effects of eviction as a punishment for breach of orders (*Observer*, 2004).

Anti-social behavior in public housing

Many public housing estates are plagued by persistent crime and disorder problems. In the United Kingdom, in addition to the schemes just described, interventions have also focused on housing providers. In Hackney in London, the local council worked with police to bring criminal and civil actions against a gang of youths known to have been involved in property offences on the Kingsmead estate, but who were not themselves tenants (Burney, 1999; see also Morris, 1998). The council sought injunctions to bar specified individuals from the estate. As a lever for third party policing, injunctions were comparatively cheap and easy to obtain (compared to eviction processes), relied on the lower civil standard of proof, and did not victimize innocent family members but only the targeted youth. However, some challenges have been brought based on the reliance on hearsay evidence against mostly unrepresented defendants, limited sanctions for breaches of injunctions by people under 18, and a practical challenge often exists in finding witnesses prepared to give evidence. Another UK study found that relatively few exclusions from social housing result from anti-social behavior (Butler, 1998), with the level being around 3 percent, but that the number increased almost four times between 1996/97 and 1997/98, probably due to legislative changes broadening the discretion of housing authorities in access and exclusion decisions.

In Australia, a similar study found that a state housing authority expressed concern about the use of eviction against public housing tenants involved in anti-social behavior, as its role was to provide housing, not evict people (Jacobs and Arthurson, 2003). In the United States, eviction is also used by public housing providers, and in 1996 President Clinton ordered the Housing and Urban Development Department Secretary to set up "zero tolerance" policies to reward public housing authorities for programs including eviction and tenant-screening procedures (Ready, Mazerolle and Revere, 1998). However, there have been successful challenges to evictions where the criminal behaviors related to the conduct of other people, and not the tenants themselves (for e.g., see Rucker v Oakland Housing Authority).

Other anti-social behavior interventions

Most other jurisdictions have not attempted such comprehensive schemes as those in the United Kingdom, and rely on ad hoc interventions to deal with localized problems, drawing on all of the legal frameworks set out in Table 4.2. Typically this will include measures similar to those used against drug offences, such as police encouraging landlords to evict tenants involved in anti-social behaviors which violate lease conditions, including excess noise or unauthorized pets (Ready, Mazerolle and Revere, 1998). Alternatively, nuisance laws might be used by neighbors to control these activities. To respond to the problem of graffiti, one intervention involved police helping young people to lobby the city council to provide graffiti walls where they could legally practice their art (Office of COPS, 1998). In another example, young graffiti "taggers" on probation were required to clean up graffiti as part of their community service (San Diego Police Department, 2000). Other interventions are directed at nuisance problems such as street prostitutes and their clients, begging, and groups "hanging out" in public space, but causing fear and apprehension to other users. In these cases, the legal lever chosen will be tailored to suit the problem, so that if the problem behaviors are caused by prostitutes' clients congregating and causing traffic, noise and other nuisances, the response is to use prostitution or other laws as a lever to control the use of space by prostitutes in the area. In San Diego, police addressed street prostitution by encouraging local residents to record and report suspect car licenses, and then following up with warning calls to their owners (San Diego Police Department, 1994). In San Bernardino, residents and businesses obtained restraining orders against local prostitutes (San Bernardino Police Department, 1999). In Buffalo, prostitutes' clients were educated about risks and exploitation issues, and had their names publicized (Buffalo Prostitution Task Force, 1999).

If the problem is caused by beggars or panhandlers harassing passers by, rather than simply moving them on or arresting them, which may not prevent the problem recurring, other levers must be sought. This may include using vagrancy, substance abuse or mental health laws to remove people to a shelter or place of treatment, in which case these laws provide the lever, and the shelter or treatment center staff become third parties in reducing the prospect of the problem recurring, by keeping transients off the streets (for example see Fontana Police Department, 1998). In another instance, police investigating service calls from neighbors of a homeless shelter identified mismanagement as a contributing factor, and pressured management into better practices (Charlotte-Mecklenburg Police Department, 2000).

Similarly, public drunkenness has been addressed through local ordinances allowing courts to issue interdictions or injunctions preventing the sale of alcohol to persons arrested for drunkenness more than five times, with notices sent to all sellers advising them of the orders (Alexandria Police Department, 1995), and through strict enforcement of liquor licensing regulations on serving alcohol to intoxicated persons (Green Bay Police Department, 2000). In these cases, the liquor retailers are inducted as third parties, through levers provided by legislative or regulatory schemes, and enforced by sanctions provided under those schemes.

In a Swedish intervention, midsummer celebrations had become marked by crowds of drunken youths, riots and confrontations with police. Measures taken to counter this included camping grounds refusing entry to likely troublemakers, town car parks being closed, and declaring the celebrations a public event meaning no alcohol could be consumed in public (Björ, Knutsson and Kühlhorn, 1992). While businesses were initially resistant to measures that could potentially reduce their profits, police persuaded them into cooperation as a precursor to maintaining order. The levers in this case included a range of regulatory and licensing schemes, and also appeals to the self-interest of businesses in minimizing events which could adversely affect them.

Another example of third parties adopting crime prevention responsibilities in a highly criminogenic site involved a police partnership with a city council to clean up a problem area, facilitate higher levels of public use, and deter criminal uses by enforcing local and environmental ordinances (San Diego Police Department, 1998). Here the levers came from existing local laws, along with council actions to physically improve the area. Other interventions involve local councils being responsible for reducing crime through environmental design and street lighting (Ditton and Nair, 1994), and using CCTV surveillance (Wilson and Sutton, 2003).

These types of interventions become third party policing when they are initiated by or with the cooperation of police, using criminal and civil laws and penalties, to respond to or deter anti-social or criminal behavior. As illustrated, they draw on the full range of legal frameworks identified in Table 4.2. The comprehensive UK scheme is an example of specific legislation setting up third party policing networks between police, local authorities and others including housing agencies, schools and parents. The possible outcomes of the levers are also specified (the orders provided for under the Acts), as are the potential targets. More ad hoc arrangements may draw on or co-opt existing regulatory schemes (building codes, prostitution laws etc), or encourage third parties to exercise rights under contract or tort (e.g. nuisance actions). In each case, police need to assess the legal levers available to them, and tailor an intervention to suit those levers.

Youth curfews

Interventions specifically directed at the actual or potential offending of young people have been another fertile source of third party policing initiatives. These interventions have taken various forms, including curfews, enforcement of truancy and anti-graffiti laws and move-on powers. In these instances, the third parties include parents who are made responsible for their children's breach of curfew or non-attendance at school; schools for enforcing attendance requirements; local councils and cities for adopting graffiti reduction strategies; and the owners of commercial premises, such as malls, for reducing other problem behaviors. The levers for intervention are found in specific curfew laws or ordinances, existing truancy laws, and other laws, for example, those dealing with police powers. This legislation generally sets out the scope of the lever and whom it can be used against (e.g. parents, schools, shop-owners).

Curfews aimed at curbing the after-hours presence of juveniles in particular places exist in some 200 American cities (Ruefle et al., 1996) and in Australian states including New South Wales and Western Australia. Curfews are meant to prevent crime by keeping young people off the streets at night, when most crimes are committed (Ruefle et al., 1996). In the United States, curfews are constituted by municipal ordinances, such as for example in New Orleans Chapter 54: Criminal Code, section 54-414. In Australia, state governments pass statutes permitting local authorities to apply for gazettal of specified areas as subject to a curfew, with police then empowered to remove children in breach of the curfew. The areas most likely to have curfews are those where juvenile crime is perceived to be at problematic levels

(Hayes et al., 1999). Also, the legislation is often couched in terms suggesting it has goals to protect at-risk children or make parents assume their supervisory duties – for instance, the New South Wales Act is called *The Children (Protection and Parental Responsibilities Act)* 1997, and the Western Australian provisions are contained in the *Child Welfare Act 1947* section 138B. But while police are empowered to remove children and return them home or to a place of safety, often no further provision is made for mechanisms to ensure the welfare of children. Usually, there is no provision for social welfare follow-up of these children (Millner, 2003), unless at the initiative of individual police officers.

Additionally, many curfews are criticized as being disproportionately targeted at minorities, both in the United States (Males and Macallair, 1999), and in Australia, where the Western Australian curfew in the suburb of Northbridge has been used primarily against Aboriginal youth (Marks, 2003). Ruefle et al. (1996) argue that there is no evidence that curfews either reduce crime or are applied consistently by police. Rob White (1996) agrees and claims that curfews may exacerbate youth victimization, criminalization and conflicts with police, are discriminatory, and breach the United Nations Convention on the Rights of the Child. While many communities seek curfews because of perceptions that juveniles are responsible for most local crime, these perceptions are often wrong, and other crime prevention measures would be more effective (Hayes, 1999). These issues are raised again in the discussion in Chapter 7 of adverse side effects of third party policing.

Truancy laws
Third party policing in this context generally involves police partnering with school or education authorities to "crack down" on chronic truancy in an attempt to control local crime problems (Baltimore Police Department, 2000). Recent activities of this type in Queensland, Australia, have led to the prosecution of sixty-eight parents in three years, with fines and good behavior bonds imposed as penalties for breaches of the truancy provisions of the *Education (General Provisions) Act* 1989 (*Courier Mail*, 2003). In the United Kingdom, under the authority of the *Crime and Disorder Act*, truancy patrols comprising teams of police and education officers patrol streets and shopping malls, stopping children of school age (even if accompanied by parents) and asking why they are not at school (*Curtis*, 2002). Truanting children and their parents are interviewed by the education authority, and face sanctions including anti-social behavior orders under the *Anti-Social Behaviour Act 2003*. So the levers in these cases are usually provided for

under legislation, generally on truancy or school attendance requirements. The laws also provide the sanctions to be used against parents and other proximate targets.

Other approaches to problem and truanting youth include "adopt a cop" style programs where police are stationed in schools to promote preventive strategies, provide resources to address social problems, and build stronger relationships with local youth (Curtis, 2002). These schemes rely less on legislation to provide their levers, and more on ad hoc and informal arrangements between police and others with some responsibility for young people. In one program, young offenders still at school were dealt with in an informal court where penalties could be waived for community service and a return to school (Penrod, 2001). In another program, probation officers were assigned to high schools and worked with police to address crimes that occurred on campus, as well as checking attendance by students on probation orders, and making visits to clients, accompanied by a police officer, to encourage school attendance (White et al., 2003).

Other interventions directed at young people
Other interventions directed at young people have focused on underage drinking as the underlying cause of problems. To counter this, liquor retailers may be policed to ensure that they strictly require proof of age from purchasers, and report purchases by older people where there is a suspicion it will be supplied to underage drinkers (Baker and Wolfer, 2003). In another intervention, a game arcade in a shopping mall was a location of crime by young people. Council ordinances were used to require re-design of the arcade, with this in turn becoming a model for use at other sites (Delta Police Department, 1997). In these cases, the framework for the intervention is most often co-opted from existing regulatory requirements, through police cooperation with other regulators or businesses. Liquor licensing authorities and councils are motivated to work with police, presumably to maintain good relationships and solve joint problems.

Similarly, in many areas of Australia chronic inhalant sniffing or chroming is seen by police as a precursor to young people's crime and disorder. Some schemes established by police and welfare agencies address this problem through police strictly enforcing laws controlling the sale of spray paint, conducting night patrols and detaining and removing young people found in possession of chroming implements, and offering them transport home or access to welfare services (Gostzyla and George, 2003). Business owners are encouraged to take further steps including the use of CCTV to prevent theft of spray cans, relocating paint cans, not selling spray cans to young people, and staff training in monitoring suspected chromers while youth organizations create alternative activity and employment programs.

Other strategies have focused on problem behaviors at school, as precursors to criminal activity. "Zero tolerance" policies apply disciplinary sanctions to misconducts typically including dress code violations, not doing homework, vandalism, absenteeism, drug use and bringing weapons to school, with police often involved at the more serious end of the misconduct scale (Dullroy, 2004). However, some reports have found that while sanctions are meant to deter misbehavior, instead they tend to lead to school dropout, subsequent delinquency, and increased opportunity for crime (Skiba et al., 2003).

Gangs

In places where gangs have been identified as a contributor to crime, third party policing interventions have been directed at non-offending as well as offending gang members. The objective is to disrupt groups that support crime, while not having to prove the involvement of all targeted individuals in specific criminal activity. Police partner with local authorities, youth workers and city governments in these interventions. Thus, in some states in the United States, laws permit prosecutors to file civil suits resulting in injunctions against gang members, preventing them from associating with each other and engaging in other prohibited behaviors (Grogger, 2002; Maxson et al., 2003). These actions target the gang as an unincorporated association, rather than requiring the collection of evidence against individual members, and can prohibit members from going to certain places or doing certain things. Breaches of the injunctions give rise to criminal penalties.

In New South Wales, Australia, the *Justice Legislation Amendment (Non-association and Place Restriction) Act 2001* also targets gang related crime, by prohibiting offenders from associating with persons and places that may increase the likelihood of their re-offending. New Zealand's *Criminal Justice Act 1985* also provides for non-association orders. The NSW Act prohibits physical association and communication, and orders may be made by court order, at sentencing, in bail, parole or leave or home detention arrangements. However, a preliminary evaluation found that eleven out of the twelve orders then granted under the Act applied to males, with three-quarters aged under thirty, five identified as Aboriginal and none of the offences which gave rise to the order were gang-related (NSW Ombudsman, 2004). This finding indicates that like many of the interventions targeted at young people (see above), these laws become vehicles for unfair, discriminatory and potentially racist policing activities, an issue taken up further in Chapter 7.

Civil asset forfeiture

Many jurisdictions have laws allowing the confiscation of assets suspected of having been acquired through criminal activity, even where no criminal conviction has been obtained. These laws are intended to weaken the economic foundations of sophisticated criminal activity that may be difficult to target by traditional criminal justice methods. Schemes are often directed at drug-related or organized crime, and impose a civil rather than criminal standard of proof, making it easier to confiscate than to convict (Warchol and Johnson, 1996). In the United States, much of this activity has been directed at drug crime (Worrall, 2001), and in some cases the confiscated assets help fund future law enforcement activities. The procedure is civil, and sometimes the burden of proof is reversed, so that the owner of an asset with a value out of proportion to that person's visible wealth and income may be required to prove that it was not gained through crime.

In terms of our analysis of legal frameworks, these types of laws are reliant on specific statutory authority to provide a lever for intervention, in the form of a civil action for forfeiture. Special legislation is required to authorize the application of civil methods to a criminal justice problem, and the removal of normal criminal justice procedural barriers such as the requirement to prove guilt beyond reasonable doubt. The scope of the lever is as set out in the authorizing Act, and in any judicial decisions interpreting the meaning and extent of that Act. The third parties include prosecutors and courts mandated by the legislation to take part in the process, and often non-offending people with some interest in the forfeited property, such as spouses, family members or banks.

In Australia, the *Criminal Assets Recovery Act 1990* (NSW) is intended to provide for the confiscation, without requiring a conviction, of the property of a person if the Supreme Court finds it to be more probable than not that the person has engaged in serious crime related activities, and to enable the proceeds of serious crime related activities to be recovered as a debt due to the Crown. Proceedings under the Act can be taken against people who have not been criminally charged, or who have been charged and acquitted. The proceedings are civil, and must relate to "serious crime related activity" which is defined as including drug and firearm offences, and other offences that are punishable by imprisonment for five years or more and involve theft, fraud, obtaining financial benefit from the crime of another, money laundering, extortion, violence, bribery, corruption, harboring criminals, blackmail, obtaining or offering a secret commission, perverting the course of justice, tax or revenue evasion, illegal gambling, forgery or homicide. Under some schemes, such as the *Criminal Proceeds Confiscation Act 2002*

(Qld), civil restraining orders can be used to protect suspect assets pending investigation. Between 1 January 2003 and 30 September 2004, $22.05 million worth of assets from 112 suspects were restrained under this scheme, including residential properties, luxury cars, bank accounts, jet skis and cash (Beattie, 2004).

These schemes have been criticized, largely because of the effect on innocent co-owners or third parties, the lower standard of proof and the infringement of civil liberties. Challenges to United States schemes led in part to the *Civil Asset Forfeiture Reform Act* 2000 (Worrall, 2001). Federal law now requires strict notice provisions for individuals subject to civil forfeiture orders, allows the filing of claims by other people with an interest in the seized property, creates uniform defenses to forfeiture claims, specifies that the government bears the burden of proof, and provides a general power in the court to determine whether the forfeiture is constitutionally excessive, based on the gravity of the offences. Disproportional confiscations are declared to be contrary to the eighth amendment of the US constitution. We take up some of these criticisms in detail in Chapter 7.

These types of actions can be classified as third party policing interventions because they involve police in formulating the suspicion that drug related or other serious crime is occurring, and the collection of evidence to suggest that assets have been illegally required. Police then partner with prosecutors, crime commissions and drug agencies to bring civil actions against suspects.

Violent crime

To prevent and control violent crimes, a range of interventions has focused on precursors to or indicators of aggression, including alcohol, guns, domestic violence and child abuse. Interventions have sought to minimize these factors, or to increase police surveillance of them. In terms of our analysis of legal frameworks, these interventions tend to co-opt existing legislative and regulatory schemes, such as those governing the licensing of alcohol sales, gun ownership and child welfare. Targeted third parties include the relevant regulatory agencies, and shop and bar owners, with the object of having them incorporate crime control functions in operating their businesses, by adopting codes and behaviors to limit their sales to problem customers. The motivating factor for the shop and bar owners is likely to be the threat of sanctions under the relevant licensing scheme – failure to cooperate may lead to loss of their license. For the regulatory agencies, the main motivator is likely to be the achievement of a regulatory objective through joint action. For example, in Canada, police were involved in the Safe Bar Initiative that trained bar owners and staff in how to deal with drunkenness and aggression, and suggested design changes to minimize misbehaviors (Graham et al., 2003). A program in Surfers Paradise, Queensland (Homel et al., 1997; Hauritz et al., 1998) was a community-based initiative aimed at reducing violence in and around licensed venues in the center of a large tourist resort. It involved forming community steering groups and task forces to address the safety of public spaces, management of venues, security and policing issues, and implementation of a code of practice regulating the responsible service of alcohol. While effective during the period of a monitored experiment, data collected two years later showed that violence had returned to pre-project levels, and compliance with the code had virtually ceased. Enforcement of the code by the liquor licensing authority did not occur, and licensees found it was not commercially viable for them to comply when their competitors did not.

Other strategies are formalized in accords. In the Australian regional city of Geelong, police, the licensing commission and bar owners signed an accord with conditions requiring bars to set entry charges for late night customers, deny re-entry to patrons who left, ban promotions using free or cheap drinks, and check identification for underage drinking (Felson et al., 1997). Police monitored compliance by bar owners, and could report non-compliance to the regulatory authority. However, a similar accord in Freemantle, Western Australia, was found to have no effect on assaults, intoxication or underage drinking, with the attributed reason for this being that bars were fearful of loss of custom if they complied, and a lack of enforcement (Hawks et al., 1999).

In Victoria, Australia, police coordinated a partnership approach to achieve the reduction of nightclub related assaults. This involved city councils, local hospitals, liquor regulators, the liquor industry association and security firms, to develop responsible alcohol policies and crowd control measures (Baker, 2004). Police and hospital reports of assault in licensed premises lead to a police visit, and possible licensing sanctions. In Western Australia, guidelines on security in licensed premises require owners to install CCTV to improve patron safety (Griffiths, 2001).

Clubs and bars can also be helped to discourage patrons seen as troublemakers. In Arlington, clubs asked problem patrons to leave, and police enforced this with criminal trespass warnings (Arlington Police Department, 1998). Breach of the notice led to arrest. Other interventions have been directed at manufacturers and wholesalers of alcohol. For example, in Merseyside in the United Kingdom, alcohol in certain areas was supplied only in plastic containers, to avoid glass being used in fights (Merseyside Police, 2001).

"Dram shop liability" has also been used to deter alcohol-related violence and crime. This refers to legislation or common law principles by which bar owners and even social hosts may be held liable for the intoxication of patrons or guests, and their subsequent criminal conduct (Ireland, 1995). In one Australian case, the victim of a violent assault by an intoxicated man successfully sued for negligence the hotel which had sold the man alcohol despite knowing of his intoxication (Speer v Nash, 1992). In addition to common law rights, the sale of alcohol to intoxicated people is generally a breach of licensing regulations, and strict enforcement may lead to prosecution. An Australian case involved the continued sale of alcohol to an intoxicated truck driver, who subsequently caused an accident in which two people died. The licensee was convicted and fined, but such action is quite unusual in Australia (Stockwell, 1997).

Some areas have created alcohol-free zones to reduce crime in problem areas, largely by using existing licensing or local authority regulation. The city of Coventry in the United Kingdom passed by-laws in 1988 creating an offence of continuing to drink in public after having been warned not to by a police officer. The restrictions applied to specific problem streets and places where alcohol was known to cause trouble (Ramsay, 1991). Police passed on the names of offenders to the city council, which conducted any prosecutions. Similar schemes were opposed in the city of Bath, which had a tradition of open-air bars and restaurants. Similarly, an alcohol-free zone was declared in Bondi, New South Wales to reduce anti-social behavior and alcohol-related assaults linked to street drinking (*Daily Telegraph* 22 January 2004). In Western Australia, provision exists under the state liquor licensing legislation to ban drinking in declared parks and reserves, and although the law has not been applied police have sought to use it during public events (*West Australian* 31 January 2004).

The sale and consumption of alcohol in Aboriginal communities in Australia is particularly problematic, resulting in extremely high levels of violent crime particularly directed at women and children (Aboriginal and Torres Strait Islander Women's Task Force on Violence, 2000). Some interventions have been aimed at limiting and controlling drinking, by restricting the hours of sale of alcohol, with these restrictions primarily enforced by police. In Queensland, these interventions depend on legislation in the form of mandated community alcohol management plans (Queensland Government, 2004). While the lever may be provided by legislation or local ordinance, the remote location of many communities means that enforcement is often by police. In two remote towns, the licensing commission imposed restrictions in consultation with community members, including the closing of suppliers on the days on which government benefits were received, limits on amounts able to be purchased by one person, and reduced trading hours (Douglas, 1998; Gray et al., 2000). Evaluations found decreases in alcohol-related harm, although consumption remained high.

Other interventions have focused on domestic violence initiatives and include the use of response teams comprising police and victim advocates, with the advocate supporting the victim in accessing services and proceeding with criminal charges (Whetstone, 2001). The goal here is for re-victimization to be reduced through increased criminalization, rather than reliance being placed only in civil restraining orders. The legal framework is usually co-opted, relying on victim support laws or voluntary cooperation by victims' service providers.

Property crime

Third party policing initiatives in response to property crime have tended to be more ad hoc than the responses to drug and violent crime and disorder described above. Most have been directed at preventing re-victimization, and reducing the opportunities for property crime to occur. Victimization schemes typically involve police or victim support organizations contacting burglary victims or other likely targets and advising them on prevention measures such as locks and alarms (Chenery, Holt and Pease, 1997). Other schemes have involved builders agreeing with police to delay the installation of appliances and other moveable property on building sites until they are ready for occupation, reducing the opportunity for theft from unoccupied building sites (Clarke and Goldstein, 2002). Some opportunity reduction schemes have included design and surveillance issues (for example, the United Kingdom car park awards scheme discussed in Chapter 6 – see Smith, Gregson and Morgan, 2003). Other interventions focus on preventing motor vehicle theft, including mandatory steering column locks (Webb, 1994) and immobilizers, mandatory vehicle identification numbers and wrecked car registers to prevent the legitimization of stolen vehicles, and multi-agency task forces comprising police, manufacturers, insurance companies and vehicle registration offices developing anti-theft systems (Hill, 1998).

In these schemes, the third party policing lever may be co-opted from legal frameworks, including existing regulatory schemes (for example licensing businesses or products, imposing manufacturing standards), or from voluntary arrangements. The incentives for voluntary cooperation by third parties such as builders, car park operators, and previous crime victims are likely to include self-interest in preventing re-victimization and maintaining good relationships with police.

Another group of interventions have targeted robberies of convenience shops. Several cities in the United States have passed "two clerk" ordinances, requiring such businesses to have at least two staff on duty, usually at night (Office of COPS, 1998). These interventions are clearly drawing on specific laws or regulations introduced to deal with this problem. In Gainesville Florida, 1986 requirements also included cleared windows so that stores were clearly visible from outside, good lighting, low cash reserves, and mandatory robbery prevention training for staff (Bellamy, 1996). In 1992, the Florida State legislature passed laws establishing minimum security standards for convenience stores statewide, including additional measures for those that had already been robbed. In Washington State, regulations inspired by state occupational safety and health laws were directed at preventing employee harm through criminal activity by requiring businesses with high risk employees (e.g. night workers in petrol stations, video rental shops and convenience stores) to implement special measures (Nelson et al., 1997). Nelson reports that the regulation was not strongly enforced. These types of interventions have attracted significant resistance, largely because of the costs to business (Bellamy, 1996).

Anti-theft measures in stores can also be third party policing interventions when police identify and advise about problem areas. In Australia, police identified that large-scale stealing from department stores was occurring because of lax refund policies – stolen goods were being taken back to the shop of origin as returned goods. The absence of a requirement to show proof of purchase was both incentive and facilitator for these crimes. Retailer associations were encouraged to develop refund guidelines to limit this problem (Challinger, 1996). While there was some resistance by businesses concerned about loss of sales, the loss through fraud was becoming so significant that it outweighed these concerns. In Victoria, Australia, similar concerns led to a new Shop Theft Infringement Notice scheme targeting the stealing of goods valued at less than $150. Police issue on the spot cautions, restitution or community service orders under the scheme, without the need for prosecution and formal proceedings. The objective is to encourage more retailers to report minor thefts, as well as diverting offenders away from formal processes (Griffin, 2001). Similarly, some schemes have targeted credit card fraud by requiring banks to improve detection and prevention policies (Webb, 1996). Generally, the levers for these interventions have not been legislative, which might be seen as too heavy-handed an interference in the conduct of the business. Instead, they have relied on industry standard setting, acting in cooperation with police in the face of a joint problem.

General crime prevention – mandatory reporting

Mandatory reporting laws require notifications by third parties of behaviors that may lead to, or evidence criminal behaviors. Examples include mandatory reporting of suspected child abuse, elder abuse or domestic violence, to police, prosecutors or other criminal justice agencies. Both the United States and Australia have schemes requiring the reporting of large-scale cash transactions, originally introduced to counter drug and organized crime money laundering, but now also used to track terrorist activities. In the United States the *Patriot Act* 2001 introduced a month after the September 11 attacks, unified and extended laws requiring banks, security dealers and others to report cash transactions, but also introduced mandatory reporting of regulated biological agents and toxins by institutes or organizations using or transferring them. Australia also requires the reporting by manufacturers or wholesalers of large-scale sales of chemicals capable of being used in weapons (Commonwealth of Australia, 2004), and in Victoria, retailers must also report thefts of prescribed substances (*Terrorism (Community Protection) Act, 2003*). Mandatory reporting may also apply in relation to some drugs – for example, in Australia, where methadone is used to treat heroin addiction, prescriptions must be authorized by and reported to the federal health department. In one scheme to combat fraud against senior citizens, bank staff were asked to report large or unusual transactions by senior citizens (Nassau County Police Department, 1998).

Mandatory reporting schemes generally rely on specific legislation to provide the lever for third party policing interventions. The legislation sets out the scope of the reporting requirement, and the sanctions for non-compliance.

Liability of local authorities, agencies and businesses to prevent crime

While most of the interventions discussed above depend on some form of legislation, federal, state or local, to provide authority for police involvement, a final category of interventions depend entirely on civil law, particularly torts liability. In these instances, potential third parties are motivated by a fear of potential liability for their actions or non-actions, into taking responsibility for reducing crime risks at their business or premises. The police role in this process may be in educating third parties about their potential liability or ways to reduce it, often within a risk management framework. The prime lever used by police in this task is likely to be court judgments and the threat of potential liability. For example, in an Australian case, *Kirtland v The Commonwealth Bank of Australia* 1993, a bank was found liable for negligence, breaching its duty of care to safeguard staff, by not reviewing security procedures after a robbery, when a second robbery occurred in similar circumstances. This case provides a persuasive tool for police, who by publicizing the threat of civil damages, may be able to convince banks to become more responsible for their own security. Similarly in *Modbury Triangle Shopping Centre v Anzil and Anzil* 2000, the Australian High Court found that a landlord may owe a duty of care to employees requiring the appropriate design, placement and use of security lighting in shopping center car parks, as a crime prevention measure. Police faced with repeated calls for service in this type of area can use the court's decision as a persuasive tool to make the property owner assume some responsibility for the crime problem. Similar duties of care may exist in a range of potential third parties, not just banks and landlords. In Australia, a line of High Court authorities on the duties of local authorities has established necessary elements including reasonable foreseeability of the likelihood of harm, a relationship of proximity, and the reasonableness of the scope of the duty (e.g. *Pyrenees Shire Council v Day* 1998, *Romeo v Conservation Commission (Northern Territory)* 1998, *Perre v Appand* 1999, *Graham Barclay Oysters Pt Ltd v Ryan* 2002). Thus a local authority, or other agencies such as prison authorities, which assume obligations on behalf of particular people, may be found to have a duty of care to take reasonable steps to protect them from foreseeable risks. Public authorities may assume responsibilities through the inspection or approval of premises in a licensing scheme, such as under building or health codes. Failure to require crime prevention measures to deal with obvious risks may lead to liability for harm caused by subsequent criminal activity.

Therefore, there is scope for civil liability for breach of a duty of care to be used by police as a level against third parties, including local authorities, regulatory agencies and private businesses. To be effective, the risk of liability needs to be formulated and communicated, along with reasonable steps that can be taken to reduce the risk. In this way, these third parties become responsible for the crime prevention measures, with police acting as communicators and advisors.

Conclusion

In this chapter we have analyzed the relaxation of barriers between criminal, regulatory and private law and remedies. This has led to a greatly expanded range of tools and outcomes being available for use in the criminal justice system (most notably the police), including non-criminal regulation and private law remedies. We have shown how there is a range of legal frameworks that provide potential levers for third party policing initiatives, including general and specific legislation and regulation, contracts and torts, and we have discussed contexts where these levers are frequently used.

Our primary conclusion from our analysis in this chapter is that the type and extent of third party policing initiative will always depend on the legal lever used in that initiative. For police involved in third party policing initiatives, that means a careful analysis of the lever is required at the very beginning of the planning stage, to identify the type of lever available, the extent of its application, potential outcomes, and appropriate third party targets. From a practical perspective, we observe that third party policing initiatives, unlike problem-oriented policing interventions, typically begin with the lever that guides and shapes its application to the particular problem, and various operational issues. The starting point and processes in problem-solving are quite different: in problem-oriented policing the police start with identifying and analyzing the problem and then match a wide and inexhaustible range of alternative responses to the problem. It is our view that the processes of third party policing are quite different. We argue that police knowledge of legal tools, options and alternatives shape and prioritize police action. We pick this point up again in our concluding chapter.

CHAPTER 5

Controlling drug problems

Measuring program performance and being able to say whether or not an intervention (e.g. third party policing) works is the bread and butter of sound policy decision-making. These days we use performance measurement for "evidenced-based policy making" or making policies based on the outcomes of well-designed and executed evaluations. In the policing arena, Sherman (1998) draws analogies with "evidence-based medicine" and defines evidenced-based policing as the use of the best available research on the outcomes of police work to implement guidelines and evaluate agencies, units and officers. In short, evidenced-based policing "... uses the best evidence to shape the best practice" (Sherman, 1998: 4).

Four categories are generally used to gather evidence and measure program performance: effectiveness, efficiency, equity and accountability. Effectiveness concerns the extent to which an objective is achieved, regardless of cost or other factors. Efficiency addresses the relationship between the cost of a program and its effectiveness (e.g. the cost of the third party policing intervention per unit of crime that is reduced). Equity (or fairness) concerns the distribution of benefits and costs. Accountability requires that the program, the intervention staff (e.g. the police) and the program participants act within the constraints set by duly constituted authority. In this chapter, we are concerned with assessing the effectiveness of third party policing initiatives aimed at drug problems. In the following chapter, we examine the evaluation literature pertaining to the effectiveness of third party policing in controlling other types of problems such as violent crimes, property crime, crimes in public places and crimes committed by juveniles. We discuss the equity and accountability issues of third party policing in Chapter 7 and lament the paucity of cost-effectiveness evidence in Chapter 8.

The questions we seek to answer in this chapter include: What evidence do we have about the effectiveness of third party policing in targeting drug problems? Does third party policing reduce drug problems? What types of third party strategies are most effective? Who are the third parties being utilized in third party policing approaches? What types of laws are most effective? In this chapter, we examine the range of third parties co-opted, the types of laws invoked and the outcome of third party policing interventions aimed to control drug problems.

Systematic reviews

From the outset, it was our intention to use a "systematic review" process to assess the effectiveness and efficiency of third party policing tactics (see Farrington and Petrosino, 2000; Farrington and Welsh, 2002; Petrosino, Boruch, Rounding, McDonald and Chalmers, 1999). Farrington and Welsh (2002) state:

> . . . systematic reviews use rigorous methods for locating, appraising, and syn-
> thesizing evidence from prior evaluation studies, and they are reported with the
> same level of detail that characterizes high quality reports of original research.
> They have explicit objectives, explicit criteria for including or excluding studies,
> extensive searches for eligible evaluation studies from all over the world, careful
> extraction and coding of key features of studies, and a structured and detailed
> report of the methods and conclusions of the review.   (2002: 9)

Consistent with the systematic review process our search for evaluations of police interventions using third party policing tactics used the following inclusion criteria:

1. There was an outcome measure of crime.
2. Third party policing, as we have defined it, was an important component of the intervention. Ideally, we wanted to examine those evaluations
   where third party policing was the only, or at least the primary, intervention tactic. However, this criterion would have precluded many important
   studies, leaving us with so few to assess that it would render our exercise
   meaningless. Thus, for our purposes, we decided to use broad inclusion
   criteria to allow us to present and discuss a relatively wide range of evaluation studies. We use these studies to discuss the outcomes, examine the
   range of third parties and describe the variety of laws used as levers in the
   third party policing activities. However, the confounding effects of including evaluations with multiple intervention tactics makes it impossible for
   us to conduct a proper, systematic review with the rigor described by

scholars in the field (e.g. see Farrington and Petrosino, 2000; Farrington and Welsh, 2002; Petrosino et al., 1999, 2000; Sherman, 2003). We return to this issue later in the chapter.

3. Ideally, Farrington and Welsh (2002) point out that the minimum design for inclusion in systematic reviews involves before-and-after measures of crime in experimental and comparable control areas (see also Cook and Campbell, 1979; Shadish et al., 2002). Our systematic search for third party policing evaluations, however, revealed an incredible dearth of high quality evaluation studies. We believe this is for a number of reasons: first, the term "third party policing" is not part of the common lexicon in criminology and not yet used as a keyword by evaluation authors; second, appropriate alternative search keywords (see below) created a wide-ranging list of potentially interesting studies. Many of these studies that we identified, however, did not use third party policing tactics and were therefore not relevant to our task. Third, the ad hoc, episodic nature of much of third party policing tactics coincides with evaluators not designing studies to isolate and capture the unique impact of third party policing interventions. As a result, we were left with a deficit of high quality evaluations of interventions that we defined as third party policing. We discuss this issue further in Chapter 8.

The following five search strategies were carried out to identify third party policing evaluations meeting our very loose criteria for inclusion:

1. Searches of on-line data bases. The following data bases were searched: Criminal Justice Abstracts, National Criminal Justice Reference Service (NCJRS) Abstracts, Sociological Abstracts, Educational Resources Information Clearinghouse (ERIC), Psychology Information (Psych-Info), Public Affairs Information Service (PAIS) International, ProQuest including ProQuest Legal, CINCH (Australian Criminology Database), Expanded Academic ASAP Plus, SwetsWise (full text electronic journals data base), Web of Science (Social Science Citation Index and ISI Current Contents Connect). These data bases were selected because the Campbell Crime and Justice Coordinating Group recommend these data bases and other systematic reviews of interventions in the field of crime and justice have used them (e.g. Braga, 2001; Farrington and Welsh, 2002; Petrosino et al., 1999).

   The following terms were used to search the data bases identified above; civil remedies, third party policing, problem-oriented policing, problem-solving policing, community policing, civil law and crime prevention, civil law and crime control, abatement, injunctions, partnership and crime prevention, partnership and crime control, quality of life policing, drugs and crime prevention/control, violent crime and crime prevention/control, juveniles and crime prevention/control, young people and crime prevention/control, property crime and crime prevention/control, public places and crime prevention/control, public space and crime prevention/control, police and partnership, asset forfeiture, restraining orders, mandatory reporting.

2. Searches of literature reviews on the effectiveness of the interventions in preventing crime including Sherman et al. (1997), Eck (2002), Poyner (1993) and Beckman, Lum, Wyckoff and Larsen-Vander Wall (2003).

3. Searches of bibliographies of reports and research articles.

4. Problem-Oriented Policing reports (e.g. Scott, 2000) and websites (e.g. Center for Problem-Oriented Policing http://www.popcenter.org, the Herman Goldstein Award Projects (part of pop center website) http://www.popcenter.org/library-goldstein.htm, the Tilley Awards: part of a general UK crime prevention website: http://www.crimereduction.gov.uk. The Tilley awards webpages are organized by year:
http://www.crimereduction.gov.uk/tilleyaward2001.htm,
http://www.crimereduction.gov.uk/tilleyaward2002.htm,
http://www.crimereduction.gov.uk/tilleyaward2003.htm, the UK Home Office website: http://www.homeoffice.gov.uk, and the COPS: Community Oriented Policing Service website: http://www.cops.usdoj.gov).

5. Contacts with leading researchers.

Both published and unpublished reports were included in the searches. We point out, that while we concentrated our search on reports and publications from 1990 onwards, we included selected studies that were conducted prior to 1990. Furthermore, the searches were international in scope and were not limited to the English language.

These search strategies resulted in the identification of 160 studies that mentioned a third party policing tactic. Of these, just seventy-seven studies were included in our review because they reported the results of an evaluation of a third party policing tactic. Most of the studies not included in the review described police use of a third party policing tactic, but reported no evaluation of the tactic. Examination of these seventy-seven studies is divided between this chapter and the next. There were twenty-one drug crime studies (Chapter 5), twenty-one violent crime studies, fifteen public disorder studies, eleven juvenile crime studies and nine property crime studies (Chapter 6).

Throughout these two chapters we utilize a scientific rating scheme developed by Sherman and his colleagues (1997) in the report "What Works, What Doesn't and What's Promising." In this report the following scheme is used:

1 = Correlational only (e.g. correlates with a program at a single point in time);

2 = Some kind of comparison but no statistical control for selection bias (e.g. program group compared with non-equivalent control; before-after intervention, no control group);

3 = Comparison with some statistical control to isolate treatment effects (e.g. experimental group and comparable control group with pre-post measurement). Includes information about background of experimental and control group and some explanation about implications of this information on results;

4 = Quasi-experimental design that compares the effects of a treatment across treatment and control conditions without the use of random allocation of subjects into treatment or control groups (e.g. experimental and control groups with control of extraneous factors by matching, pairs, etc.);

5 = Use of random allocation of subjects to treatment and control groups to isolate treatment effects.

We note, from the outset, however, the dearth of high quality evaluations of third party policing. This lack of sound, scientific evidence makes it difficult to provide definitive answers as to the effectiveness and cost-effectiveness of third party policing. Nonetheless, we provide an analysis of effect sizes for those studies with sufficient information.

In this chapter we present the results of our review for studies with a drug outcome. We included twenty-one drug crime evaluation studies in our review. There are three primary domains where the police have used third party policing tactics to control drug problems. These include strategies to pressure residential property owners tactics to coerce business owners and efforts to influence the operations of public housing authorities. There are also several emerging areas of drug control where third party policing practices have been utilized and evaluated. These include third party policing using medical practitioners as levers for the control of drug problems and tactics that target entertainment promoters. We discuss each of these categories of third party drug control in turn.

Residential property owners

The most common application of third party policing in efforts to control drugs is through targeting residential property owners. This section presents the results of our review that examines the effectiveness of third party policing in controlling street-level drug problems at residential locations, using residential property owners as third parties. Table 5.1 presents a summary of twelve studies that have evaluated what we would classify as third party policing initiatives used to control street level drug problems at residential targets.

Table 5.1 reveals twelve studies that targeted residential property owners using third party policing tactics (Clarke and Bichler, 1998; Higgins and Coldren, 2000; Eck and Wartell, 1998; Fergusson and Fitzsimons, 1990; Green, 1996; Hope, 1994; Joliet Police Department, 2000; Lurigio et al., 1998; Mazerolle, Kadleck and Roehl, 1998; Mazerolle, Price and Roehl, 2000; Ramker, 1999; and San Diego Police Department, 2000). Across these studies there were six legal levers used including abatement laws, eviction procedures, code enforcement, council by-laws, the Safe Streets NOW Act, and a rental inspection ordinance.

An example of a comprehensive third party policing program is the Beat Health Program of the Oakland Police Department in California (Green, 1996; Mazerolle, Kadleck and Roehl, 1998; Mazerolle, Price and Roehl, 2000). This third party policing program is aimed at both residential and commercial property owners (see later), but primarily residential properties. The program uses Drug Nuisance Abatement Laws and a series of local housing, building and fire codes to control drug problems at residential properties. Beat Health officers coordinate site visits by the Specialized Multi-Agency Response Team (SMART) that comprises a group of city inspectors. Depending on preliminary assessments made by the police, representatives from agencies such as Housing, Fire, Public Works, Pacific Gas and Electric, and Vector Control (a government agency that deals with rodent infestations) are invited to inspect a problem location and, where necessary, enforce local housing, fire, and safety codes. About half of all targeted locations have SMART inspections and about two-thirds of the targeted sites are cited for at least one code violation from a city inspector: the most common type is a housing code violation. The police department also draws upon its in-house legal expertise and, as needed, uses a variety of civil laws to bring suit against the owners of properties with drug problems. For example, the Uniform Controlled Substances Act makes every building where drug use occurs a nuisance,[1] thus allowing the city to use the civil law to eliminate the problem by fining the owner or by closing or selling the property. About 2 percent of cases result in formal court action against a property owner.

Like the Beat Health Program, Eck and Wartell (1998) describe a San Diego Police Department initiative known as DART (Drug Abatement

Table 5.1 *Residential property owners as third parties in drug control*

Cite	Third party(s)	Target	Legal basis/lever used to coerce third parties	Scientific rating	Outcome
Fergusson and Fitzsimons (1990)	Property owners	Drug dealers and users	Abatement and eviction laws	1	In its first two years, the program resulted in over 625 actions against crack houses; over 90 percent were resolved through owner action.
Hope (1994)	Property owners	Drug dealers and users	Evictions, building codes, council by-laws	2	Calls for service declined by 95% in targeted block and by 70% in adjacent blocks.
Green (1995; 1996)	Property and business owners	Drug dealers and users	Health and Safety, building codes, fire, rodent, housing codes	3	34% reduction in narcotics arrests, 4% reduction in narcotics calls and 59% reduction in field contacts at SMART sites relative to changes city-wide. 37.1% of SMART sites revealed improvement in outdoor appearances after SMART intervention. Little evidence of displacement (Green, 1995).
Clarke and Bichler (1998)	Slumlords	Drug dealers and users	Building codes, Health and Safety codes, housing codes, abatement	3	Properties owned by slumlords attracted 60% more calls for service than neighboring properties properly managed; number of arrests in apartment block reduced by over 75% in two years following intervention forcing slumlord to improve his property.
Eck and Wartell (1998)	Property owners and managers	Drug dealers and users	Evictions, nuisance abatement	5	Following meeting with Drug Abatement Response Team (DART) 60% reduction in crime in experimental group. Following letter only from DART, 13% reduction in crime in experimental group.

Study	Target owners	Target	Ordinance/law	No.	Findings
Lurigio et al. (1998)	Property owners	Drug dealers	Civil abatement	3	Residents aware of evictions on blocks targeted for abatement but they reported small reduction (5%) in perceived drug dealing; physical observations by researchers indicated a reduction in drug dealing and closing of several drug houses.
Mazerolle, Kadleck and Roehl (1998)	Property and business owners	Drug dealers and users	Health and Safety, building codes, fire, rodent, housing codes	5	Statistically significant reduction in males selling drugs and signs of disorder at experimental sites.
Ramker (1999)	Property owners and managers	Drug dealers and users	Chronic nuisance and nuisance abatement ordinance	2	Narcotics arrests increased by 600%; narcotics seizure increased by 300%.
Higgins and Coldren (2000)	Property owners and managers	Drug dealers and users	Gang and drug house abatement ordinance	3	Number of narcotics offenses decreased by 72% in targeted buildings and 31% in surrounding areas.
Mazerolle, Price and Roehl (2000)	Property and business owners	Drug dealers and users	Health and Safety, building codes, fire, rodent, housing codes	5	Reduced drug calls at experimental sites by 7.7% compared to an increase in drug calls at control sites by 54.7%; Beat Health intervention reduced drug calls for service at the residential experimental sites by 13.2% whereas the control residential sites increased by 14.4%.
Joliet P. D. (2000)	Property owners	Tenants	Rental Inspection Ordinance	2	Calls for service for drug-related activities reduced by 55%; calls for service related to quality of life also decreased.
San Diego P. D. (2000)	Property owners	Drug dealers	Safe Street Now Act, abatement, evictions	2	Average numbers of calls for service in apartment block and neighboring blocks decreased from twenty-three to two per month.

Response Team). The DART program uses nuisance abatement statutes and evictions to control drug problems at residential properties. In the first instance, DART members send a letter to the owner to inform them of the drug activity on their property and to warn them that under California Law, if repeated drug dealing is found, the City of San Diego can take the owner to court. If this occurs, the property could be closed for up to one year and the owner fined up to $25,000. As part of the DART program, officers from the Code Compliance Department, the police and the landlord meet to develop a plan for preventing future drug dealing (Eck and Wartell, 1998).

Other studies such as Hope (1994) and Clarke and Bichler (1998) and Ramker (1999) report on similar third party policing initiatives involving enforcement of housing, building and safety codes and, in Hope's (1994) study, council by-laws. These studies, like the evaluations by Green (1996), Mazerolle and her colleagues (1998, 2000) and Eck and Wartell (1998), emphasized code enforcement as the legal lever to ensure compliance from the third party.

The Cook County Drug Abatement program described in Lurigio et al. (1998) is slightly different in that it involves a specialized Narcotics Nuisance Abatement Unit (NNAU) that is administered by the Cook County (Chicago) State's Attorney's Office. The NNAU uses three approaches to controlling drug problems at commercial establishments: voluntary abatement, prosecutorial abatement and community outreach. The program and legislative basis is similar to the DART (San Diego) and SMART (Oakland) initiatives.

Lurigio et al. (1998) describe the legislative basis to the Cook County initiative, which parallels the history and context of many other abatement initiatives across the US (e.g. New York's "Padlock Law Enforcement Program" [see Ward, 1987] and a drug abatement program in Seattle, Washington [see Ferguson and Fitzsimons, 1990]). They write:

> Statutory provisions for the abatement of drug houses existed prior to the NNAU's creation. In 1915, the state legislature adopted the Lewdness Public Nuisance Act, Chapter $100\frac{1}{2}$, sec.1-13, Illinois Revised Statutes. Although this legislation did not specifically address drug houses, it provided the statutory impetus for civil and criminal abatement of public nuisances. In the amendments added to this statute in 1957, and in the enactment of the Illinois Criminal Code of 1961, Chapter 38, sec 1, provisions for the abatement of drug houses were specifically mentioned for the first time in Illinois law. Subsequent amendments to these statutes and to the Cannabis Control Act, Chapter $56\frac{1}{2}$, sec 701-719 and the Controlled Substances Act, Chapter $56\frac{1}{2}$, sec 1100-1603, advanced the possibility of nuisance abatement as a means for reducing drug houses. This early legislation neither conformed to current definitions and methods of abatement nor clearly provided for circumstances in which property owners had no knowledge of the nuisances.

Hence, provisions in the earlier statutes existed only for voluntary owner abatements, subject to penalties if alleviation of the nuisance did not occur; but all of this was directed at property owners who knew of the nuisances. Furthermore, no clear provisions were available for forfeiture of properties gained through illicit drug and drug paraphernalia profits. In 1982, the legislature adopted the Narcotics Forfeiture Act, Chapter $56^1/_2$, sec 1651-1660, which outlined forfeiture of real and other properties obtained from the receipts of illicit drug profits. The Drug Paraphernalia Act Chapter $56^1/_2$, sec 2101-2107 took effect in 1983 and applied forfeiture of illegal drug paraphernalia but not of real property. Amendments in 1990 and 1992 to Chapter $100^1/_2$ provided greater statutory clarification for both the abatement of drug houses and the encouragement of voluntary abatement by property owners subject to civil prosecution. Also clarified was the definition of a drug house: any property where two arrests for illicit drug activity have occurred within a 12-month period.   (Lurigio et al., 1998: 193–194)

As this passage suggests, drug nuisance abatement statutes have undergone several key changes, particularly in recent years, to increase their specificity and provide clear avenues for the police (and others, such as prosecutors) to act against properties with drug problems. It is also interesting to note the ease with which police can initiate legal proceedings against properties with suspected (or known) drug problems. For example, the specification that a drug house is a property "where two arrests for illicit drug activity have occurred within a 12 month period" makes it very easy indeed for the police to justify action against the property owner. That is, it is very easy for the police to make two arrests at properties with even low levels of drug activity (see Weisburd and Green, 1995; see also Green, 1996, pp. 90–93).

The next study by Higgins and Coldren (2000) evaluated the effect of the intensive enforcement of the Chicago Gang and Drug House Abatement Ordinance enacted. In one district of the city, attorneys teamed up with council inspectors for intensive targeting property owners and applying administrative sanctions against those who did not improve the management of their property and dealt with criminal tenants.

The Joliet Police Department (2000) and San Diego Police Department (2000) third party policing initiatives aimed at residential properties introduced two new legislative levers to control drug activity. In Joliet, the police used a city rental inspection ordinance that required property owners of two or more rental units to pass a maintenance inspection and to maintain a rental inspection certificate for each property. The certificate, which can be revoked for cause, must be renewed every two years. The city used to enforce certification only in response to complaints from tenants and neighbors and the police used the ordinance to teach landlords to identify problem tenants, to screen prospective tenants, to enforce illegal drug clauses in leases and to evict problem tenants. At police request, the city council passed an ordinance requiring landlords to cooperate with police once they were notified that their property was involved in criminal activity. If they failed to cooperate, they could be forced to vacate their property.

In San Diego, the police used the Safe Streets Now Act to pressure landlords to reduce drug problems. The Safe Streets Now Act is designed to demand better management from landlords whose properties attract drug activity and other crime. Neighbors gather evidence on properties they suspect is used for illegal activity. Then they send a demand letter to the property owners asking them to clean up the property and evict the problem tenants. If the property owners fail to comply or fail to resolve the problems, the people go to a small claims court and argue that the owners are maintaining a public nuisance by allowing illegal activity to occur on their property. Under the rules of the small claims court, each neighbor is eligible to claim for damages. The threat of huge financial penalties often compels the owners to step in and take care of the problems.

Program outcomes for residential targets

The evaluations reviewed in this section used a variety of measures to assess the program outcomes. Calls for service data were used by Green (1996), Mazerolle and her colleagues (1998, 2000), Clarke and Bichler (1998), Hope (1994), the San Diego Police Department (2000) and the Joliet Police Department (2000). Arrest data were used by Green (1996), Clarke and Bichler (1998), and Ramker (1999) who also used a narcotics seizure measure. Eck and Wartell (1998) and Higgins and Coldren (2000) used police data detailing the number of reported offenses. Lurigio and his colleagues (1998) examined perceptions by landlords to assess the impact the strategy had on targeted drug problems.

On face value, the outcome results are surprisingly consistent across every study examined. As a result of the third party policing initiative, calls for service were reduced, arrests went down and perceived drug dealing went down (see Table 5.1). For example, Green (1996) shows that the SMART (Specialized Multi-Agency Response Team) approach, involving intense site visits by teams of local inspectors (including housing, health and safety, building, rodent control and fire), had a positive and significant effect in alleviating the level of drug nuisance problems at targeted sites. The results reveal a 34 percent reduction in narcotics arrests, 4 percent reduction in narcotics calls and a 59 percent reduction in field contacts at the targeted sites. More than a third of the targeted sites showed improvement in the outdoor appearances after SMART intervention. In short, the study demonstrates that a third party drug-control strategy that aims to clean up the physical conditions of drug nuisance places can significantly reduce the amount of drug-related activity (Green, 1996).

In a follow-up study of the same program Lorraine Green Mazerolle and her colleagues (2000) demonstrated, under experimental field trial conditions, that street-level drug dealing places targeted using a third party policing strategy improved relative to control sites. Police used traditional law enforcement tactics to deal with the street-level drug problems at the control sites. The results show that the Beat Health intervention reduced drug calls for service at the residential experimental sites by 13.2 percent whereas the control residential sites increased by 14.4 percent. There was also a statistically significant reduction in males selling drugs and fewer signs of disorder at the residential experimental sites than at the residential control sites following the intervention (Mazerolle, Kadleck and Roehl, 1998). The experiment also found some improvement in catchment areas surrounding the experimental residential sites, but a possible displacement of drug problems in and around both the commercial experimental and control sites (see later).

Similarly, Eck and Wartell (1998) show that third party policing efforts that sought to improve the place management of rental properties with drug dealing problems led to a sizable reduction in reported crime within six months of the intervention. They report that following meetings with the Drug Abatement Response Team (DART) there was a 60 percent reduction in crime in the experimental group. For the group that received just a letter (and not a meeting), there was a 13 percent reduction in crime at the experimental group drug dealing places.

In their Chicago study, Higgins and Coldren (2000) also reported a positive effect of the intensive abatement program. In the experimental district, the number of reported narcotics offences reduced by 72 percent in the buildings specifically targeted, and 31 percent in the catchment area surrounding these buildings, in the year following the intervention. The number of narcotics offenses also diminished in the control districts but at a rate 10 to 23 percent lower.

Not surprisingly, some of the scientifically weaker evaluation studies reveal even more dramatic results. Hope (1994) reports that calls for service declined by 95 percent in targeted blocks and by 70 percent in adjacent blocks. Clarke and Bichler (1998) show that properties owned by slumlords attracted 60 percent more calls for service than neighboring properties which were properly managed. They also found that the number of arrests was reduced by 75 percent in the two years following any intervention that had forced slumlords to improve their properties. Ramker (1999) reported that in the year following the enactment of the Nuisance Abatement ordinance narcotics arrests went up 600 percent and drug seizure increased 300 percent, as police were able to focus law enforcement on pressing problems identified by residents.

The Joliet Police Department (2000) and the San Diego (2000) studies provide additional evidence that third party policing tactics are effective in reducing crime problems. In Joliet, calls for service for drug-related activities were reduced by 55 percent and calls for service for quality of life complaints also decreased (Joliet Police Department, 2000). In San Diego, the Safe Streets Now Act enabled police to reduce the average number of calls for service in targeted apartment blocks and neighboring blocks from twenty-three per month down to two per month.

In a descriptive analysis of drug abatement programs (not included in Table 5.1), Davis and Lurigio (1998) report that most property owners complied with directives and that drug problems subsided in 85 percent of cases. Property owners, while agreeing that abatement was successful, however, argued that it was unfair to place the burden on them and mentioned instances of retaliation by evicted tenants. We explore the pros and cons of abatement laws in Chapter 7. For now, however, our point is that third party policing initiatives, aimed at property owners with a view to control drug problems in residential settings, reveal impressive and consistent crime control benefits.

Commercial property owners

From the outset, we expected that the documented success of third party policing tactics aimed at residential property owners (see above) would be more pronounced in commercial settings. Commercial property owners generally have more to lose (at least financially) from legal action taken against their property than perhaps residential property owners. As such, we expected the impact of third party policing action taken against commercial properties to result in greater declines in drug and drug-related activities than the declines reported above against residential properties. Indeed, Green (1996) reports that the median value of commercial properties targeted by the Beat Health Program was greater than the median value of targeted residential properties.

Table 5.2 presents the results of two new studies that we identified in the literature as reporting evaluation results depicting interventions involving third party policing against commercial properties. The new studies include

Table 5.2 *Commercial property owners as third parties in drug control*

Cite	Third party(s)	Target	Legal basis/lever used to coerce third parties	Scientific rating	Outcome
Weisburd and Green (1995)	Business owners	Drug dealers and users	Housing codes, liquor licensing laws	5	Statistically significant reduction in disorder calls for service reduced in the experimental sites compared to control sites.
Green (1996) [REPEAT]	Property and business owners	Drug dealers and users	Health and Safety, building codes, fire, rodent, housing codes	3	34% reduction in narcotics arrests, 4% reduction in narcotics calls and 59% reduction in field contacts at SMART sites relative to changes city-wide. 37.1% of SMART sites revealed improvement in outdoor appearances after SMART intervention.
Indiana State P. D. (1997)	Local businesses	Drug manufactures	Mandatory reporting of sale of legal chemicals used in drug chemistry	2	Thirty-nine clandestine labs shut down in the three years following the initiative; major supplier of ephedrine shut down.
Mazerolle, Kadleck and Roehl (1998) [REPEAT]	Property and business owners	Drug dealers and users	Health and Safety, building codes, fire, rodent, housing codes	5	
Mazerolle, Price and Roehl (2000) [REPEAT]	Property and business owners	Drug dealers and users	Health and Safety, building codes, fire, rodent, housing codes	5	Beat Health intervention led to 45.2% increase in drug calls for service at the commercial experimental sites compared to a 1,306% increase at the commercial control sites. Disorder decreased by 12.1% at the commercial experimental sites compared to a 37.1% increase at the commercial control sites.

David Weisburd and Lorraine Green's (1995) experimental evaluation of a drug law enforcement program in Jersey City, New Jersey and the Indiana Police Department's (1997) problem-oriented policing evaluation involving a mandatory reporting initiative of businesses selling legal chemicals. We also re-examine Lorraine Green Mazerolle's evaluation of the Beat Health Program in Oakland in 1996 and the experimental evaluation reported in 2000 (and also identified in Table 5.1) that targeted both commercial as well as residential targets.

The Indiana problem-oriented policing study reported in Table 5.2 involved local businesses in south-central and southwest Indiana reporting the sale of legal chemicals used in drug manufacture (e.g. toluene, xylene, muratic acid, battery acid and items such as tubing). Although there was no specific law or statute requiring reporting (hence technically violating our criteria of what should be included as "third party policing"), the study reports that the police managed to "convince" the (legal) suppliers of the drug chemicals to report sales to the police. In one case, the police managed to convince the local supplier of ephedrine tablets to stop selling the drug. It appears the supplier might have been pressured by police as the article mentions, "after several checks of his record by Drug Enforcement Administration agents and a single visit to his establishment by uniformed Indiana State Police officers, the business owner decided to be part of the solution." This particular supplier was eventually shut down. In 2003 a new law was passed that made it easier for retailers to report suspicious sales of chemicals (including providing them with immunity from prosecution).

Lorraine Green Mazerolle and her colleagues (2000) designed an experimental evaluation of the Beat Health Program in Oakland that created statistical "blocks" to enable close examination of the potential for differential impact of Beat Health on residential and commercial properties. They used a blocked randomized experimental design and assigned commercial properties to one block and residential properties into a second block. Randomized block designs, which allocate cases randomly within pairs or groups, minimize the effects of variability on a study by ensuring that like cases are compared with one another (see Lipsey, 1990; Neter, Wasserman and Kutner, 1990; Weisburd, 1993).[2] Mazerolle and her colleagues randomized cases in the study within statistical blocks because they believed there were substantial differences between drug dealing activities at commercial and residential properties (see Mazerolle, Price and Roehl, 2000; see also Green, 1996) and that law enforcement efforts would differentially affect drug problems at commercial and residential properties. All incoming cases were verified as being either commercial or residential properties.

Residential properties were allocated within the "residential block" and commercial properties were randomly allocated to the control or experimental treatment within the "commercial block."

Like the Oakland drug law enforcement experiment, an earlier field experiment by David Weisburd and Lorraine Green also used a block randomized design that sought to assess the differential impact of innovative drug law enforcement tactics (1995). In the Weisburd/Green experiment, however, the statistical blocks were created based on the size of the drug market, rather than on the type of target. Analysis of a series of videotapes made of the targeted sites reveals that 79 percent of the sites targeted in the Jersey City experiment involved a commercial target. Analysis of Weisburd and Green's experiment as a third party policing "tactic" is further confounded because the intervention involved a step-wise approach to closing down street drug markets of which one step in the program was to "closedown" drug dealing locations using third party policing tactics. Other steps in the intervention included a "preparation" set of interventions, crackdowns and a maintenance step. As such, the experimental evaluation by Weisburd and Green (1995) technically cannot illuminate whether or not the "closedown" tactic contributed more or less to reductions in crime than other "steps" in the program intervention. We include the Weisburd and Green (1995) study in this section because of the preponderance of commercial sites in the drug markets targeted.

Weisburd and Green (1995) compared the effectiveness of unsystematic, arrest-oriented enforcement based on ad hoc target selection (the control group) to a treatment strategy involving analysis of assigned drug hot spots, followed by site-specific enforcement and collaboration with landlords and local government regulatory agencies and concluding with monitoring and maintenance for up to a week following the intervention. The specific interventions used in the Jersey City drug law enforcement experiment included a step-wide intervention program including crackdowns and closedowns. Crackdowns generally lasted only a few hours and were determined by the social and physical characteristics of the hotspot, the number of offenders at the site, and the types of drugs sold. "Closedowns" (or what we would now regard as third party policing) were conducted when bars, restaurants, or stores were considered as involved in drug activity. At these sites, the police coordinated efforts with local government agencies such as sanitation, fire and building departments to cite the businesses for violating regulations related to health or to alcohol and beverage licensing. Obviously, it was this closedown tactic of the Jersey City experiment that interests us most and motivated us to include this study in our review.

Program outcomes for commercial targets

Across the five studies included in this section, calls for service, arrests and incident reports were used to measure the outcome of the interventions. The results reveal some important findings. The Indiana "mandatory" reporting study reports that thirty-nine clandestine laboratories were shut down in the three years following implementation of the project. The scientific weakness of the evaluation precludes us from being able to estimate whether or not the results are strong or weak and whether or not the shut downs resulted from the initiative or not. The results are merely suggestive that the initiative was instrumental in reducing drug manufacturing in parts of the State of Indiana.

The results from the Jersey City and Oakland experiments are more instructive. Mazerolle and her colleagues (2000) reporting on the Oakland Experiment compared the experimental and control treatments ("type") as well as the "block" effects (commercial versus residential) across four categories of calls for service incidents: violent, property, disorder and drugs. They used the street block as the unit of analysis and compared the effects of the interventions using percent change for the number of calls over a twelve-month pre-intervention period compared to the number of calls over a twelve-month post-intervention period. We note that there were just fourteen commercial sites in the commercial "block", perhaps creating some limitations in the interpretability of the block findings. The results revealed that the experimental commercial experimental sites experienced a 45.2 percent increase in drug calls, compared to a 1,306.2 percent increase in drug calls at the commercial control sites. For disorder calls for service there was a 12.1 percent decrease in the commercial experimental sites and a 37.1 percent increase in drug calls to the commercial control sites. Both differences were statistically significant.

Mazerolle and her colleagues (2000) also found a possible displacement of drug problems in and around both the commercial, experimental and control sites. Notably, the displacement effect was most pronounced in the commercial control sites. While the density of drug calls increased for both experimental and control commercial properties, the increase was very large (282.2 percent) for the control commercial properties. In short, the Mazerolle third party policing experiment in Oakland reveals that third party policing tactics (at least those tactics used against the commercial properties) were not as effective at the commercial sites as they were against the experimental residential sites. Importantly, however, the Beat Health tactics at the commercial sites appear to at least have contained the escalation of more serious drug problems far better than traditional drug control tactics such as arrests and preventive patrolling that were used against the control commercial sites.

The Weisburd and Green (1995) experiment created statistical blocks around the size of the drug market activity. Their results reveal that the treatment drug hot spots, compared to the control drug hot spots, fared better with regard to disorder and disorder related crimes. Importantly, most of the reduction in drug and disorder problems in the experimental drug hot spots stemmed from the high-activity drug-market locations that contained commercial targets such as liquor stores, bars and convenience stores. The study, however, cannot isolate whether the crackdown, closedown or some combination of the two tactics contributed most to the reductions in drug activity at the experimental targets.

Overall, the results of the studies described above suggest third party policing tactics used to control drug problems at commercial properties are probably more beneficial than routine, preventive patrolling. We are still left wondering, however, as to how much in crime control benefit is gained by implementing third party policing strategies aimed at controlling drug problems at commercial targets. We pick up this point again in Chapter 8.

Public housing

Public housing sites are another type of place where drug problems prevail. We identified five evaluation studies that involved third party policing practices in public housing settings (see Table 5.3). These include an evaluation of a problem-oriented policing program across six public housing sites in Jersey City (Mazerolle et al., 2000) coupled with a related study of evictions from public housing sites by Justin Ready and his colleagues (1998) using data from the Jersey City Public Housing Problem-Oriented Policing project (see Mazerolle et al., 2000), a case study of an initiative by the local police and Hackney Housing Department in London (Morris, 1998), a study by Deborah Weisel (1990) and a report by Simpson (1999). In each of these studies, the police partnered with the local public housing authority and used legal provisions to create pressure on leaseholders to reduce drug problems in their apartment or face eviction. In most cases, the ultimate targets of the action were children or relatives of the leaseholder.

The legal levers identified in these studies include a special council eviction ordinance (Simpson, 1999), drug free zone legislation (see Weisel, 1990), injunctions (Morris, 1998), evicting residents, creating and enforcing new housing policies (Mazerolle et al., 2000) and administrative "notices to cease" citing public housing lease conditions that could lead to eviction if

Table 5.3 *Third party policing to control drug problems in public housing*

Cite	Third party(s)	Target	Legal basis/lever used to coerce third parties	Scientific rating	Outcome
Weisel (1990)	Public housing authority; leaseholders	Drug using tenants	Evictions, building codes, housing codes, drug-free zone	1	Striking decrease in drug dealing; improved well being in complex; 55% decrease in violent crime; street sale of drugs declined.
Morris (1998)	Public housing authority; leaseholders	Drug involved tenant	Injunctions	1	Domestic burglaries fell by 82%, robberies by 79% and vehicle crime decreased by 55% following the injunctions and evictions of criminal tenants.
Ready et al. (1998)	Public housing authority; leaseholders	Tenants	Lease conditions	4	"Notices to cease" (evictions due to violations of lease conditions for non-criminal behaviour) are a powerful tool to control tenants' activities and target criminal tenants who pay their rent and avoid arrest; their use should be monitored to avoid abuse.
Simpson (1999)	Public housing authority; leaseholders	Drug using tenants	Council eviction ordinances	1	Within two months of ordinance being enacted, four people have been evicted for drug-related activities and a fifth one is being investigated.
Mazerolle, Ready et al. (2000)	Public housing authority	Tenants	Lease conditions	4	25% decrease in serious calls for service across the six public housing sites but no decrease for public disorder calls.

violated (Ready et al., 1998). Sheridan Morris, for example, reporting from a third party policing case study in Hackney, London describes the use of injunctions on housing estates. He states that the injunctions were used to ". . . provide interim relief from anti-social and criminal behavior, and to try and counter witness and victim intimidation on the Kingsmead Estate" (Morris, 1998: 340). The injunctions were taken out under Section 222 of the Local Government Act of 1972 which provides local authorities with very broad powers to prosecute where a local authority considers it expedient for the promotion and protection of the interests of the inhabitants of their area (see Morris, 1998).

In the Jersey City project, Ready and his colleagues (1998) describe the use of the Anti-drug Abuse Act of 1988 (Public Law 100-690) that states that criminal activity, including drug use, is cause for termination of tenancy (1998: 309). More recently, the Housing Opportunity Program Extension Act of 1996 gave public housing managers the authority to evict suspected offenders after an administrative hearing, without having to wait for a criminal conviction. The housing authority in Jersey City issued "notices to cease" when tenants were in violation of public housing policy (e.g. occupancy violation such as housing "boarders," throwing objects from a window, unsanitary conditions and unruly behavior) or when they were in violation of administrative conditions (e.g. failure to file occupancy forms, inspection noncompliance and failure to attend meetings). These notices to cease formed the basis of eviction proceedings being brought against public housing tenants (see Ready et al., 1998: 315).

Program outcomes for public housing sites

A variety of measures were used to assess the effectiveness of the third party policing activities in public housing settings. As with residential and commercial sites, researchers used calls for service, reported crime incidents and arrests as indicators of change following implementation of third party policing initiatives. Ready et al. (1998) used data gathered from public housing lease records to differentiate the factors most likely to lead to eviction from public housing.

Results from the evaluation studies reveal that third party policing activities can be highly effective in reducing drug problems in public housing sites. Weisel (1990) for example, reports that there was a striking decrease in drug dealing, improved well-being in the complex, a 55 percent decrease in violent crime and a significant decline in street drug sales. Morris (1998) reports that domestic burglaries fell by 82 percent, robberies declined by

79 percent and vehicle crime decreased by 55 percent. Simpson (1999) reporting the results of the council eviction ordinance states that within two months of the ordinance being enacted the level of drug problems had been reduced and that four people were evicted for drug related activities and a fifth tenant was being investigated.

The Jersey City Public Housing Project revealed that the quantity of problem-oriented policing activities led to reductions in calls for service concerning interpersonal violent crimes (robberies, assaults, domestic assaults), property crimes (burglary), and vehicle crimes (auto theft). Mazerolle and her colleagues (2000) did not find that the problem-oriented policing activities reduced public disorder calls (e.g. drugs, morals, nuisance and suspicious persons). Overall, there was a 25 percent decrease in serious calls for service across the six public housing sites in our study: a decline in calls that was not mirrored in the wider community.

The Jersey City Public Housing evaluation also found that the greater the volume of problem-solving activities, the greater the crime control benefits. Moreover, the study revealed that the crime control benefits accrued more as a result of police problem-solving activities (such as arrests, enforcing warrants) than as a result of public housing authorities problem-solving activities (such as serving "notices to cease," evicting tenants). This effort at disentangling the unique contributions of direct and third party policing activities tends to suggest, therefore, that the direct, police activities are more powerful in reducing crime problems in public housing settings than those third party policing activities mobilized by the public housing authority.

Overall, the research into third party policing and its effectiveness in controlling drug problems in public housing settings is suggestive of crime control benefits at best. The results suggest that third party policing activities were not the most effective strategy in reducing crime problems in public housing sites. Indeed, the Jersey City Public Housing Project (Mazerolle et al., 2000; Ready et al., 1998) found that violations of lease conditions were a crucial factor leading to tenant evictions from public housing sites and that ". . . notices to cease appear to be an important and direct tool used by site managers to control the activities of public housing residents" (Ready, 1998: 321). When the role of these administrative complaints were examined in the context of the overall evaluation findings (see Mazerolle et al., 2000) the results suggest, however, that evictions did not seem to be a proximate and important factor in reducing drug problems in particular and other categories of crime in general. The results tend to suggest that the coercive authority of the police was more effective in controlling crime in public housing than the types of problem-solving activities (e.g. notices to cease) that were available to public housing employees.

Medical practitioners

One new avenue for controlling drug problems is police partnering with medical practitioners and creating incentive-based systems for doctors to report drug prescriptions. A study reported by Read and Tilley (2000) identifies a lever that requires doctors to report drug prescriptions (see Table 5.4). In the UK, doctors can prescribe methadone as they see fit and some doctors used to prescribe enough for several days. Some doctors were renowned for their "generous" prescriptions. The prescribed methadone could then be resold by the person to whom the treatment was originally prescribed. Police analyzed the problem and pressured the Health Authority to do something about this; the Health Authority in turn pressured doctors to change their methadone prescription regime. A voluntary ban on methadone tablets (more likely to be misused than ampoules) was put in place in November 1998 and strong guidelines on prescribing were issued to doctors (e.g. prescribe only the daily dose, pharmacists to supervise the taking of the drug). Pharmacies' dispensing of methadone was monitored and doctors who continued over-prescribing were contacted and reprimanded by the Health Authority.

Since this time, the UK government has been looking at changing the laws regulating doctors' prescribing of drugs. Following a report by the Advisory Council on the Misuse of Drugs in 2000, the Department of Health has been setting up a system to organize and monitor the delivery of methadone. For instance, tablets and ampoules would no longer be available (since they can be taken away and sold). Instead, people would visit the chemist daily and ingest the dose there. Other recommendations include reporting doctors who over-prescribe to the General Medicine Council (GMC), the medical practitioners' registering body. The Chief Medical Officer issues guidelines to doctors and all doctors are supposed to follow these guidelines. The Read and Tilley (2000) study shows the changing prescription practices from January 1998 to June 1999. The amount of ampoules and tablets being prescribed went down and the trend correlated with a decrease in 1998 of methadone-related death. In 1999 no methadone-related deaths occurred. In conclusion, they report a ten-fold reduction in prescription of methadone tablets

Table 5.4 *Third party policing, medical practitioners and the control of drug problems*

Cite	Third party(s)	Target	Legal basis/ lever used to coerce third parties	Scientific rating	Outcome
Read and Tilley (2000)	Doctors	Drug users	Monitoring of drug prescription	2	In UK, ten-fold reduction in prescription of methadone tablets, which reduced overdosing and trafficking and eliminated methadone-related deaths.

and describe how this third party policing measure reduced overdosing and trafficking and eliminated methadone-related deaths (see Read and Tilley, 2000).

Function promoters

Another strategy that is gaining popularity with the police is when they enlist function promoters as third parties and then threaten to use injunctions, search warrants and city ordinances against the function if the promoters do not adhere to standards set out by the police aimed at decreasing drug use at Rave Parties and similar events that typically involve illicit activity and drug use. One example is a recent promotion of a concert in Florida where the promoter was advertising that a live, on-stage suicide was to take place during the concert. The council intervened by using an injunction against the promoter and stopped the concert from going ahead (*Courier Mail*, 2003).[3]

Similarly, in a report prepared by the National Drug Intelligence Center (2001), authors report the results of "Operation Rave Review" that was initiated in New Orleans in January 2000 (see Table 5.5). This program targeted rave party promoters in an effort to control illicit drug use by party goers. The Drug Enforcement Authority (DEA) and the New Orleans police noticed that drug overdoses requiring emergency room visits usually occurred during rave parties. They decided to target rave party promoters who allowed open and widespread drug use during the parties. Police used

Table 5.5 *Third party policing, function promoters and the control of drug problems*

Cite	Third party(s)	Target	Legal basis/ lever used to coerce third parties	Scientific rating	Outcome
National Drug Intelligence Center (2001) –	Rave promoters	Party goers	Injunctions; search warrants; city ordinances.	2	Operation Rave Review resulted in a 90% decrease in drug use at rave parties and eliminated overdoses.

a federal statute (21 USC s. 856) to investigate rave promoters and gather evidence that some promoters allowed distribution and use of drugs during their events. This statute is known as the "crack house" law and was designed to combat the use of rented houses as drug houses and illegal labs. It stipulates that it is unlawful to knowingly maintain, rent, lease or make available for use any place for the purpose of manufacturing, distributing, or using any illegal drugs. Any person who violates this statute is liable for up to twenty years' jail or a $500,000 fine.

Following the initiative in New Orleans three promoters were arrested and indicted in January 2001. According to a CNN report it was the first time that the federal "crack house" law had been used to prosecute rave party promoters. The operation drew upon injunctions, search warrants and city ordinances against the rave party promoters. The report states that Operation Rave Review resulted in a 90 percent decrease in drug use at rave parties and eliminated overdoses (National Drug Intelligence Center, 2001). Again, the scientific integrity of the study is low (scientific rating of 2), thus raising questions as to whether or not this third party policing initiative is as powerful as reported.

Asset forfeiture (including homes, cars and boats)

One area of third party drug control that warrants special mention is civil asset forfeiture. The most well known application of asset forfeiture laws is directed against property – boats, houses, cars etc – used in the commission of drug trafficking or narcotics use. Mary Cheh describes asset forfeiture as an "in rem action, that is, a proceeding directed against a property and not against any person having an interest in property. It is based on the legal fiction that property used in or derived through violations of law is 'guilty' and may be confiscated" (Cheh, 1998: 48). Forfeiture is authorized in over 140 federal laws and all states [in the United States] have one or more statutes permitting seizure of assets (Kessler, 1994). Worrall (2001) suggests that civil asset forfeiture is designed to weaken the economic foundations of the illicit drug trade and assist law enforcement in reducing drug-related crime. It is used widely by drug law enforcement agencies.

Through our systematic search of the research literature, we were unable to uncover an evaluation of the use of civil asset forfeiture and its impact on drug markets or use, despite the fact that some authors claim that asset forfeiture is one of the most effective tools to combat drug trafficking (Warchol and Johnson, 1996). However, its widespread use by law enforcement agencies to control drugs makes it an important third party activity to acknowledge. There have, however, been numerous challenges to the use of civil asset forfeiture for crime control purposes (see Chevy, 1996; Hakala, 1997; Jensen and Gerber, 1996; Miller and Selva, 1994; Worrall, 2001). These challenges have been discussed in more depth in Chapter 4.

Quantitative review

From the outset, our goal was to conduct a meta-analysis of third party policing interventions. The meta-analytic technique is a collection of systematic quantitative procedures employed to synthesize the research findings of multiple studies testing the same hypothesis (Lipsey and Wilson, 2001). Through the calculation of effect sizes, studies varying in terms of design and methodological procedure can be meaningfully compared. Effect size is a parameter of the magnitude of the effect of a specific intervention, independent of the sample size of a study. Generally, effect sizes are combined to calculate mean effect sizes, allowing an inference to be made regarding the overall effect of the intervention. Formulas are subsequently employed to test the homogeneity of the studies (Q statistic) (Lipsey and Wilson, 2001). Typically, to allow for such an analysis to be meaningful, the meta-analyst must have a sufficient number of studies testing the same general hypothesis and employing the same or highly similar outcome variables and operationalizations (Lipsey and Wilson, 2001).

A comprehensive meta-analysis of our third party policing studies was not possible for two basic reasons. First, a lot of the studies included in the narrative review (see above) did not report sufficient quantitative information to allow the calculation of an effect size statistic. Second, those studies reporting sufficient data to calculate an effect size were extremely hetero-geneous in terms of the type of crime targeted (i.e. drug sellers, drug users, drug manufacturing, places with drug problems) and outcome variables (arrests, calls, observations). As such, it was our judgment that the degree of heterogeneity of the outcomes was too great to conduct a meaningful meta-analysis.

The good news, however, is that several methods exist for systematically examining groups of studies and providing important insights about pro-gram outcomes without taking the extra step of combining the outcomes in a formal meta-analysis. In this section, we present the results of a quan-titative review of eight of the twenty-one drug crime studies included in the narrative reviews described earlier in this chapter.[4] Typically, there are three approaches to the calculation of an effect size: (a) standardized mean difference, (b) correlation, and (c) odds-ratio (Lipsey and Wilson, 2001). The present quantitative review predominately uses the odds-ratio effect size statistic, which allows a comparison between two groups (the inter-vention and comparison groups), pertaining to the change in the rela-tive odds of an outcome (i.e. arrest, incident, call for service) occurring as a result of the implementation of an intervention (Lipsey and Wilson, 2001; Wilson, personal communication; Welsh and Farrington, 2003). Welsh and Farrington (2003) outline the appropriateness of using the odds-ratio effect size when the data most commonly reported by studies to be analyzed is incident data for intervention and comparison groups/areas, pre-post intervention.

The odds-ratio effect size is calculated using the following formula:

$$OR = \frac{f_{post_c}/f_{pre_c}}{f_{post_e}/f_{pre_e}}$$

Where: f represents the frequency of the outcome variable for the con-trol/comparison (c) and experimental/intervention (e) groups at pre- and post-intervention.

One of the fundamental advantages of the odds-ratio is the ease of interpretation – for example, an odds-ratio of 1.37 represents that the control/comparison group experienced a 37 percent increase in the out-come variable in comparison to the intervention/treatment group (due to the fact that the mean of $OR = 1$). Conversely, the effect of the intervention on the experimental group can be assessed by calculating the inverse of the odds-ratio, using the formula below:

$$\text{Inverse of OR} = \frac{1}{OR}$$

That is, in the previous example, the inverse of the odds-ratio would be $1/1.37 = 0.73$, which would represent a 27 percent decrease in the outcome variable in the intervention group compared to the control group (again due to the fact that the mean of $OR = 1$). The odds-ratio effect size statistic can also be interpreted as such: odds-ratios below one suggest a negative intervention effect, while an odds-ratio above one is indicative of positive intervention effects.

Another advantage of the odds-ratio is the fact that the equations used to derive such an effect size take into account the possible effects of pre-intervention non-equivalence between the intervention and control groups. For instance, in Green (1996), the number of calls for service, pre- and post-intervention, for the intervention group (target sites) were 28 and 27 respectively, while for the comparison group (City-wide comparison data) the figures were 807 and 898 respectively. Thus, the odds-ratio allows for the calculation of effect size that is independent of group non-equivalence. Table 5.6 below presents the results of the odds-ratios calculated for sixteen outcomes across seven third party policing evaluation studies targeting drug-related crime. We do not present graphed results for two outcomes for two of the studies (Mazerolle et al., 1998 and Clarke and Bichler, 1998) due to their large confidence intervals.

As Table 5.6 shows, there were sixteen outcomes calculated (fourteen appearing on the graph). Desirable effects were found in eleven of the sixteen outcomes analyzed (69 percent). Of the eleven desirable effects, nine (56 percent of the total) were found to be statistically significant at either the $p < .05$, $.01$, or $.001$ level. Conversely, five of the effects were in an undesirable direction. Of the five undesirable effects, none were statistically significant. That is, none of the interventions produced statistically significant negative effects. These results suggest that third party policing efforts aimed at controlling drug problems are generally quite successful.

The standardized mean difference approach was utilized for one of the drug evaluation studies (Eck and Wartell, 1998) whose effect sizes could not be calculated employing the odds-ratio approach: in this study only post-intervention data were reported, thus negating the ability to calculate an odds-ratio statistic. The formula for calculating the standardized mean difference is as follows:

$$d = \frac{M_C - M_E}{S_{pooled}}$$

Where: d is the standardized mean difference effect size, M_C is the control/comparison group post-intervention mean, M_E is the

Table 5.6 Odds ratio results for third party policing strategies targeting drug-related crime[a]

Citation	Year	Effect name	Effect	Lower	Upper	P Value		
Clarke	1998	Calls for service	6.566	4.817	8.951	.000		
Green	1996	Field contacts	1.920	1.026	3.595	.038		
Green	1996	Calls for service	1.154	.674	1.975	.601		
Green	1996	Arrests	1.232	.737	2.059	.425		
Green	1995	Arrests and contacts	1.849	1.659	2.062	.000		
Higgins	2000	Narcotic offences	2.440	1.295	4.598	.005		
Mazerolle	2000	CFS violence related	.982	.850	1.134	.806		
Mazerolle	2000	CFS property crime related	.929	.783	1.104	.404		
Mazerolle	2000	CFS drug related	1.661	1.390	1.985	.000		
Mazerolle	2000	CFS disorder related	.989	.917	1.068	.782		
Weisburd	1995	CFS violence related	.960	.880	1.046	.350		
Weisburd	1995	CFS property crime related	.920	.805	1.051	.218		
Weisburd	1995	CFS nuisance related	1.112	1.042	1.187	.001		
Weisburd	1995	CFS drug-related	1.324	1.116	1.571	.001		

Graph axis: 0.1 0.2 0.5 1 2 5 1

Undesirable effect — Desirable effect

[a] The "arrest" outcome (97.44% decrease in number of arrests in treatment compared to control site; statistically significant and desirable) from the Clarke and Bichler-Richardson (1998) study, as well as the "males selling drugs" (84.85% decrease in males selling drugs in treatment compared to control sites; statistically significant and desirable) from the Mazerolle (1998) study were excluded from the above graph given their extremely large confidence intervals. (Confidence intervals were 6.78–224.38 for the arrest outcome in Clarke and Bichler (1998) study and .86–50.54 for the "males selling drugs" outcome in the Mazerolle et al. (1998) study.)

Table 5.7 *Standardized mean difference results of third party policing strategies targeting drug-related crime*

Citation	Year	Effect name	Effect	Lower	Upper	P value	−1.00	−0.50	0.00	0.50	1.00
Eck	1998	Reported crimes	.322	−.115	.759	.140					
Eck	1998	Reported crimes	.375	−.078	.828	.097					

Undesirable effect Desirable effect

intervention/treatment group post-intervention mean, and S_{pooled} is the pooled within standard deviation of the intervention and comparison groups, calculated:

$$S_{pooled} = \sqrt{\frac{s_1^2\,(n_1 - 1) + s_2^2\,(n_2 - 1)}{n_1 + n_2 - 2}}$$

Where: s represents the respective standard deviations of the intervention and comparison groups and n are the respective sample sizes.

It is a little more problematic when interpreting standardized mean difference effect sizes (d). As a guideline for interpretation, Cohen (1977) tentatively suggested standardized mean differences of approximately .2 as representing small effects, .5 medium effects and .8 large effects.

Table 5.7 presents the results for the Eck and Wartell (1998) study. Standardized mean differences were calculated to assess the effect of both levels of the DART intervention (letter only versus letter plus meeting with DART representative) on rates of reported crime at thirty-month post-intervention. The results show that there are relatively small effects (not statistically significant) of the third party policing intervention for both the levels of intervention for crimes reported.

Conclusion

This chapter has provided a review of the research evidence involving third party policing tactics used to control drug problems. Our review suggests that the majority of evidence collated about third party policing involves property owners (residential property owners in particular), as third parties and that the weight of the evidence suggests that third party policing approaches used to control drug problems are generally quite successful. We point out, however, that our inability in some of these studies to disentangle the effects of the third party interventions from other interventions implemented at the same time confounds the results. In Chapter 8 we discuss the need for future researchers to design evaluations of third party policing that allow for the unique contribution of third party policing interventions to be isolated from the contributions of other tactics implemented at the same time.

In short, the answer to our question about the effectiveness of third party policing is that it appears, at least on the surface, that third party policing is an effective mechanism to control drug problems. Using third parties and legal levers (many of which were not intended for crime control purposes) seems to be an effective tactic to expand the responsibility for crime control, sometimes even among unwilling third parties.

CHAPTER 6

Controlling crime problems

Third party policing has wide applicability across a variety of different settings (places, situations and people) and across a variety of different types of crime. In this chapter, we continue presenting the results of our systematic review of third party policing interventions (described in Chapter 5), concentrating on four specific crime categories: tactics geared to reduce violent crime problems, third party policing strategies used to reduce juvenile offending, third party policing aimed at property crime and, finally, third party policing that seeks to reduce a generic set of problems in public places. For each of these four categories we examine the range of third parties co-opted, the types of laws invoked and the outcome of the third party policing interventions.

Violent crime problems

This section examines the effectiveness of third party policing in controlling a variety of violent crimes including assaults, robberies, domestic disputes and gun crimes. Our systematic review reveals five domains where the police have used third party policing tactics to control violent crime problems. These include third party policing tactics that engage businesses (e.g. bars, nightclubs), victims, public officials (e.g. school administrators, probation officers, local council officers), professional service providers (e.g. medical practitioners, lawyers, accountants), and finally, not-for-profit service providers (e.g. victim advocates, social service providers). In this section, we discuss each of these areas of third party policing that seeks to control violent crime.

Business owners

Table 6.1 shows fifteen studies that we have identified as evaluating third party policing tactics aimed at working with business owners and making them take some crime control responsibility to control violent crime problems. These studies include the Arlington Police Department (1998) problem-oriented policing project that used trespass laws to pressure nightclub managers into controlling the behavior of assault perpetrators; an experimental evaluation conducted by Anthony Braga and his colleagues (1999) of twenty-eight violent crime places where police used council ordinances, building codes and evictions to pressure business owners into controlling both robbery and assault problems; a quasi experimental study by Putnam, Rockett and Campbell (1993) who evaluated the effectiveness of a server intervention program in reducing assault injuries on licensed premises; an experimental evaluation of the Safer Bar Program conducted in Canada by Kate Graham and her colleagues (2003) that sought to reduce physical aggression in bars; a community intervention that relied on a responsible beverage service program and Liquor Licensing laws to alter drinking patterns and lower alcohol-related violence, evaluated by Holder et al. (2000) using a quasi-experimental design; a community Safety Action Project in Surfers Paradise by Homel and his colleagues (1997) who examined the effect of a Code of Practice adopted by nightclub owners; evaluations by Felson, Berends, Richardson and Veno (1997) and Hawks et al. (1999) of Police-Licensee Accords which are agreements between police, the Liquor Licensing Commission and publicans to reduce drunkenness and the associated street disorder and violence; a study by Hauritz and her colleagues (1998) in Cairns, Townsville and Mackay (North Queensland) that used liquor licensing laws to pressure bar owners to prevent bar patrons from getting into fights; a study by Alison Warburton and Jonathon Shepherd in Cardiff, Wales (2003) that saw Emergency Department personnel and police partner together to pressure bar owners to reduce assaults; a study by the Halton Police Department in Canada (2002) that used liquor licensing laws, fire safety laws and underage drinking laws to reduce violence among nightclub patrons; the recent Cardiff Tackling Alcohol-related Street Crime (TASC) project by Maguire and Nettleton (2003) where nightclub owners were required to implement environmental crime prevention measures and staff training in their establishments to reduce violence; two studies by Douglas (1998) and Gray, Saggers, Atkinson, Sputore and Bourbon (2000) that evaluated whether liquor licensing restrictions imposed on licensed premises in outback Australian towns were

Table 6.1 *Third party policing, business owners and controlling violent crime*

Cite	Third party(s)	Target	Legal basis	Scientific rating	Outcome
Putnam et al. (1993)	Licensed premises owners	Bar patrons getting into fights	Code of Practice liquor licensing laws	4	Hospital admission for assault-related injuries declined by 21% in treatment area compared to an increase of 4% in control areas.
Bellamy (1996)	Local council, Convenience shop owners	Robbers	Local city ordinance requiring the presence of two staff members at all times	1	The annual robbery rate fell 62% from previous year. In the five years preceding the ordinance, eighteen serious injuries including death were recorded; in the five years following the ordinance, only one serious injury recorded as the result of a robbery.
Felson et al. (1997)	Pub owners	Bar patrons getting into fights	"The Accord", agreement between publicans, police and Liquor Licensing Commission	2	Rates of serious assault in Geelong, Vic, were 52% higher than in six comparable cities; during the implementation of The Accord, rates fell to the same level as the other cities, and in the following three years decreased to 63% of the comparison rates.
Homel et al. (1997)	Nightclub owners	Disorderly nightclub patrons	Code of Practice, liquor licensing laws	2	Decrease in level of patrons' intoxication. Security data reveal the number of reported incidents decreased by 64% in six months following initiative; police data show a 34% drop in number of reported assaults.

Study		Assault perpetrators			Findings
Arlington P. D. (1998)	Nightclub manager	Assault perpetrators	Trespass law	2	Over two years the average number of calls for service per day has dropped 33%.
Douglas (1998)	Bar and bottle shop owners	Violent patrons	Restriction of hours of sale of alcohol	2	Fall of 18% in total number of charges laid by police two years after start of restrictions.
Hauritz et al. (1998)	Bar owners	Bar patrons getting into fights	Liquor licensing	3	Aggression (physical and verbal) and violence decreased 75–81%; decrease in level of male patrons' intoxication.
Braga et al. (1999)	Business owners, Local council, Property owners	Robbery and assault perpetrators	Council ordinances, Building codes, Evictions	5	Number of calls for service and reported criminal incidents significantly reduced in experimental group: social disorder alleviated in 91% of experimental places.
Hawks et al. (1999)	Licensed premises owners	Bar patrons getting into fights	"The Accord," agreement between publicans, police and Liquor Licensing Commission	3	No change in the recorded number of assaults to which police were called.
Gray et al. (2000)	Bar and bottle shop owners	Violent patrons	Restriction of hours of sale of alcohol	2	Decrease in the number of persons taken in police custody on the day of the restrictions from 20% of weekly total down to 8.5%.
Holder et al. (2000)	Licensed premises owners	Violent patrons	Staff training, liquor licensing laws	4	Level of assault injuries in emergency departments reduced by 43% compared to the control area.

(cont.)

Table 6.1 (*cont.*)

Cite	Third party(s)	Target	Legal basis	Scientific rating	Outcome
Halton Regional Police Service (2002)	Nightclub owner	Violent nightclub patrons	Liquor licensing laws, fire safety laws, Search and ID checks	2	Assaults reduced by 75%.
Graham et al. (2003)	Bar owners	Aggressive patrons and staff	Managers and staff training	5	The Safer Bar Program resulted in a modest (around 5%) but significant decrease in aggression in experimental bars especially for intentional aggression by patrons. Aggression by staff did not change.
Maguirre and Nettleton (2003)	Nightclub owners	Aggressive patrons and staff	TASC project	3	Violent incidents reduced by 4%; expected level of violent incidents reduced by 8%.
Warburton and Shepherd (2003)	Bar owners	Assault perpetrators	Liquor licensing	4	Emergency department data used by the police associated with a significant reduction in venue assaults (27%) compared to police intervention alone. But increase of 105% in street assaults.

effective in reducing the rate of assaults; and finally a review by Bellamy (1996) of Florida laws that require that two staff members be on duty at all times in convenience shops in order to reduce the risk of robberies.

With the exception of the Jersey City violent crime places experiment (Braga et al., 1999) and the Bellamy (1996) review, the studies we have identified in this category of third party policing tactics all focus on licensed premises as the venue for violent crime activity. The legal levers used in the studies include trespass laws, building codes, fire codes, evictions, liquor licensing laws and codes of practice. The measures used to assess the programmatic outcomes include observations, calls for service data, incident, emergency room presentations and arrest data.

The outcome results are interesting. The Safer Bar program was a randomized field trial involving twelve control bars and eighteen experimental bars matched on factors such as location, type of bar (e.g. dance club, sports bar, gay bar), ethnicity and age of patrons and size of bar. Before and after observations were conducted where "aggressive incidents" were coded by independent raters. The intervention included the police identifying the bars with the most problems and providing an "Assessment Booklet" for bar owners alerting them to the problems on their premises. Managers and bar staff members were trained in how to deal with drunkenness and aggression. For example, bar staff were trained to identify intoxicated persons lining up to get into the bar and lining up to be served alcohol and then to understand their legal position to refuse entry to intoxicated persons and decline to serve alcoholic beverages to intoxicated patrons. The results show a modest (around 5 percent), but significant decrease in aggression in the experimental bars, especially for intentional aggression (Graham et al., 2003).

Putnam and her colleagues (1993) used a quasi experiment design to evaluate the effects of a training program targeted at bar staff in three communities (one experimental and two control) matched on socio-economic factors, age of residents, community stability, alcohol-related injuries and injury death rates. The intervention consisted of a server intervention program based on a written service policy for licensed premises followed by training of bar staff in enforcing liquor licensing laws, responsible sale of alcohol, and recognizing drunken patrons in order to refuse service. The number of hospital emergency room injuries due to assaults was recorded for eighteen months prior to the program and for eighteen months following the intervention. Hospital admissions for assault-related injuries declined by 21 percent in the experimental community but increased by 4 percent in the control communities. While it was not possible to determine if alcohol was a factor in the assaults that caused the injuries, the authors are confident that the results could be attributed to the effect of the intervention.

The community-based intervention evaluated by Holder et al. (2000) used similar levers but, in addition to voluntary compliance, police were able to apply sanctions against businesses not adhering to the responsible beverage service practices. This tactic is consistent with Stockwell's (2001) general observation suggesting that programs aimed at lifting standards of alcohol service to reduce harm were more effective when legal sanctions could be applied to ensure the cooperation of licensed business owners. In the Holder et al. (2000) study, researchers collected data from hospital emergency rooms in two matched control and treatment communities. In the two years following the introduction of the program, less binge drinking occurred and assault injuries recorded in emergency departments reduced by 43 percent in the experimental community compared to the control community. These results were attributable to the intervention.

The study by Alison Warburton and Jonathon Shepherd (2003) in Cardiff, Wales examined assaults resulting in emergency department treatment. In this study, Accident and Emergency Department (AED)-derived assault injury data were provided on a monthly basis to the police, city authorities and the local media. The police used these data to oppose, on injury grounds, drinks/entertainment license applications in an effort to reduce assaults in nightclubs. The results reveal a 27 percent reduction in assaults in bars, yet a huge 105 percent *increase* in street violence, largely attributed both to a displacement of the assault problem away from inside the bars to outside on the streets as well as to an aggregate rise in the influx of licensed premises in the city center. We discuss this issue of displacement of crime and third party policing further in Chapter 7.

Three other similar studies (Halton Regional Police Service, 2002; Hauritz et al., 1998; Homel, Hauritz, Wortley, McIlwain and Carvolth, 1997) used scientific evaluation methods inferior to the studies outlined above. In both the Homel et al. (1997) study and the replication study by Hauritz et al. (1998), researchers used unobtrusive observational data of aggressive and violent incidents to assess the impact of using liquor licensing laws to restrict the sale of alcohol to intoxicated patrons. In the Halton Regional Police Service (2002) study, police data and a public survey were also used to assess the impact of using liquor licensing laws, fire safety laws and identification checks. The results reveal impressive outcomes. For example, Homel and his colleagues (1997) report that the atmosphere in nightclubs became friendlier and more relaxed, and that drinking rates and drunkenness decreased. As a result, assaults declined by 52 percent, verbal abuse by 82 percent and arguments by 68 percent. Similarly, Hauritz and her colleagues (1998) report a 75–81 percent decrease in physical and verbal aggression and an overall decrease in the level of male patrons intoxicated. In the Halton study, assaults were reported as being reduced by 75 percent.

In Maguire and Nettleton's (2003) TASC project, nightclub owners cooperated with police to implement changes such as installation of CCTV, training, registration and regulation of door staff, and ServeWise, a training program for bar staff. In the twelve months following the implementation of the program, combined data from police records and hospital emergency rooms indicated a rise of 49 percent in street disorder incidents paralleled by a 4 percent decline in violent incidents. The authors pointed out that the rise in disorder incidents had started before the intervention but had demonstrated a marked slow down after the start of the intervention. The decline in violent incidents was accompanied by a 10 percent increase in licensed premises capacity and the authors were able to estimate that the project has helped to reduce the expected level of violence by 8 percent. They also noted that in the rest of South Wales, in the same period, the number of violent assaults increased by 2 percent compared to Cardiff.

In a study by the Arlington Police Department (1998) a somewhat different legal lever was used to deal with aggressive bar patrons. In this study, trespass laws were used to send a message to potential troublemakers that the club did not want or need their business. All persons arrested at the club were given a Criminal Trespass Warning and advised that returning could result in prosecution. Under Texas law, a person may be arrested for Criminal Trespass if they are warned away from a location in the presence of a Peace Officer. Calls for police service were used as the outcome measure and reportedly dropped by 33 percent over the two-year study period.

In the Felson et al. (1997) study, bar patrons were also the target of the initiative, but the aim was to reduce disorder in the city streets. Felson et al. (1997) used police data to examine the rate of serious assaults in Geelong, following the implementation of "The Accord," an agreement between police, the Liquor Licensing Commission and local publicans designed to reduce pub hopping and the ensuing disorder and violence created by intoxicated patrons moving from pub to pub. The Accord required that publicans follow a uniform policy that included: charging an entry fee, stopping alcohol promotion such as "happy hours," and strictly enforcing Liquor Licensing laws especially in regard to underage drinking. The Liquor Licensing Commission could enforce sanctions against publicans not following The Accord. During the year prior to The Accord, the rate of serious assault in Geelong was 52 percent higher than in six comparable Victorian cities. As The Accord was implemented, the rate fell to the same level as these other cities, and in the three years following continued falling to only 63 percent of the comparison rates.

An evaluation by Hawks et al. (1999) of a similar accord was conducted two years later in Fremantle (Western Australia). This study was more rigorous than the previous study as it involved a control district where no accord was in place. It failed to replicate the positive results of the Felson et al. (1997) study as the police records of the number of assaults that happened in or near licensed premises in the twelve months following The Accord *increased* by over 40 percent in both experimental and control districts.

Liquor licensing restrictions were the legal levers used in the study by Douglas (1998) in Halls Creek (Western Australia) and Gray et al. (2000) in Tennant Creek (Northern Territory). In both studies, the hours of sale and the amount and strength of alcohol sold per customer were curtailed. Douglas (1998) reported that, in the two years following the imposition of the restrictions, the number of hospital presentations for domestic violence injuries did not change; however, police data revealed a drop of 18 percent in the total number of charges laid (for all types of crime). Gray et al. (2000), relying on police data recording the number of people taken in custody and of reported offences, focused on Thursdays, the day the restrictions were the most severe, twelve months pre and twenty-four months post intervention. He reported that the level of most commonly reported offences (assaults, break and enter and criminal damage) fell by 7 percent in the post period, with a marked reduction from 19 percent to 9 percent of weekly total for the average number of assaults on Thursdays. Overall, the number of people taken into custody increased but decreased on Thursdays, from 20 percent to 9 percent of the weekly total. Furthermore, despite objections from licensees, the measures received support from the majority of community members including Aboriginal people.

The Bellamy (1996) study reports results of an evaluation of a third party policing tactic targeting robbery problems, concentrating on convenience stores that open until late at night. In the period from 1981 to 1985, Gainesville, Florida had the highest crime rate in the state with 96 percent of convenience stores being robbed at least once, resulting in eighteen serious injuries including the death of a clerk. In 1986 the council passed a series of ordinances requiring that storeowners implement situational crime prevention measures including clearing windows and making the cash register visible from outside, good lighting inside and outside the shop, CCTV and robbery prevention training for the staff. One ordinance made it mandatory for storeowners to have two staff on duty at all times.

While shopowners objected to the law on the ground of costs, the annual robbery rate in Gainesville fell by 62 percent compared to the previous year and in the period 1987 to 1993 only one serious injury resulting from robbery was recorded.

The Jersey City violent crime places experiment (Braga et al., 1999) is the final study in this group of evaluations of third party policing measures used to target violent crime problems. This study targeted mainly outdoor robbery and assault problems in what were defined as "violent crime places" scattered throughout the city (Braga et al., 1999). The twenty-eight target sites were carefully matched into pairs and then randomly allocated to a control or experimental group. Interviews, observations, incident reports and calls for service records were examined to assess the impact of using a problem-oriented policing approach to solving the problems at the violent crime places. That is, detectives were assigned to sets of violent crime places. They spent several weeks analyzing the problems at the places and then designed tailor-made responses to deal with the unique problems identified at the places. Of particular interest to us in this book is the use of city council ordinances and building codes to co-opt commercial property owners into taking action to reduce the violent crime problems occurring either inside or in close proximity to their businesses. Police officers believed that the violence associated with some of the places were linked to the disorder in the street. Therefore, they attempted to clean up the environment and improve the physical appearance of these places. Storeowners were required to clean their storefronts and increase security by adding locks; property owners were required to remove graffiti from buildings, evict troublesome tenants and improve lighting. Provisions under the building codes were used to force property owners to fence and clean up their vacant lots, or board or demolish their derelict buildings. The results show that the number of calls for service and the number of reported crime incidents declined significantly in the experimental group and observed social disorder was greatly reduced in 91 percent of the experimental places (Braga et al., 1999).

Victims
The use of third party policing where the police "partner" with victims of violent crime is arguably the most controversial of all third party policing tactics. In some cases, the victims might be willing "partners." But in other cases, the police may coerce, convince or pressure victims of domestic violence into taking out restraining orders against their violent perpetrators. Some may argue that it is unfair that the victim becomes the burden-bearer of the responsibility to deal with the problem. It is clear, however, that restraining

orders give the police an added legal lever to deal with the problem of domestic abuse. Whatever the line of argument one may follow, the use of restraining orders to prevent or control domestic violence fits the criteria of third party policing because it involves the use of a legal provision used by a "third person" (victim) to have some control over the behavior of an ultimate target (the abuser). Table 6.2 presents the results of our review of third party policing approaches that seek to control violent crime problems with victims as "third parties."

We note that the term "third party" is an unfortunate label in our example of domestic violence. Some may also recoil at the notion that the victim might be used as a lever to enable the police to gain control. Obviously, we are very sensitive and aware of the negative image of victims being defined as "third parties" and we do not seek to further marginalize victims from the adversarial nature of the two-party criminal justice system that characterizes many western cultures.

Restraining orders are a unique category of laws insofar as the police generally are not entitled to issue a restraining order on behalf of the victim. Rather, it must be the victim's "initiative" to proceed with taking out a restraining order (we discuss the legal conditions of restraining orders in Chapter 4).

Throughout our search of studies that fit the criteria of "third party policing" we were unable to locate studies that systematically researched and reported the process by which police coerced or pressured victims into taking out restraining orders. But the nature of the interaction and the potential for coercive force to be used by the police in convincing a victim to take out a restraining order is important for developing our understanding of third party policing. Observations, however, reveal that the police are regularly called to domestic disputes, the police diffuse the situation and talk to the victim, gently suggesting that she (or he) might want to consider taking out a restraining order. At the time of the dispute, the police are protecting the victim and shielding her from any immediate harm. The victim is in a powerless position and typically willing to do anything at that time to avoid further physical injury.

The research evidence is not especially supportive of use of restraining orders to reduce domestic violence. The study by Klein (1996) examined the criminal records of 663 male abusers who had been issued with a restraining order for domestic violence by the Quincy Court (see Table 6.2). During the two years following the issuance of the restraining order, re-offending was measured by the number of subsequent official reports of abuse by the same victim. Almost half the abusers (48.8 percent) re-abused their victims within two years and 14 percent of the abusers had new restraining orders taken

Table 6.2 *Third party policing, victims and controlling violent crime*

Cite	Third party(s)	Target	Legal basis	Scientific rating	Outcome
Harrell and Smith (1996)	Victims of domestic violence	Batterers	Domestic violence restraining orders	2	60% of women who had taken a restraining order against an abusive partner reported incidents of re-abuse within a year following the RO (incl. severe violence, threats of violence and psychological abuse). Nearly 25% of women reported they had received death threats, 15% reported they had been stalked.
Klein (1996)	Victims of domestic violence	Batterers	Domestic violence restraining orders	2	Almost half the abusers (48.8%) were officially reported by the same victim within two years following the Restraining Order. 14% of abusers had new ROs taken against them.

against them. A similar study was conducted by Harrell and Smith (1996). In this study 355 women were interviewed who had been abused and taken out temporary or permanent restraining orders against their abuser. The study reveals that 60 percent of the women reported that the man named in the restraining order re-abused them during the year following the issuance of the restraining order (including severe violence, threats of violence and psychological abuse).

Professionals

One area of third party policing that is entirely under-researched is the use of mandatory reporting by professionals (such as doctors, lawyers, psychologists) to reveal suspected incidences of violence, particularly against young children. For example, if a child is brought to a hospital with injuries that are suspected to be the result of intentional harm, doctors in most democratic countries are compelled through notification laws to report the suspicious circumstances of the injuries. Our systematic review was unable to locate any studies that have reported or evaluated the use of mandatory reporting and its effect on crime outcomes (notably violent crime outcomes).

Public officials

The use of public officials such as school administrators, probation officers, local council officers and housing authority administrators to gain a crime control benefit is another popular category of third party policing practice. In our review of evaluation studies we identified three studies that used legal levers to involve public officials in an effort to control violent crime problems. A summary of these studies is presented in Table 6.3. The National Crime Prevention Council (1996) describes an initiative where the police worked with school administrators in the US to introduce mandatory wearing of school uniforms in order to reduce tension and violence due to clothing (e.g. as an expression of gang membership), develop a feeling of community and help build an atmosphere conducive to learning. The uniform greatly contributed to school safety as gang members and youths who did not belong to the school were immediately recognized. Parents cooperated with police to ensure the plan's success.

Table 6.3 also describes a study by White and his colleagues (2003) and Grogger (2002). In these studies, incident reports and arrests were used to assess the impact of the third party policing activities.

In the study by White and his colleagues (2003) the police worked with a number of public officials in an effort to reduce homicides (see Table 6.3). The strategy involved a number of enforcement and non-enforcement

Table 6.3 *Third party policing, public officials and controlling violent crime*

Cite	Third party(s)	Target	Legal basis	Scientific rating	Outcome
National Crime Prevention Council (1996)	School administrators, Parents	School aged assault perpetrators	Mandated wearing of school uniforms	2	51% decrease in fights.
Grogger, J. (2002)	Local councils	Gang members	Civil injunctions	4	5–10% decrease in violent crime.
White et al. (2003)	Schools, Probation officers, Housing authorities	Homicides	Gun control laws, car registration, building codes, Adopt a School program	3	Outdoor homicides dropped by 37%; drive-by shootings dropped by 64%; homicides involving female victims dropped by 61%; gun related homicides dropped by 43%; drug related homicides dropped by 59%.

policing initiatives aimed at stopping the "paths that frequently lead to homi-cide" (p. 202) rather than reacting after-the-fact. The intervention was multi-faceted. For instance, local, state and federal authorities were co-opted to identify, locate and arrest violent fugitives in the area. Probation officers were assigned to high schools and worked with police to address crimes that occurred on school campus. They also checked probationers' daily school attendance and made after-hours visits to clients, accompanied by a police officer to encourage them to attend school. The local public housing authority was pressured to improve the physical conditions of their housing stock and design a model lease agreement that obligated tenants to avoid involvement with drug and crime or risk eviction. Based on the assumption that gang activities such as drive-by shooting are dependent on having easy access to vehicles, "Tow Nights" were initiated when cars were stopped to verify registration and drivers' license status, as well as searched for guns. Cars that were not properly registered or whose driver failed to produce a current license were impounded for thirty days. Police and legal advocates worked together to enlist the cooperation of victims of domestic violence in an effort to stop escalation to extreme violence and possibly murder. Police and school principals developed a non-punitive program to reduce truancy, assist at-risk youths, and promote positive interaction between police and youths. The results show that outdoor homicides dropped by 37 percent, drive-by shootings dropped by 64 percent, homicides involving female vic-tims dropped by 61 percent, gun related homicides dropped by 43 percent and drug related homicides dropped by 59 percent (White et al., 2003).

In a study by Grogger (2002) the police worked with local council officials in an effort to induce the councils to take out civil injunctions to control the violent crime behavior of gang members. The outcome results are instructive especially given the scientific rating of the study of four. In this evaluation, Grogger (2002) found that there was between a 5 and 10 percent decrease in violent crime following the introduction of civil injunctions by the local council.

Service providers

The final category of third party participants in crime control efforts initi-ated by the police involves co-opting of service providers to control violent crime problems. One example of this category of third party policing is legal provisions that mandate the presence of domestic violence advocates at domestic violence scenes to which the police have been called. Whetstone (2001) describes an evaluation of a program that involved a coordinated response between a victim advocate team and the police (see Table 6.4).

Table 6.4 *Third party policing, service providers and controlling violent crime*

Cite	Third party(s)	Target	Legal basis	Scientific rating	Outcome
Whetstone (2001)	Victim advocates	Domestic violence perpetrators	Coordinated response team	4	Increase of 41% for arrest and prosecution; 20% increase in conviction of perpetrators compared with control group.

In this study specialized uniformed police officers teamed up with victim advocates to respond and follow up all incidents of intimate partner domestic violence. Police officers were trained to enhance their investigative and interview skills. The victim advocates focused on the victim's needs including medical assistance, counseling, access to service providers and provided support during court appearances. Probation and parole officers assisted them to ensure greater compliance by the perpetrators with court-ordered sanctions and limitations. The evaluation involved an experimental and an equivalent control district. Data were collected during one year preceding the intervention and for eighteen months following the intervention. Data consisted of the number of calls for service relating to domestic incident received by the police, number of arrests of perpetrators, and number and types of court dispositions. Clients' satisfaction with the program was assessed through survey forms, which revealed that the majority of victims (82 percent) showed overwhelming support for the program, especially the sustained assistance they received from the victim advocates. The research also showed a 41 percent increase in arrest and prosecution and a 20 percent increase in conviction of perpetrators compared with the control group. These results suggest that the investigation and preparation of the case were improved and that this had an impact on the court outcome. Repeat offending was not measured in this study.

Controlling crime and disorder in public places

Criminological theory has typically been divided into two lines of inquiry: first, those theories that seek to explain the etiology of criminal offenders and second, those theories that seek to explain why some places experience

more crime problems than others. In the early years of criminological theory, the ecological approach to understanding crime tended to focus on the
distribution of crime across countries, regions and other large geographic
areas. In recent years, however, criminological interest in the relationship
between crime and place has, as Taylor (1998) describes it, traveled down
the cone of resolution. These days, criminologists tend to take a more micro-
level approach to understanding the relationship between crime and place.
Indeed, "places" are defined as "specific locations . . . that can be as small
as the area immediately next to an automatic teller machine or as large as a
block face, a strip shopping center, or an apartment building. Often places
are thought of as addresses, specific types of businesses, or blockfaces" (Eck
and Weisburd, 1995: 3).

In this section, we review the research literature that explores the effectiveness of third party policing activities that seek to control or prevent
crime problems in small places. We present a summary of studies that have
evaluated third party policing initiatives used to control a variety of crimes
occurring in small places including shopping malls, hot spots, public parks
and car parks.

Our systematic review of the literature reveals two common crime control partners with whom the police work to control crime problems in small
places. First, the police often team up with local councils to get them to use
their legal levers to control place-oriented problems such as drug dealing,
gang activity and disorderly behavior. Second, business owners are another
common group of third parties with whom the police work to control problems such as prostitution, public drunkenness and disorderly behavior. In
this section we discuss these two categories of third parties to control crime
in public places.

Local councils
Local councils are important levers and partners in third party policing.
Through delegated legislation (see Chapter 4), local councils have the
authority to create ordinances and regulations that match the problem to
a solution. In our review of the literature, we identified eight studies that
evaluated programs where the police teamed up with local councils in an
effort to control problems in public places (See Table 6.5).

The first study by Ditton and Nair (1994) evaluated a program involving the extensive relighting of public streets in Glasgow. Improved lighting was also one of the tools used in the study by Dennis Budz (1998)
who reports how the police worked with the Gold Coast City Council and
Queensland Rail to redesign a local railway station in an effort to reduce

Table 6.5 *Third party policing, local councils and controlling problems in public places*

Cite	Third party(s)	Target	Legal basis	Scientific rating	Outcome
Ramsay (1991)	Local council	Drunk and disorderly members of the public	Alcohol-free zone	2	No change in the number of offences recorded by police. No change in number of self-reported assaults and mugging. Self-reports of insults by stranger dropped by 32%.
Björ et al. (1992)	Local council	Drunk and disorderly members of the public	Short term council ordinances	2	Number of arrests decreased by 64% compared to previous year. 95% of local community members perceived an improvement compared to previous year.
Spelman (1993)	Local council	Gang members Drug dealers Prostitutes	Building codes, Unsecured building ordinances	1	83% of unsecured abandoned buildings show signs of illegal use compared to only 34% of secured abandoned buildings. Crime rate in blocks with unsecured abandoned buildings was double the crime rate of blocks with secured or no abandoned buildings.
Ditton and Nair (1994)	Local councils	Street crime perpetrators	Relighting of public streets	2	Number of victimization self-reports decreased by 63% following the relighting. Car victimization decreased by 96%.
Herlihy (1995)	Community members Local council	Drunk and disorderly persons	Night patrol	2	Police reported that alcohol-related crime decreased by 43% following the creation of the patrol.
National Crime Prevention Council (1996)	Local councils	Gang members	Injunctions	1	Noticeable improvement in quality of life for residents, increase in business trade, neighborhood improvement, drive-by shootings stopped.
Budz (1998)	Gold Coast City Council	Railway station disorder	Duty of Care	2	Decrease of 27% in number of calls for service following redesign of station and implementation of security system.
Vancouver Police Dpt (2000)	Dog pound	Drug dealers	Unleashed dogs ordinance	2	Reduction of 83% in the number of calls for service to the park.

disorderly, menacing behavior. In this study, the police impressed upon the Rail Authority and local council that they had a "duty of care" to create public space that was safe for commuters (we have discussed the legal arguments around "duty of care" in Chapter 4). A further three studies in this category of third party policing examined the impact of council by-laws on neighborhood crime, disorder and threatening behavior in public space: a study conducted by the Vancouver Police Department (2000) which involved an evaluation of an unleashed dog ordinance that was implemented in an attempt to control gang activity in a local park; the Coventry alcohol-free zone experiment (Ramsay, 1991); and Spelman's (1993) study, which does not evaluate a specific intervention but examines the relationship between abandoned buildings and crime rates, and the potential effect of the strict enforcement of council building codes.

The Swedish evaluation by Björ, Knutsson and Kühlhorn (1992) describes the cooperative efforts by police and local council to prevent and control collective disturbances associated with the celebration of Midsummer Eve. The National Crime Prevention Council (1996) reports how local councils were pressured by the police to initiate injunctions against gang members frequenting public places. In the last study in this section, Herlihy (1995) reports on a partnership between the aboriginal community, the local council and the local police that resulted in the creation of the Julalikari Night Patrol in Tennant Creek (Northern Territory).

In the studies by Budz (1998) and the Vancouver Police Department (2000), the authors used calls for police service as a means to assess the outcome of the programs. Herlihy (1995) relied on police reports for alcohol-related crime. Björ et al. (1992) used the number of arrests and residents' perception and Spelman (1993) used observational and police data as outcome measures. In the studies reported by Ditton and Nair (1994), the National Crime Prevention Council (1996), and Ramsay (1991), residents' perceptions were used to assess the outcome of the third party intervention.

In order to assess the effects of an environmental design initiative, Ditton and Nair (1994) interviewed a representative sample of adult householders in two residential districts three months before and after the council relighting program. In both districts self-reported victimization declined by an average of 63 percent following the street relighting. The decline was particularly striking for car victimization, which fell 96 percent (from twenty-three incidents before to only one incident after).

In the study by Dennis Budz (1998), the police presented the problem of disorderly behavior at a local railway station to the Gold Coast City Council and Queensland Rail. Up until this time, the police had not worked cooperatively with outside agencies about these types of matters and relied on reactive strategies in past operations. When the police first met with the Ward Councilor from the local council and representatives from Queensland Rail (QR), the police impressed upon the Council and QR their obligation to create a "safe" environment. In the background to these conversations were the "duty of care" obligations that the rail authority and council had to create a safe environment for commuters. The police attended these early meetings armed with suggestions to improve the physical environment of the railway station and ideas for blocking opportunities for disorderly behavior disrupting the lives of regular commuters. Researchers report that the impression of legal action taken against the city council and rail authority was the crucial lever that mobilized these parties to take action (Budz, private correspondence). An evaluation of the initiative reveals that there was a 27 percent decrease in the number of calls for service following re-design of the station and implementation of a security system (Budz, 1998).

The evaluation of the unleashed dog ordinance by the Vancouver Police Department (2000) is interesting in so far as these types of local council ordinances (loud radios, loitering, disturbing the peace, littering, graffiti removal, juvenile curfews, drug and/or alcohol free zones, prostitution free zones, traffic control and traffic flow, panhandling, street and mall design and lighting requirements) are used frequently in problem-oriented policing (see Scott, 2000). Despite their frequent use, there are limited evaluations of their contribution to crime control perhaps because local council ordinances are rarely used as the mainstay of intervention efforts. It is the singular use of a specific local council ordinance by the Vancouver Police that makes the "unleashed dog" example interesting. The goal of utilizing the unleashed dog ordinance was to disperse gang members from hanging out in a local park. The gang members would bring their dogs to the park to hang out and let them off their leash, causing fear amongst other park goers. Following zero tolerance enforcement of the unleashed dog ordinance, the Vancouver Police reported an 83 percent reduction in the number of calls for service to the park.

Ramsay (1991) examined the impact of a Coventry Council by-law that declared the streets and public spaces in central Coventry an "alcohol-free zone." Although the by-law gave the local police an opportunity to engage in order maintenance (by warning drinkers to stop their behavior), it did not itself carry any power of arrest; instead, offenders were prosecuted by the city council. Police data recording the number of offenses and respondents' self-report of assaults and mugging did not change following the alcohol-free zoning; however, 89 percent of respondents agreed that the city center had become more pleasant and that insulting behavior by strangers had dropped significantly (by 32 percent).

Spelman's (1993) study was based on a matched cohort design and involved comparing illegal use of building and crime rate in blocks with unsecured abandoned buildings (vacant buildings with open access), secured abandoned buildings (vacant buildings with no open access) and no abandoned buildings. Observational data reveal that of all abandoned buildings, 83 percent of unsecured abandoned buildings showed signs of illegal use (e.g. drug use and dealing, prostitution, use by gang members) compared to only 34 percent of secured abandoned buildings. Police data, based on the number of calls for service, showed that blocks with unsecured abandoned buildings had a crime rate double the rate of blocks with secured abandoned buildings or no abandoned buildings. Spelman (1993) suggested that enforcing building codes promptly to effectively secure abandoned buildings was likely to reduce the crime rate both in the abandoned buildings and in the neighborhood.

In the Björ et al. (1992) study, a range of preventive measures including refusal to accept those likely to cause trouble on camping sites, the closure of parking lots, and restrictions on the serving of alcohol were introduced during the three days of the Midsummer Eve celebration by the police, council and community in an effort to prevent drunken and disorderly behavior. Compared to the previous year celebration, the number of arrests for disorderly conduct dropped by 64 percent. Despite initial opposition by business owners fearing a loss of profit, 95 percent of local key community members expressed the view that the initiative had resulted in an improvement of the situation.

According to Herlihy (1995), the Julalikari Night Patrol is "unique in that it addresses major Aboriginal concerns in a culturally acceptable way, yet is able to operate in tandem with modern law enforcement" (pp. 6–7). The program is staffed by volunteers (mainly women) with seniority in the aboriginal community. Night Patrol staff picks up intoxicated people who are causing disturbances and endeavor to diffuse conflicts and potential incidents. The next morning disputes are mediated and perpetrators are admonished in a culturally appropriate way, during a community meeting. Three years after the creation of the Night Patrol the police reported a decrease of 43 percent in the level of alcohol-related crime. While there has been no substantial increase in the number of reports to police from the Night Patrol, researchers report there has been a significant increase in the number of disputes and disturbances being resolved without the need to call the police.

The National Crime Prevention Council (1996) evaluation reports that residents perceived a noticeable improvement in the quality of life for themselves, an increase in business trade and that drive-by shootings stopped altogether. We note that the scientific integrity of these studies was very low (score of 1 or 2).

Business owners

Police targeting business owners is a common theme throughout the third party policing literature. In the case of controlling crime problems in public (as opposed to private) space, the use of business owners as third parties is perhaps most controversial. We identified seven studies in the literature that evaluate the use of legal levers and businesses as third parties taking some responsibility for the activities occurring in public spaces (not including their business space). These spaces may be the sidewalk immediately outside of a local store or a park adjacent to a business. Controlling street prostitution, public drunkenness and disorderly behavior is the ultimate goal of this category of third party policing. Table 6.6 summarizes the studies in this category.

The first study in Table 6.6 reports the results of a 1994 program implemented in San Diego to control street prostitution. In this example, the police convinced business owners to take out restraining orders against named street prostitutes stipulating they could not be within a certain distance of the store without being in breach of the restraining order (San Diego Police Department, 1994). The San Bernardino Police Department (1999) and the Prostitution Task Force of Buffalo (1999) describe similar uses of restraining orders taken out by business owners to control street prostitution. Calls for service, arrests and observations were used to evaluate the effectiveness of this tactic.

In the fourth study, the Alexandria Police Department pressured licensed premises owners to become vigilant (or suffer the consequences of health or fire inspection) about using a statute prohibiting sale of alcohol to intoxicated persons. The goal was not so much to reduce the disorderly behavior occurring *inside* the licensed premises (although the businesses were the target of the intervention) but rather the goal was to reduce disorderly behavior occurring outside the licensed premises, on the street outside and on nearby streets. The number of court appearances for public drunkenness was used to evaluate the outcome of the program.

In the fifth study, the Green Bay Police Department (2000) partnered with local inspectors to enforce ordinances on open consumption of alcohol, trespassing in and eviction from city parks and lewd and lascivious behavior.

Table 6.6 *Third party policing, business owners and controlling problems in public places*

Cite	Third party(s)	Target	Legal basis	Scientific rating	Outcome
San Diego P. D. (1994)	Business owners	Street prostitutes	Restraining orders	2	In the targeted area number of prostitutes decreased from 8 to 25 per night to 0 to 2 on any given night.
Alexandria P. D. (1995)	Licensed premises owners	Drunks on the street	Statute prohibiting sale of alcohol to interdicted persons	2	80% reduction in court appearances for public drunkenness.
Prostitution Task Force of Buffalo (1999)	Business owners	Street prostitutes	Restraining orders	2	Reduction of 60% in number of calls for service relating to prostitution.
San Bernardino P. D. (1999)	Business owners	Street prostitutes	Restraining orders	2	In the targeted street prostitution was reduced by 84%, indecent exposure by 39% and drug-related arrest of prostitutes by 100%.
Green Bay P. D. (2000)	Business owners, liquor licensing authority	Disorderly behavior	Enforcing public ordinances, evictions from city parks, increase liquor licensing	2	65% decrease in total calls for service; 86% in disorderly conduct calls; 91% decrease in calls for rescue services for injuries (1993–99).
Katz et al. (2001)	Property owners	Street disorder	Building codes Housing codes	2	Calls for service relating to public morals decreased by 34%; physical disorder calls decreased; no effect on violent and serious crime; residents noted a general improvement in the neighborhood.
Stokes (2002)	Commercial property owners	Street disorder	Customer Service Representatives	1	Patrons and customers reported an increased feeling of safety (from 44% to 77% of respondents feeling safe) and improvement of the general atmosphere of the business district.

Police instructed bar owners to refuse service to habitual drunkards and new ordinances were passed that made it possible to suspend the liquor license of those who did not comply. The liquor licensing authority also increased its activities to reduce disorderly behavior on the streets. Similarly, an evaluation by Katz and his colleagues (2001) report on the use of building and housing codes to cite property owners in the quest to control street disorder.

The last study (Stokes, 2002) describes an original initiative by the Philadelphia Center City District (an association of commercial property owners). The association decided to employ Customer Service Representatives (CSR) to patrol the district and ensure public safety and crime prevention. CSRs were unarmed but wore a distinctive uniform; their role was more than security guards as they also acted as public relations and marketing agents. Their task was varied and included: general patrolling and calling police if required, reporting public damages to relevant authority, dealing with panhandlers, writing up zoning violations by commercial owners and generally assisting the public.

Whilst the scientific integrity of the evaluations reported in this section are fairly weak (scores of 2 or 1), the results from these studies reveal a consistent story. The three evaluations of the use of restraining orders to control street prostitution show marked reductions in street prostitution. The San Diego Police Department study (1994) reports from an observational study that the number of prostitutes in the targeted area before the intervention ranged from between eight to twenty-five women. In the post-intervention period, there were between zero and two prostitutes observed on any given night. In the San Bernardino Police Department (1999) study the targeted street prostitution was reduced by 84 percent, indecent exposure by 38 percent and drug related arrests of prostitutes by 100 percent. An evaluation of a similar program in Buffalo revealed a 60 percent reduction in the number of calls for service relating to prostitution (Prostitution Task Force of Buffalo, 1999).

The Alexandria Police Department (1995) evaluation of the third party policing strategy used to reduce the number of drunks on the streets revealed an 80 percent reduction in court appearances for public drunkenness. Finally, the use of ordinances against property owners to control street disorder appears to be equally effective. The Green Bay Police Department (2000) study reported a 65 percent decrease in total calls for service, an 86 percent decrease in disorderly conduct calls, and a 91 percent decrease in calls for rescue services for injuries from 1993 through 1999. The Katz et al. (2001) study reveals that calls for service relating to public morals decreased by 34 percent, physical disorder calls decreased, but there was no effect on violent and serious crime. Additionally, in this study, residents noted a general improvement in the neighborhood. In the Stokes' (2002) study, a non-probability survey of property owners and patrons over five years following the introduction of CSRs revealed a continued increase in feelings of safety (from 44 percent to 77 percent of respondents feeling safe) and improvement in the general atmosphere of the business district (from 67 percent to 87 percent of respondents reporting improvement). The local police rated the CSRs' performance positively and reported a productive relationship.

Again, whilst we reiterate the weakness of these evaluation studies, the results seem to consistently show that the use of legal levers and the co-opting of business owners as third party crime control agents is particularly effective in dealing with public space problems.

Controlling juveniles

One of the common ultimate targets of third party policing is young people. The activities, behaviors and public visibility of young people are commonly perceived as a crime control problem (White, 1998). This section focuses on crime control attempts that involve third parties in controlling the activities and behaviors of young people including curfews, anti-gang laws and parental responsibility laws. Proximate third party targets include parents and guardians, schools, property owners and housing authorities and community organizations. Business owners and local governments may also be involved, often through their operation of surveillance technology such as CCTV, or pressure applied to them to cooperate in the prosecution of young people for minor misdemeanors on their property. We note that many of the studies that we have described earlier in this chapter, particularly those pertaining to the control of drugs and disorderly behavior in public space, have relevance to the control of young people. We included them in the earlier discussions, however, because they did not specifically state that the tactic was designed to target young people.

As with all third party policing, one important issue is effectiveness: is there any evidence that these techniques actually work to change the undesirable behaviors of the young people being targeted? In this section, we examine four categories of third party policing directed at controlling juvenile behavior including levers that target businesses through tactics that utilize provisions available to licensing authorities and strategies to coerce parents to take on more responsibility, including youth curfews and efforts to engage school administrators to enforce truancy laws; housing authorities; and initiatives by Aboriginal communities who ran night patrols as a tool for juvenile crime prevention.

Business owners

The first category of third party policing efforts used to control problem behaviors by young people are those tactics used to coerce and convince business owners to take some crime control responsibility. Table 6.7 summarizes the results of four studies that have reported evaluation results of third party policing interventions used to control youth behavior. The Delta Police Department (1997) in Canada specifically identified young people as the target of their third party policing activities. The police department partnered with the local council to pressure a shopping mall management group to control the unruly behavior of young people hanging out in malls. In this study, the police worked with the local council to create a series of council by-laws that required the mall to redesign the shopping complex, especially the video game arcade, to reduce the patterns of youth unruly behavior. The redesign included: placing the game machines around the periphery of the arcade instead of in the center to allow good visibility; an internal wall that was blocking the view for the cashier was removed in order to allow a clear and open view from the outside; clear instead of tinted windows were fitted; extra lighting was installed inside the arcade and on access routes and parking areas. Calls for service and reported crime statistics were used to evaluate the effectiveness of the intervention. The Delta Police Department (1997) report that the number of calls for service were reduced by 150 percent in the first year, by 5 percent in the second year and the number of calls remained low for four subsequent years. They also report a 24 percent decrease in reported crime after the first year following the intervention.

Licensing authorities are another important lever used frequently by the police to control the activities of businesses in an attempt to reduce crimes committed by young people. We identified two evaluations (see Table 6.7) that assessed the effectiveness of liquor licensing laws (Baker and Wolfer, 2003) as well as provisions available through the Bureau of Alcohol, Tobacco and Firearms to reduce gang violence, particularly among young people (Braga et al., 2001). In the Baker and Wolfer (2003) study researchers and police officers partnered to solve problems of vandalism and harassment in a suburban community. Some solutions included: trimming vegetation in a nearby park and installing fences, removing a phone booth where nuisance calls originated and alerting the youths' parents. The analysis, however, revealed that drug and alcohol consumption by young people exacerbated

Table 6.7 *Third party policing, business owners and controlling juveniles*

Cite	Third party(s)	Target	Legal basis	Scientific rating	Outcome
McNees et al. (1980)	Convenience store owners	Elementary school-age children	In-store reward program	2	Number of stolen items decreased 58% and profits increased 42% during the program.
Delta P. D. (1997)	Mall management	Youth hanging out in malls	Creation of council by-laws to redesign shopping center	2	Number of calls for service reduced by 150% in 1st year, 5% in 2nd year and remained low for four subsequent years; 24% decreased in reported crime for 1st year.
Braga et al. (2001)	Bureau of Alcohol, Tobacco and Firearms, Parole and probation officers	Gang members	Probation and parole conditions	3	Operation Ceasefire aimed to reduce homicide victimization. 63% decrease in homicide victimization for youth under 24 years.
Baker and Wolfer (2003)	Liquor dealers	Underage drinkers	Liquor licensing laws	4	Time series shows drunk and disorderly conduct decreased by 32% and fear of crime decreased 30%.

the problem, as older members of the group were able to buy alcohol for the underage youths. Police persuaded the local liquor dealers to strictly enforce underage liquor laws by checking identification and reporting young adults who purchased large amounts of alcohol. The evaluation was designed as a quasi-experiment and involved surveying two randomly selected groups of residents from the affected neighborhood (experimental group) and from another district in the city (control group). Levels of victimization and fear of crime were measured both before and after the intervention.

Boston Operation Ceasefire (Braga et al., 2001) aimed at controlling and reducing serious gang violence. One of its main elements was a partnership between the police and the Bureau of Alcohol, Tobacco and Firearms (ATF) to target firearms traffickers supplying youth with guns. The ATF focused on the types of guns most used by gang members and the traffickers supplying the city's most violent gangs. A tracking system was put in place to trace guns used in crimes and reduce the supply of firearms. Another element of the operation was a coordinated criminal justice response that disrupted the activities of gangs, particularly those using violence. Data used to evaluate the effectiveness of Operation Ceasefire were the monthly number of homicides victims aged twenty-four and younger. Statistics were provided by the Boston Police Department. In order to assess the impact of the operation, youth homicide trends in Boston were compared with similar trends in other US major cities. The comparison suggested that the large reduction in the number of youth homicides in Boston was not related to a national trend and could be attributed to Operation Ceasefire. The scientific integrity of both of these studies is quite high: the Baker and Wolfer (2003) study is rated as a four and the evaluation of Operation Ceasefire reported Braga et al. (2001) is rated as a three.

The time series analysis conducted by Baker and Wolfer (2003) shows that drunk and disorderly conduct as reported by the residents in the area targeted by the intervention decreased by 32 percent and fear of crime decreased by 30 percent. In the study by Anthony Braga and his colleagues (2001) the Operation Ceasefire intervention led to a 63 percent decrease in homicide victimization for youth under twenty-four years of age.

The last study by McNees, Kennon, Schnelle, Kirchner and Thomas (1980) described an ingenious initiative by a convenience storeowner to reduce shoplifting by young children. In this study, the shopowner had put in place a program in which elementary school-age children, who paid for all their items and displayed appropriate behavior received tokens exchangeable for little gifts. As the number of items stolen in the shop decreased, the rewards increased. The baseline for the number of the most commonly stolen items (candies) was recorded for six weeks, then for another six weeks during the program, and finally for ten days after the program had stopped. During the program a 54 percent reduction in losses of merchandise was achieved, accompanied by a 42 percent increase in shop profits. The authors pointed out, however, that the program was successful while in place but that shoplifting resumed to higher levels after the completion of the program. They suggested that to remain effective the program needed to be maintained, and was likely to be effective with young children but probably not with older age groups.

Parents
One of the key third parties utilized to control the behavior of young people is the parent. We identified six studies that evaluated third party policing strategies using parents as the third party (see Table 6.8). In the first study, Penrod (2001) reports on the results of Operation CleanSWEEP where students and their parents appeared in an informal court where they could be fined up to $400 for minor crimes on school campus such as graffiti, vandalism, petty theft and underage smoking. They could avoid the fine if the young person agreed to improve their school attendance or grades, provide community service and attend diversionary programs such as anger management. Statistics collected by police showed a decline in suspensions and exclusions from school and a decreased in crime in areas adjacent to the school. Parents reported that the program enabled them to regain some control over their teenage children. We also include an evaluation by the Baltimore Police Department (2000) that reports an evaluation of a truancy abatement program. In the other studies by Ruefle and Reynolds (1996), Males and Macallair (1999) and Reynolds and his colleagues (2000), youth curfew laws are described and evaluated. Youth curfew laws create a burden on parents in certain areas of a city (or sometimes across the entire city) to control the times that young people are out in public places.

Most juvenile curfew laws restrict the time when young people (upper age limit varies according to the jurisdiction from twelve years to seventeen years) can be out in public places during nighttime hours; some jurisdiction, however, enforce daytime curfews as well in an effort to reduce truancy from school. A young person found in breach of the time curfew is usually not prosecuted but warned and sent home or to the curfew center. Sanctions apply to the parents who become vulnerable to being fined, ordered to attend counseling or to perform community service. The descriptive study by Ruefle and Reynolds (1996) (see Table 6.8) reports that 73 percent of 200 American cities with populations of 100,000 or more had enacted some

Table 6.8 *Third party policing, parents and controlling juveniles*

Cite	Third party(s)	Target	Legal basis	Scientific rating	Outcome
Ruefle and Reynolds (1996)	Parents	Young people	Juvenile curfews	Descriptive study only	73% of 200 American cities with population of 100,000 or over had enacted some sort of juvenile curfews; surge in enactment of curfew laws between 1990–95.
Males and Macallair (1999)	Parents	Young people	Youth curfews	3	No correlation between strength of curfew law enforcement and rates of juvenile crime or victimization.
Baltimore P. D. (2000)	Parents and school administrators	Young people	Truancy abatement	2	The Canton Middle School Project found overall attendance increased by 5%; chronic truancy (absence for more than 20 days) decreased by 24%; overall daytime crime in neighboring school area decreased by 26%.
Reynolds et al. (2000)	Local council	Youth offenders	Juvenile curfew	2	Juvenile victimization, all ages victimization and juvenile arrests did not decrease after the curfew was implemented.
Penrod (2001)	Parents	Young people	Parents fined	2	Following Operation CleanSWEEP police calls for service to schools declined by 12 to 50%; suspensions and expulsions declined by up to 70% in participating schools.
Bullock and Jones (2004)	Parents, Housing authority	Young people engaging in anti social behavior	Acceptable Behavior Contracts	2	For the six months of the contract fewer people came to the attention of the police for criminal offences than in the previous six months (62% prior compared to 43% during contract).

sort of juvenile curfew and that there was a surge in enactment of curfew laws between 1990 and 1995. Calls for service, crime incident reports, victimization reports and arrests are used to assess the impact of curfew laws.

The study by Reynolds and his colleagues (2000) has a scientific rating of a two. In this study archival data spanning the year before and the year following the implementation of the curfew laws were collected from the New Orleans Police Department. Data included official records of victimization (detailing type of offence and age of the victim) and the number of juvenile (under age seventeen) arrests. Both sets of data were coded according to whether they occurred during curfew hours or non-curfew hours. The strength of police enforcement of the curfew laws overtime was also recorded and other factors (e.g. seasonal crime pattern) that could influence the results were controlled for. The results suggest that juvenile victimization, victimization of all age groups and juvenile arrests did not decrease after the curfew was implemented. This result seriously questions the effectiveness of youth curfews as an effective strategy in controlling crime. The study by Males and Macallair (1999) has a scientific score of three. Males and Macallair (1999) used the California Department of Justice crime data to examine and compare crime rates, number of arrests and victimization levels across California cities over a seventeen-year period. For the cities that had implemented juvenile curfew laws, the strictness of police enforcement was included in the analysis. The results suggest that there was no correlation between the strength of curfew law enforcement and the rates of juvenile crime or victimization either absolutely or relative to adults (who are not subject to curfew laws) by location, city or type of crime.

Activating truancy laws is another common third party policing tactic that uses parents as the targets to control the behavior of young people. The Baltimore Police Department (2000) reports the results of an evaluation of the Canton Middle School Project. In this study, the police department partnered with the local school administrators to "crackdown" on the patterns of chronic truancy in the school district in an attempt to control some local crime problems. Up to 30 percent of students were away from school each day. In relation to their population, juveniles were experiencing a disproportionate level of victimization and they were also committing a large number of crimes such as graffiti, vandalism, petty theft, joy riding and daytime burglary. The results show that overall attendance at school increased by 5 percent, chronic truancy (absence for more than twenty days) decreased by 24 percent and overall daytime crime in the neighboring school area decreased by 26 percent.

The last study by Bullock and Jones (2004) evaluates the effectiveness of Acceptable Behavior Contracts (ABCs) as a tool to curb anti-social behavior by young people. Anti-social behavior incorporates a broad range of acts from looting to intimidating behavior to low-level offending. ABCs are aimed at young people aged ten to eighteen years who have been identified as having engaged in persistent anti-social behavior that has impacted on the quality of life of local residents. The contracts are written agreements between the young person, the local housing authority or social landlord, and the local police, signed in the presence of the young person's parents or guardians, in which the youth agrees not to carry out specific behaviors defined as anti-social (e.g. damage property, verbally abuse passers-by, threaten, congregate in groups). The Housing Authority usually monitors the ABC and serious breaches can result in the family being evicted. Authors used police data to evaluate the impact of the ABCs on the behavior of the young people. For the six months of the contract, fewer of the young people came to the attention of the police than in the previous six months (62 percent prior down to 43 percent during the ABCs). The overall number of anti-social acts committed by the youths decreased by around half in the same period. Among the ninety-four young persons on ABCs there had been eighty-five arrests for criminal offences prior to the study (some had been arrested several times); during the length of the Contracts, only thirty-four arrests were recorded. The evaluation concluded that ABCs can reduce the amount of anti-social behavior committed by young people for the duration of their contracts, as well as the likelihood of them committing criminal acts.

Community members

The use of community members as third parties is often discussed in the crime prevention literature, but our systematic review revealed just one study that had conducted an evaluation where community members were directly described as levers in controlling juvenile delinquency. Table 6.9 summarizes the study results.

The site of the study was in New South Wales (Australia) where four pilot programs involving night patrols by indigenous and non-indigenous community members were evaluated (Blanchard and Lui, 2000). These four night patrols aimed to support young people, regardless of ethnicity, to move from "at risk" situations by transporting people affected by drugs or alcohol

Table 6.9 *Third party policing, community members and controlling juveniles*

Cite	Third party(s)	Target	Legal basis	Scientific rating	Outcome
Blanchard and Lui (2000)	Aboriginal community members	Young people	Night patrols	1	Fall in the rates of crime such as malicious damage and street offences. Car theft decreased by 50% followed by a return to pre-patrol levels when the patrol was suspended.

to a safe place and providing young people who are in public places at night with a range of street-based youth services. Results showed a reduction in juvenile crime rates on the nights the patrols operate including for offenses such as criminal damages and street crime. In one town, police recorded a 50 percent drop in car thefts during the three months the patrol operated. When the patrol stopped, car theft rates returned to their pre-patrol levels.

Property crime

This final section examines the effectiveness of third party policing in controlling property crime problems. Table 6.10 presents a summary of studies that have evaluated third party policing initiatives used to control a variety of property crime problems including auto-theft, theft, fraud and property damage.

As Table 6.10 shows, there are three primary domains where the police have used third party policing tactics to control property crime problems. These include strategies used against business owners, manufacturers and insurance companies. We discuss each of these areas of property crime control in turn.

Business owners

Business owners again feature prominently in our examination of the effectiveness of third party policing. We identified five evaluations of third

Table 6.10 *Third party policing, businesses and controlling property crime*

Cite	Third party(s)	Target	Legal basis	Scientific rating	Outcome
Van den Berg (1995)	Business owners	Thefts	Improve security systems Hire security guards	1	50% decrease in thefts on industrial site.
Challinger (1996)	Retailers Retail staff	Refund fraudsters	Cash refund policy	2	Number of detected refund frauds and the monetary value of detected refund fraud decreased sharply following the implementation of the policy.
Webb (1996)	Retailers, Banking sector	Credit card thieves	Credit card policy Hot Card File	2	Overall monetary losses attributable to plastic card fraud have reduced by 41%.
Clarke and Goldstein (2002)	Builders	Thefts	Delaying installation of appliances	3	Construction site theft reduction of 50% with no displacement and diffusion of benefits.
Smith et al. (2003)	Car park owners	Thefts	Secured Car Park Award Scheme	2	Mixed results but improvement made in order to obtain the Award can help reduce levels of vehicle crime and fear of crime especially when targeted at high crime car parks.

party policing where businesses were specifically targeted to reduce property crime problems. The first study by Smith et al. (2003) is an example of third party policing used to create direct and tangible incentives to business owners. The Smith study reports the results of an incentive scheme to induce car park owners to improve the conditions of their car parks. Known as the Secured Car Park Award Scheme, the goal of the program was to create incentives to car park owners to create physical conditions in their car parks that met crime prevention standards. The Secured Car Park (SCP) Award was established in the UK in 1992 and was designed to encourage car park operators to improve security as a means of reducing criminal activity and fear of crime. Car parks are assessed by police officers on a number of criteria known to be associated with crime reduction and including: surveillance, design of parking area, access, lighting, security staff and management practices. Car parks that achieve high standards on these criteria are given the award, which lasts for one year. Award recipients are able to publicize the fact their car parks provide a high level of security and attract more customers. We discuss the use of incentives such as described in this program further in Chapter 7.

In the study presented by Van den Berg (1995) business owners requested increased police presence in a Dutch industrial estate; police, however, concluded that improving security systems and hiring security guards would be more effective and time-efficient as police would not have to visit the site in the case of false alarms, and a formal partnership was launched. The project included various elements: police officers trained unemployed people as security guards; the site physical environment was improved (better lighting, litter removed, vegetation trimmed back); a central alarm system was set up; and preventive surveillance overnight and around the clock during weekends and holidays was established. The outcome of the project was measured using the number of reported incidents pre- and post-implementation.

Clarke and Goldstein (2002) tested an initiative designed to reduce the theft of kitchen appliances from building sites. Following a sharp increase in thefts from building sites, police recommended that builders delayed the installation of appliances until just after the occupants had moved into the new house (effectively removing the target until a capable guardian is present).

The last two studies in Table 6.10 describe initiatives aimed at retailers. Challinger (1996) examined the effect of a strict refund policy devised by the major Australian retail company Coles Myer Ltd on cash refund fraud. The policy, adopted in 1994, was implemented in 1,700 outlets including supermarkets, discount stores and department stores. Under the new policy, customers asking for a refund were required to produce a proof of purchase and some identification, and exchange of goods or credit vouchers were always offered in preference to cash refund; cash refunds were given in some circumstances but only if the goods had been paid by cash in the first place. Webb (1996) described measures, introduced in 1992 by the banking industry in the UK, to prevent plastic card fraud and which required the cooperation of retailers. First, banks lowered the value of transactions at which bank authorization is required (retailers were required to ring the bank to obtain authorization more often). Second, a "Hot Card File" system was implemented to allow banks to transmit very quickly the details of lost or stolen cards to retailers, in order for them to refuse the card.

Based on interviews with car park operators and car park users, and recorded crime data from the police the Smith et al. (2003) study found that the Secured Car Park Award Scheme reduced levels of vehicle crime and fear of crime, especially when the car park owners of high crime car parks took up the incentive offer. In the Van den Berg (1995) evaluation, the study reports a 50 percent decrease in thefts from industrial sites. Clarke and Goldstein (2002) revealed that, although the procedure was not always followed consistently in the twelve experimental sites, theft declined by 50 percent. No displacement of crime was recorded. Diffusion of benefit occurred with a number of adjacent control sites recording some decrease in theft. Challinger (1996) relied on fraud data provided by the retail company to assess the effect of the new refund policy. While exact figures were not provided, as they constituted commercially sensitive data, Challinger (1996) reported a sharp decline in both the number of detected refund frauds and the monetary value of detected frauds. Webb (1996) used data provided by the banking industry that calculated the financial loss incurred nationally from plastic card fraud. The results indicated that since the introduction of the measures the overall loss attributable to plastic card fraud had reduced by 41 percent.

Manufacturers

Manufacturers are a second group of third party targets that are often used by the police to control property crime. Our review of the literature uncovered just two evaluations of what we would consider to be a third party policing intervention that used manufacturers as the third party to control property crime (see Table 6.11). The study by Gant and Grabosky (2000)

Table 6.11 *Third party policing, manufacturers and controlling property crime*

Cite	Third party(s)	Target	Legal basis	Scientific rating	Outcome
Webb (1994)	Car manufacturers	Car thefts	Mandatory steering column lock fitted on all new cars	2	In Germany, car thefts decreased 20% following the introduction of compulsory steering column lock. In Britain and the US, new cars fitted with the device were less likely to be stolen than older cars.
Gant and Grabosky (2000)	Car manufacturers Insurers Car repairers Media	Car thefts	Inbuilt car security, Report suspected insurance frauds, Register of parts, Register of wrecked vehicles, Public education	2	Between July 1991 and June 1992 car theft declined by 25%, producing an average saving of $A50 million.

describes the manner in which police used car manufacturers to reduce auto thefts. Car manufacturers were encouraged to make more readily identifiable parts through component marking. In this study, other tactics were used that confound the results of the third party initiative. Other tactics such as the use of the media to increase public awareness of auto-theft, the partnering with insurance companies to report to the police suspected insurance frauds and the registering of wrecked vehicles and auto parts were used in conjunction with the third party tactic. As such, the evaluation is unable to isolate the effects of the third party intervention. Nonetheless, the study serves as a useful example of how manufacturers can be brought into help control property crime problems. The overall results suggest that between July 1991 and June 1992 car theft declined by 25 percent, producing an average saving of AUD$50 million.

Webb's (1994) study is instructive in its assessment of mandatory government regulations on car theft (see Table 6.11). Regulations making mandatory the fitting of steering column locks in all new cars were introduced as a compulsory measure in Germany in 1961, and in Britain and the US in 1971. Car thefts in Germany fell 20 percent following the introduction of the measure. In Britain, in 1973, new cars (i.e., fitted with the steering column lock) represented 21 percent of all cars but only 5 percent of stolen cars indicating they were less likely to be stolen than older cars not fitted with the device. In the US in 1974, new cars fitted with the device represented 58 percent of cars on the road, but only 45 percent of vehicle stolen in that year, suggesting those cars were less at risk of being stolen. The author suggests that the introduction of the compulsory steering column lock had a beneficial and lasting positive effect in reducing car thefts, especially the casual taking of the car for temporary use.

Vehicle owners

We only located one study (Forbes, 2000) where owners were required to take measures to prevent the theft of their vehicles. Forbes (2000) reports that on 1 July 1999 an amendment to the *Road Traffic Act 1974* was passed by the Western Australia government making the installation of an engine immobilizer a prerequisite for registration and transfer of ownership of a car. This scheme was different from the mandatory steering column lock legislation (Webb, 1994) as it targeted transfer and renewal of registration for older cars, not just brand new ones. Vehicle owners were given $40 when purchasing the device. Although the scientific rating of this study is low (rating 1) because the WA Department of Transport did not have the resources to implement systematic data collection on car theft, Western

Australia is the only Australian state to record an overall reduction of 12 percent in the number of car thefts. This reduction correlates with the estimation that 60 percent of all vehicles in WA are fitted with an immobilizer compared with only 30 percent nationally. Abru (2001) also reported that the similar but voluntary Immobilise Now! schemes in Victoria and Tasmania led to car-theft reduction of 5 percent and 21 percent respectively. It is worth noting that as a result of market demand around 85 percent of all new cars are fitted with an immobilizer as standard equipment.

Insurance companies

One of the most powerful third party partners in dealing with property crime is an insurance company (see Roach-Anleu, Mazerolle and Presser, 2000). While insurance companies are widely recognized as an under-utilized resource for controlling crime, there are very few evaluations that examine the impact of crime prevention or crime control schemes involving insurance companies. One study by the National Motor Vehicle Theft Reduction Council (1999) evaluates the New South Wales Written-Off Vehicle Register (WOVR) and its impact on professional car theft. In order to legitimize the sale of stolen cars professional thieves need to apply a legitimate Vehicle Identification Number (VIN) to a stolen vehicle of the same make, model and age. Written-off cars sold for parts at auction provide a way of obtaining a legitimate VIN. In NSW, a comprehensive register of all written-off vehicles, based on mandatory reporting by insurance companies and parts dealers, is a means to prevent thieves obtaining VINs. The register is maintained by the Road and Traffic Authority and permits the VIN of vehicles that are not repairable to be cancelled, thus making it impossible to "re-birth" stolen cars using these VINs. Using police data and data obtained from insurance companies and vehicle auctioneers the study reported that the WOVR did not have an impact on the overall number of car thefts in NSW; however, following the introduction of the register, a decrease in the number of unrecovered vehicles was recorded as well as a decrease in the price of written-off vehicles at auction, suggesting the register had an impact on professional car theft in NSW. It was likely that the impact of the scheme was reduced because other states did not keep such a register; therefore, cars stolen in NSW could be transported to adjacent states for re-birthing. The NMVTRC (1999) recommended that such a register should be implemented nationally in order to reduce professional car theft. The register, however, is unlikely to have an effect on casual car theft for "joyriding" purposes.

Quantitative review

Consistent with our quantitative review of third party policing efforts to control drug problems (see Chapter 5), we also sought to conduct a systematic review of third party policing efforts used to control the other categories of crime covered in this chapter. Our goal was to identify a collection of studies with high scientific integrity and create a standardized effect size to enable comparisons of the impact of the interventions across a variety of different studies. Unfortunately, unlike the drug intervention evaluations, many of the evaluations that targeted other categories of crime using third party policing tactics were of insufficient scientific integrity to calculate an effect size (see Chapter 8). Indeed, just two of the violent crime studies, none of the disorder studies, just one of the juvenile studies and just one of the property crime studies provided sufficient statistical data to create effect sizes using the odds ratio or standardized mean differences. Tables 6.12 and 6.13 summarizes the effect sizes and confidence intervals for selected studies reporting the results of third party policing efforts used to target property and violent crime problems. The four studies included in our quantitative review include the experimental evaluation of the Safer Bar Program that sought to reduce physical aggression in bars conducted in Canada by Kate Graham and her colleagues (2003); the Grogger (2002) study that evaluated police partnerships with local council officials in an effort to induce the councils to take out civil injunctions to control the violent crime behavior of gang members; the Baker and Wolfer (2003) study that examined police efforts to persuade local liquor dealers to strictly enforce underage liquor laws by checking identification and reporting young adults who purchased large amounts of alcohol; and the evaluation of the Secured Car Park Award Scheme in the UK conducted by Smith and her colleagues (2003). The Car Park Award Scheme sought to create incentives to induce car park owners to improve the physical conditions of their car parks.

The results presented in Tables 6.12 and 6.13 reveal some mixed findings. Of the five effect sizes calculated, three revealed desirable outcomes and the other two (both from the Baker and Wolfer study) revealed undesirable outcomes. Baker and Wolfer's (2003) results show a 17.17 percent increase in the number of reported break and enter offenses and a 9.0 percent increase in the number of property theft offenses in the treatment sites compared to the control sites. We note, however, that both of these undesirable outcomes were not statistically significant. In contrast, both the Graham et al. (2003) and the Grogger (2002) studies targeting violent crime problems reported statistically significant and desirable effect outcomes. The Graham et al.

Table 6.12 *Third party policing strategies targeting other crime (odds ratio)*

Citation	Year	Effect name	Effect	Lower	Upper	P Value	0.1	0.2	0.5	1	2	5	10
Baker	2003	Incidence property theft	.917	.441	1.907	.817							
Baker	2003	Incidence break and enter	.853	.375	1.944	.706							
Graham	2003	Observed aggression	1.754	1.102	2.792	.017							
Grogger	2002	Violent crimes	1.061	1.021	1.104	.003							

Undesirable effect   Desirable effect

Table 6.13 *Third party policing strategies targeting other crime (standardized mean difference)*

Citation	Year	Effect name	Effect	Lower	Upper	P Value	−2.00	−1.00	0.00	1.00	2.00
Smith	2003	Reported car crime	.644	−.483	1.770	.213					
								Undesirable effect		Desirable effect	

(2003) study revealed a 43 percent decrease in the number of observed incidents of aggression and the Grogger (2002) study showed a 5.78 percent decrease in the number of violent crimes in the treatment sites compared to the control sites. Smith and her colleagues (2003) revealed a moderate and desirable outcome for the third party policing interventions that targeted reported car thefts from car parks.

Concluding comments

In this chapter we presented the results of our review of 56 studies reporting evaluation results of third party policing interventions aimed at violent crime problems, property crimes, juvenile crimes and crimes in public places (excluding drug problems). The interventions that we identified primarily targeted business owners, much like our review of drug problems revealed in Chapter 5. The business owners are targeted as third party "partners" to work with the police in dealing with violent crime problems in bars, property crime problems in unsecured car parks, drunk and disorderly behavior in public places and street prostitution. But our review also revealed a range of other categories of regulatory "nodes" (or third parties) in the ongoing trend towards expanding responsibility for crime control beyond the police. Parents, school administrators, domestic violence victims, liquor licensing authorities, car manufacturers, local councils and public housing authorities are all co-opted in third party policing to utilize the legal levers that are either available to them (e.g. restraining orders, council by-laws, liquor licensing laws) or designed to punish them (e.g. parents) for failing to control the behavior of the ultimate targets (e.g. children). The general message from these systematic reviews is clear: there is a trend towards widening the "net" of crime control agents where legal levers are being utilized, designed and targeted by third parties to control a wide variety of crime problems.

Some of the third party initiatives are more effective than others. We suggest that third party efforts designed to target business owners tend to result in the best crime control outcome. This is likely to be the result of a longer tradition of police-business owner partnerships. But as the range of third party partners continues to widen, strengthen and become more institutionalized, we would expect the results to become more favorable towards third party initiatives.

CHAPTER 7

Equity, side effects and accountability

In previous chapters we have introduced the notion of third party policing, described its dimensions, and surveyed both its legal status, tools and effectiveness. These chapters have given a snapshot of how third party policing works in various situations, and of what we know about its effectiveness in preventing or responding to crime. We have shown that the use of third party policing is largely episodic, hidden and outside of most police programmatic responses. Despite this, and based on the limited evaluative evidence available, it appears that third party policing is a highly effective tactic.

But to examine only the effectiveness of third party policing is to consider only half the equation – despite its apparent effectiveness, there has been limited examination of the side-effects, fairness and equity of third party policing. We need to examine the intentional and unintentional, positive and negative, impacts of third party policing on the partners who work with police (regulators, property owners, business owners), as well as on other groups in the community (schools, community groups), on the ultimate targets and their families and communities, and even on the police organizations themselves. How does third party policing affect the community in which it is practised? How equitably does it affect different communities, both internally and in comparison to other communities? Just as importantly, who is held accountable for the outcomes and impacts of third party policing, and how? Are traditional police accountability mechanisms adaptable to take account of this new way of doing business, or is there a need for new mechanisms to be developed? Overall, is third party policing an ethical practice?

This chapter begins by examining side effects of third party policing. Positive effects can include contributions to social efficacy and cohesion in neighborhoods, the establishment of mutually helpful partnerships with regulators and service providers, and the fostering of broader responsibility for crime control and prevention. Negative effects can include the disproportionate allocation of police and regulator resources creating both over-policing of some areas and under-policing of others, the spatial, temporal or tactical displacement of crime problems, intensifying problems in already disadvantaged areas, the cooption of regulator resources and agendas away from their primary purposes, and the cooption of law and legal instruments for purposes other than those originally intended. We examine how these side effects arise in practice, how they can be predicted and managed, and suggest some creative approaches to reducing adverse consequences and increasing positive outcomes.

The chapter moves on to consider accountability for third party policing. The management and accountability of police generally is still an area of dispute and research, given the nature of police discretion and their legitimate use of force (Reiner, 1993; Loveday, 1996, 2000). But third party policing brings special challenges, especially given the potential severity of its intended and unintended side effects. We discuss some of the challenges raised by third party policing and potential solutions to them, such as the need to establish policies and protocols for the coercive use of legal levers against third parties, and for the monitoring and reporting of initiatives. We suggest the police work through a side-effect and accountability check list when planning third party policing initiatives.

Side effects of third party policing

Third party policing brings with it both positive and negative side effects. To date much third party policing has been ad hoc and episodic, and therefore these side effects have been largely unconsidered in the planning and operational stages of interventions. By identifying the types of positive and negative side effects that can potentially occur, we can ensure that these effects are considered in the planning stage of new initiatives and that steps are taken to maximize appropriate positive outcomes while also reducing the prospects of negative effects.

Positive side effects

One category of positive side effects from third party policing involves the enhancement of social, community and organizational factors within the neighborhood. This can include the creation of collective efficacy and social cohesion within some neighborhoods as the community becomes more involved in task-specific activities that seek to control and prevent crime (Sampson et al., 1997), the establishment of positive relations between the police and local service providers, the creation of some responsibility within otherwise negligent organizations, and more satisfied police officers who are directly involved in creative problem solving rather than routine reactive responses.

Another category of side effects from third party policing is the possibility of a diffusion of crime control benefits that go beyond the targeted place, person or situation (Clarke and Weisburd, 1994). This "diffusion of benefits" occurs when crime control measures not only reduce crime opportunities at targeted places or situations, but also reduce crime at other places or times not the subject of the crime control efforts, as positive effects "spill over" from the initial action, either through deterrence, discouragement or incapacitation, or a combination of these factors (Ratcliffe and Makkai, 2004). For example, using building codes to shut down drug houses in one street may lead to surrounding streets experiencing less drug related nuisance and crime as dealers and users re-locate or are permanently closed down. Establishing responsible alcohol-service protocols in nightclubs can not only limit street-based violence in the immediate area, but also have spill over effects on subsequent domestic violence caused when drunken patrons return home. Ratcliffe and Makkai (2004) refer to this as "positive displacement," but say it is rarely considered in law enforcement planning because the effect is not well known, benefits are not guaranteed, and there is always a risk of crime displacement as opposed to more positive effects. But they go on to suggest advantages of this type of policing, including the gains in crime reduction over and beyond a particular project as a way of justifying the project's expense, the achievement of political approval and increase in public support, and the deflection of criticism if the original project produces unsatisfactory results (2004, 1).

These outcomes are difficult to measure, particularly if appropriate research designs have not been employed (Weisburd and Green, 1995; Ratcliffe and Makkai, 2004). But third party policing, by its very nature, is likely to produce both of these types of side effects when the intervention is well planned and operationalized. The process of consultation with third parties such as local regulators and community groups is likely to produce improved relationships and greater cohesion, regardless even of the success of the intervention itself. The key is that the intervention is based on consultation – unnecessary use of coercion is likely to lead to counter-productive resentment and non-cooperation. The development of team approaches can lead to lasting improvements in service delivery and neighbourhood amenity, again regardless of the success of the actual intervention – cleaning up derelict buildings and removing fire and health hazards are positive outcomes in themselves, as is reducing excessive alcohol consumption. Cleaning up local crime problems can help revitalize commercial and business activities in nearby areas as the locality is seen as safe to visit and shop in. These effects are difficult if not impossible to measure (although see Caulkins, 1998), but are likely to flow on from most well planned projects. We discuss the planning process further below.

Negative side effects – adverse social consequences

It is well recognized that crime prevention initiatives can generate unintended adverse consequences, social costs, or "negative externalities" (Grabosky, 1996). These initiatives can either make the original problem worse, or have side-effects that are as bad or worse than the original problem. Grabosky (1996) has catalogued side-effects including the escalation of the original problem (through labelling, enticement, self-fulfilling prophecies, etc), displacement, creative adaptations (to develop new and original forms of offending), over-deterrence of basically useful activity, the creation of perverse incentives and of moral hazards both as incentives to offend and to victimization. In third party policing the main negative side-effects fall into three groups – adverse social consequences arising from police coopting other organizations and individuals to deal with crime, the possibility that third party policing only displaces crime into other areas or times, and the impact of third party policing on regulatory systems, legal rights, civil liberties and laws.

Dealing first with the possible adverse social consequences of third party policing, the broadest argument here is the leftist critique of misdirection (Mazerolle and Prenzler, 2004; see also White, 1998) – that strengthening the policing focus on traditional targets continues to ignore the social causes of crime. Resources spent on the third party policing effort, on this view, would be better targeted at the fundamental causes of the problem, such as drug addiction, poverty and social inequality. Third party policing can be seen as too reactive, dealing with the consequences and not the causes of serious social problems. Thus the poor, homeless, minorities, addicted or otherwise disadvantaged risk being doubly victimized by both their inherent disadvantage and then the implementation of third party policing. Not only does this misuse resources, but it may also have a net-widening effect, drawing into the criminal justice system more and more of the socially disadvantaged, simply because they live in or are otherwise associated with a risky area or group. So for example, as already discussed in Chapter 4, an evaluation of a new system of on-the-spot penalty notices dealing with low-level disorder offences in the United Kingdom, found a significant net-widening effect, with between a half and three quarters of notices classified as "new business", issued to people who would not otherwise have been cautioned or prosecuted (Home Office, 2004). Similarly, the breach of a curfew by an otherwise non-offending juvenile can lead to police attention and confrontation, and ultimately arrest for disorder offences (White, 1998).

This argument is to some extent borne out by the types of third party policing we have found to be predominant, which focus on drug problems, public order issues and public housing, rather than the white collar crimes of the middle and upper classes. However, to some extent the lack of research into third party policing in areas such as taxation, financial services, and information technology regulation may contribute to this perceived bias. Further research may indicate that the focus on street and drug crimes in the literature is not a fair representation of the true prevalence patterns of third party policing practice.

There are also counteracting arguments that suggest that marginalized groups are also victimized by the effects of crime in their neighborhoods, and third party policing by addressing these effects can actually help to improve their quality of life. This improvement comes not just from the closing down of crack houses and targeting of alcohol fuelled violence, but from the flow-on effects of better housing and more peaceful schools caused by the stricter enforcement of regulatory codes. On the one hand, the proliferation of third party policing might work towards making middle and upper class property owners more responsible for their housing stock and thus improve the conditions for lower class residents. On the other hand, however, third party policing has the potential to add additional (and more complex) burdens on already over-policed groups in society and to diminish perceptions of police legitimacy through the effects of differential policing. For example, recent changes to the law in the United Kingdom re-classified cannabis so that possession is no longer automatically an arrestable offence. Police enforcement guidelines stipulate that there should be a presumption against arrest for simple possession, except where the person is smoking in public view, a repeat offender, under 17, or where the local authority has an identified local policing problem (the *Independent*, 2004). Camden, London has a drug problem, and on the basis of this identified problem police have adopted a zero-tolerance policy for cannabis possession, so that on crossing the (unmarked) border from one local authority to another, quite different policing practices apply, in a way that has not been publicized or advertized.

This sort of differential outcome is very likely to arise under third party policing given its localized nature, and can undermine confidence in and legitimacy of the law.

As well as being further victimized by third party policing, it is also possible that socially marginalized groups can be victimized by a *denial* of the benefits of third party policing activities, caused by the disproportionate allocation of policing and resources to one particular area or problem, at the expense of others. How police choose to target their third party policing activities could act to entrench or alleviate inequalities in the distribution of criminal justice and regulatory resources. Again proper planning and consultation are keys to avoiding this negative effect.

Other social side effects of third party policing are somewhat more nebulous to measure. For example, consideration needs to be given to the impact on communities, families and organizations of eviction, retaliation from domestic violence perpetrators, retaliation from displaced or arrested drug dealers, and strained relations with service providers and local regulators (e.g. building inspectors, local council code enforcers etc). Issues of legitimacy also arise here. Tracey Meares (1998) for instance argues that drug crackdowns, by removing people from the community and increasing family disruption and the loss of family providers, also impact adversely on law abiding citizens, and detract from their perceptions of police legitimacy. Curtis (2000) describes how intensive policing operations such as "buy and bust" initiatives are generally supported in neighborhoods where drug dealers are outsiders; but when dealers are small operators who live in the neighborhood and are friends or relatives to the residents (and the drug dealing is not a source of violence), residents resent the police intervention because it disrupts the community and breaks up family life.

Some police actions risk serious public health side effects. Maher and Dixon (1999) have described the consequences of police crackdowns on drugs on public health and the health of drug users. As a result of a crackdown in Cabramatta, in Sydney, Australia, dealers took more risks and started storing heroin caplets in their mouths. If subject to police attention, they would swallow the caplets, risking overdose. Injecting drug users in the crackdown area started to inject more quickly, in unsafe places, using unsafe practices such as sharing and re-using needles, risking HIV and blood borne diseases. They stopped frequenting needle disposal centres and discarded used needles in the street, creating public health hazards.

Another potential adverse side effect of policing initiatives is to drive offenders into developing better and more effective ways to offend. For example, a project aimed at the aerial eradication of cannabis crops in

Kentucky was hailed initially as successful, but has had the side effect of growers moving to hydroponic methods, which are actually more effective and harder to detect than outdoor cultivation (Potter, Gaines and Holbrook, 1990).

Many of these potential, adverse social side effects are not specific to third party policing, and can arise under any police intervention as Grabosky (1996) suggests. But these examples highlight the need for such possibilities to be considered and taken into account in the planning stage of third party policing interventions.

Negative side effects – displacement

While the adverse social consequences it can cause comprise the first group of possible negative side effects of third party policing, the second group is concerned with the extent to which these interventions may lead to problems being displaced to nearby places (spatial displacement) or to some other time (temporal displacement), being committed in another way (tactical displacement), or being transformed into some other kind of offense (target displacement) (Cornish and Clarke, 1987; Gabor, 1978, 1990; Reppetto, 1976). These negative displacement effects happen when a police intervention reduces a crime problem at one place, or in one particular situation, but fails to protect other nearby places or situations from offenders who are not discouraged or deterred from committing a crime. However, recent interventions that have directly measured the wider spatial effect of crime opportunity-reducing measures, have shown that reductions in crime can be achieved with little displacement (Clarke, 1992).

Concern about displacement in third party policing is no different to the concerns about displacement for other crime control or preventive interventions. We raise the issue to highlight the general lack of concern to date in the evaluation literature using third party policing tactics to measure and monitor the possibility of displacement. The key issue here, as with avoiding adverse social consequences of third party policing, is for careful consideration to be given to these factors prior to starting the intervention.

Negative side effects – impact on regulation, law, rights and justice

Apart from adverse social consequences and displacement, the third set of possible negative side effects from third party policing relates to its impact on regulation, rights, law and justice. By this we mean that because so much of third party policing involves the cooption of other things (regulatory systems, statutes, private legal rights) and other people (regulators, city inspectors, property and business owners, parents and schools) for crime control purposes, there can be an unintended but detrimental effect on the coopted tool or person. In addition, the process of cooption can cause a distortion of public policy (Grabosky, 2004), as the main goals and purposes of the coopted person or scheme are diverted or even undermined.

For example (see Mazerolle and Ransley, 2005), police efforts to use land-lords and business owners to deal with crime problems may lead to them coming under pressure as proximate targets, in what Sherman (1990) would characterize as a localized crackdown. Previously these burden-bearers had escaped police scrutiny because of their nominal legitimacy. As society and criminology increasingly draw a link between lifestyles and episodic offend-ing, and target conditions that give rise to criminal events, the rules shift and so do perceptions: nominal legitimacy comes under greater scrutiny, and is denied/rejected until compliance with police requests (represent-ing a larger community notion of order) is achieved. While individuals, such as landlords and business owners, may find themselves increasingly the burden-bearers for crime control, there can also be adverse effects from third party policing on regulators coopted by police. Third-party policing can be an intrusion into the routinized activities of regulatory agencies, in effect making burden-bearers out of nominal partners. The normal compli-ance model is suspended in favor of a more enforcement-oriented approach, disturbing the presumptively cordial relationship between regulator and regulated. Third-party policing also skews the resource allocation of the regulatory agencies, albeit temporarily, and often does so without any fore-seeable reciprocation (though such reciprocation can often be found at the line level, as street-level bureaucrats in one agency help and ask help of their counterparts in others).

On the other hand, police enlistment of regulatory actions under the third-party policing rubric may actually enhance the regulatory powers. Practitioner war stories teem with anecdotes about the fiction of routinized inspection: enforcers and compliance agents alike know of the fringe ele-ments – the likely proximate targets of a third-party action – whose businesses are out of compliance on a seemingly full-time basis. When the mail gives them advanced notice of the pendency of an inspection, they take minimal actions to assure that their business will be in compliance on the day the inspector arrives, and at the conclusion of the inspection return to business as usual. In conjunction with their community partners, police act as "eyes and ears" of the regulators, identifying the small number of non-compliant clients. As "the complaint" gives the police access to normally private areas (Reiss, 1971), the police identification of a problem provides inspectorial partners with the justification to act outside the routinized (and politically comfortable) standard practices. Like the police, the agents are no longer taking action on their own authority, but act with the express authority of the community.

One problem with this depiction of the relationship is that the move to responsive regulation makes it less and less likely. In that case, rather than a detailed code enforced by inspection and prosecution, regulation involves a process of negotiated compliance, rewarded by positive incentives as well as sanctions for non-compliance. The intrusion of police into this relationship can disturb the balance of incentives and sanctions, and diminish the trust between regulated and regulators that inadvertent breaches will not lead to heavy sanctions.

Just as regulators can find their activities disrupted by police cooption in third party policing, so too can the law and legal instruments be adversely affected. The broadest issue here is concern with the cooption of civil law for criminal justice purposes. As discussed in Chapter 4, civil and criminal laws have traditionally been regarded as having quite different purposes and rationales, leading to different levels of rights and protections. Civil laws generally rely on a lower standard of proof in establishing breaches, do not assume that targets are legally represented, and use a different system of sanctions and penalties. Traditionally those penalties did not involve the threatened loss of personal liberty through imprisonment, and therefore a lower standard of protection seemed justified. Some contemporary civil laws, however, have closed this traditional divide – not just by allowing for jail sentences for serious breaches (in Australia for example, under environmental protection and corporate regulation), but also such severe penalties as the loss of a licence to pursue an occupation, and the confiscation of possessions. Criticisms arise when these serious sanctions are sought not necessarily to further the aims of the regulatory scheme the civil law relates to, but as a way around the problems and protections developed in the criminal law. Cheh (1991) suggests that:

> Police and prosecutors have embraced civil strategies not only because they expand the arsenal of weapons available to reach anti-social behaviour, but also because officials believe that civil remedies offer speedy solutions that are unencumbered by the rigorous constitutional protections associated with criminal trials. (1991: 1329)

The main issue then is not that police are seeking to use civil laws, but their motivation for doing so – that the criminal law is too hard, too encumbered by protections, too ineffective. Cheh (1998) is also particularly concerned with new forms of civil law, such as civil asset forfeiture and injunction laws, specifically developed to overcome these perceived shortcomings of the criminal law. Forfeiture facilitates incapacitation, not by jailing perpetrators, but by locking up their assets and proceeds of crime, removing both their capacity to continue offending and their motivation for doing so. Similarly, injunctions can target problem sites or groups, without the necessity of proving particular individuals to have been responsible for particular acts of wrongdoing or nuisance. The issue is not with the effectiveness of these mechanisms, but with their capacity for injustice if misdirected, and the lack of legal protections applying to their use. In many cases, laws permit these types of actions in the absence of the target, or of legal representation, and based only on a probability rather than certainty of misbehaviour. Further, even if accurately directed, these laws can have a broad brush effect extending far beyond the original targets of action, to include for example the spouses and children also affected when a home is confiscated as an asset, or the other family members evicted along with an offending tenant.

There are two distinctly different scenarios that could arise if the trend to using civil laws in criminal justice continues. The first is that courts will become increasingly concerned at the impact on civil liberties, and begin to impose stricter controls, as occurred with criminal laws in the 1960s and 1970s, and was seen with the United States Supreme Court gang law cases in the 1990s (see discussion of *Morales* case in Chapter 4). There is little indication of this occurring to date in other third party policing areas (see Cheh, 1998). The second scenario is that the trend will continue until checked by political and legislative action, caused by some misuse of power by police, and in turn leading to legislative reform. Such a series of events led in the United States to federal reforms to civil forfeiture laws (see Chapter 4). Police can avoid this scenario and maintain what can be very useful tools by careful consideration and use of those only in appropriate circumstances.

Michael Buerger (1998) alludes to another side effect of this type when he talks of the potential for the loss of legitimacy for police actions (see discussion in Chapter 4). The argument is that public respect and authority for the police role is largely derived from the tradition of call for service policing – the public invites police participation in a problem and therefore legitimizes their involvement and if necessary use of force. Buerger (1998) suggests this legitimacy may not extend to more proactive forms of police involvement in communities, particularly where police do not even use the criminal law but instead coopt regulatory or civil systems. Any undermining of authority for the police role in such cases can only be countered by factors we have already stressed – the need for extensive community and agency consultation and cooperation before beginning a third party policing initiative. If a nightclub code is introduced with the active involvement and agreement of all nightclub operators in the area, plus alcohol rehabilitation service providers and other stakeholders, then it attracts a new form of negotiated legitimacy, akin to that existing between regulators and the regulated in responsive systems. This legitimacy involves active participation, and in many ways is likely to lead to stronger positive outcomes than the old imposed forms of authority.

Creative approaches to dealing with the side effects of third party policing

How then, should police go about maximizing the positive outcomes of third party policing initiatives, while limiting negative side effects? We suggest four main approaches. First, there must be a high level of consultation by police with other stakeholders, particularly regulators and other third parties. This requires joint discussion and analysis of the particular problem and the legal lever being used to address it. Third parties need to be able to contribute to the design of the intervention to ensure that it fits with their own regulatory or other goals, and to ensure the legitimacy of the proposed police action. Some writers suggest that the notion of joint ownership of interventions will always be problematic, because of the police desire for ownership and control of what is happening. Johnston (2003) describes the struggle in "plural policing" between other government agents of social control and the police desire to monopolize policing. The result is the gradual drawing in to the "police family" of these other agencies, so police can be sure of managing the process. Similarly, Barton and James (2003) describe a case study of plural policing that effectively was subverted to exclude community goals and considerations and to focus on the goals of the public police. In addition, police need to ensure that as with responsive regulation, they take a tiered approach to the use of incentives and sanctions to achieve compliance with their own objectives, and not use coercion as a first strategy. As regulators build compliance pyramids, police need to work through their own pyramid of responses. At the base of the pyramid, the first level response might be to find and appeal to common interests in the object of the intervention. For example, if the object is to close down drug houses, police might be able to show how compliance with building and health codes in certain areas is poor, but unlikely to improve because inspectors feel physically unsafe in taking any action. Police could suggest that joint teams could lead to greater protection for inspectors, who can then achieve their regulatory goals. If the objective is to remove children from high call-for-service incidence shopping malls, police can point out to mall managers the lack of local activities for children, and suggest potential services the mall could provide.

If suggestions and appeals to common interests don't work, then police need to work up the pyramid of coercive techniques, perhaps beginning with identifying consequences of non-cooperation, such as adverse publicity or the possibility of high-cost legal suits ensuing from the victims of non-action. Only when these tactics fail should police resort to more coercive methods. These methods will vary from case to case, depending on the type of third party and the legal tool. The requirement is for police to develop a graduated pyramid of responses applicable to each situation.

After improved consultation and a pyramid of increasingly coercive levers, our second suggestion for third party policing practice is that there needs to be a focus on developing policies and protocols for these interventions, rather than relying on often poorly articulated street level deals. Relationships and responsibilities need to be set out clearly in writing, along with reporting requirements and accountability provisions (discussed below). This not only clarifies roles and expectations, but also sets up models that can be applied elsewhere if the intervention proves successful.

Third, there is a need to identify positive incentive schemes to motivate entry into third party partnerships, rather than relying always on threats and coercion. Just as regulators may use incentives for their regulated communities, police need to identify positive motivators for regulators, landlords, parents and schools, to make them want to take on some crime control and prevention responsibilities. As discussed, positive motivating factors serve not only to improve the prospects of compliance and success, but also add to the overall legitimacy of the project. They also mean less police use of force, and therefore less need for the development of elaborate accountability mechanisms designed to oversee that use of force.

Positive incentives may also work in areas where deterrence and the threat of punishment have failed. Grabosky (1995) suggests that when choosing between negative sanctions (deterrents) and positive incentives, relevant factors for regulators to consider include: likely effectiveness of the instruments, its cost efficiency and social impact (including on individual liberty, democratic participation and accountability). The positive incentives may be awarded based on the role of the recipient (target of regulation or third party reward) and they may be material rewards or symbolic (Grabosky, 1995).

Positive incentives are common in regulatory schemes. They can include grants, bounties, fees, tax credits, loan guarantees, prizes or awards, favorable administrative consideration, praise, inducements, incentives, indulgences and compensatory power (Grabosky, 1995). So for example taxation departments may agree to waive fines and penalties and simply charge interest for overdue taxes where taxpayers come forward and comply with tax laws within a stipulated period. Environmental regulators may allow corporations with good records to trade pollution credits from one manufacturing site to another, compensating for below target performance at one site with good compliance at another. Corporations with strong internal audit committees may be subject to less intrusive external audits or compliance checks, on the strength of their good compliance. In Australia, corporations that have engaged in illegal cartel activities may receive more lenient treatment for blowing the whistle and giving evidence about other participants (ACCC, 2004). Makkai and Braithwaite (1993) described how nursing home inspectors using praise as a positive sanction contributed to improved compliance with regulatory standards. In the same industry, bonus payments to nursing homes were paid when improvement in patient health outcomes were achieved (Grabosky, 1995). Other examples of direct incentives to the target of regulation (Grabosky, 1995) include grants or subsidies to industries for research and development, and price preferences by government purchasers for environmentally friendly products. Incentives for third parties include rewards for information, and also the widespread availability in the United States of *qui tam* actions, or actions under the *False Claims Act*, which allow private citizens to prosecute regulatory breaches in return for a share of any damages.

There are many advantages of positive incentives over negative sanctions: they are less alienating, have increased legitimacy, can help with the learning of the desired behaviour, are more likely to lead to cooperation and assistance, and can foster pride in the organization (Friedrichs, 2004; Grabosky, 1993, 1995, 1996). But there are also disadvantages in offering what are essentially bribes for cooperation, in that they can sometimes be easily manipulated, costly, vulnerable to fraud and can foster distrust.

It is difficult to think of examples of criminal justice system equivalents to these regulatory incentives. One possibility is plea-bargaining, where offenders are offered incentives of more lenient treatment in return for evidence against co-offenders. Another is whistleblowing schemes, where statutory protection against reprisals might be seen as some kind of incentive for individuals to come forward with evidence of wrongdoing. A third example is the payment of informants for information leading to prosecutions. Apart from these examples, negative sanctions are far more common than positive incentives in dealing with crime. Criminal justice responses are typically structured as punishment for misbehaviour rather than incentives for compliance. So instead of promising a repeat juvenile offender a reward for not offending further, the criminal justice system is generally structured to wait and respond to misbehaviour, whether by cautioning, prosecuting or using restorative justice options.

A challenge for third party policing is the development of a range of positive incentives to encourage cooperation by third parties, which will vary according to the situation and the lever being used. The only example we came across in our review for this book was the UK car park awards scheme, discussed in Chapter 6. Here, a police sponsored award for safe practice operated as a positive tool to get operators to comply with crime prevention objectives. Police need to consider the range of incentives that can be used in each third party policing situation they are involved in.

Accountability

In the previous section we identified three main types of negative side effects from third party policing (adverse social consequences, displacement and impact on legal rights and laws) and finished our discussion of each by arguing they could be managed through careful police planning and usage. The issue of accountability is central to this, because it is through accountability for their decision-making that police use of third party policing interventions can be assessed. How police are to be controlled and managed is a continuing area of dispute, theorizing and research (Reiner, 1993; Loveday, 1996, 2000). The issue has traditionally been framed around the notion that police, as recipients of a monopoly over legitimate force, have a special need and duty to account for the use of that force. The literature therefore, has focused on the control of corruption, excessive force and discrimination in policing, and whether accountability should be overseen by agencies internal or external to police organizations. From these notions have developed the traditional models of police accountability.

But many of these assumptions about the role and nature of police work are threatened or weakened by developments such as private and pluralized policing, partnerships and risk assessment. The monopoly on police use of force is being broken, as coercive powers are extended to other agencies and officials. Jason-Lloyd (2003) writes of new forms of quasi-policing, where not only have police functions been devolved to other agencies, but so too have some of their powers. He describes the powers now given in Britain to, among others, non-police involved in airport security, courts' security, prison custody, immigration centres, channel tunnel security, civilian enforcement officers under the *Access to Justice Act* 1999, civilians employed by police organizations and private security. Similar trends are occurring in Australia. For example, in the Brisbane city district of South Bank, the *South Bank Corporation Act* 1989 empowers private security guards, in certain circumstances, to forcibly detain, search and exclude visitors from defined areas of public space, even where no offences have been committed.

How these quasi-police are to be held accountable for their actions and use of force is problematic, and so too is the notion of accountability for third party policing interventions. The most fundamental issue is who is to be held responsible, the police or their proximate targets including regulators, landlords and families? What standards should apply? The notion of police partnerships with other organizations, particularly where the partnerships are ad hoc, informal and localized, does not necessarily sit well with traditional notions of democratic governance, ethics and accountability. Legal and institutional mechanisms directed at controlling and making accountable police uses of power do not necessarily affect other providers of policing functions, particularly those that are not state agencies. Similarly, while third party policing holds promise of improved efficiency and effectiveness, how are managers to be held accountable for individual projects and their expenditure and outcomes, particularly when some of the resources are actually coopted from other agencies and individuals? Where agencies are mandated, or choose, to work together towards crime prevention and control, who bears ultimate responsibility for the success or failure of their decisions? Particularly problematic is the issue of ethics and accountability in making decisions not to become involved in controlling or preventing some crime problems – to focus on one housing estate or shopping centre at the expense of another. That is, the decision to under-police can be even more significant than the decision to over-police.

Much of the concern with accountability derives from the breadth and flexibility of police discretion in these areas – the discretion to enter into third party policing arrangements, to decide where to target them, against which targets, for the benefit of which groups, and using which legal or regulatory levers. This discretion is responsible for much of the usefulness of third party policing, enabling local level police to identify local problems and targets and develop community-based solutions, so accountability should not be directed at removing or stifling discretion. Instead, what is essential is as much transparency and openness as possible in these processes, and in the exercise of police discretion. It is important that there are some formalized means of community input into these processes and openness to scrutiny through public complaints mechanisms and other mainstream police accountability devices.

The major accountability implication for third party policing is the need for proper consideration of other agencies and of the individuals involved as proximate and ultimate targets. Police coordinating these types of interventions need to consider the full scope of which agencies might be involved in reaching a solution for the particular crime problem at hand, and considering those methods which least contribute to re-victimizing the already socially disadvantaged, or spreading the adverse consequences beyond immediate targets. For example, are there housing agencies that can be involved to help re-locate tenants from premises shut down for building code violations as part of a crack down on drugs, or are people simply left to fend for themselves?

Mazerolle and Prenzler (2004) suggest a checklist to be used by police planning third party policing interventions, to ensure the use of their discretion in an ethical and accountable way. The checklist covers such issues as the inclusion in the planning group of all possible stakeholders, the prioritizing of negotiation and persuasion over threats, assessment of the impacts of the intervention including displacement and re-victimization, consideration of whether benefits outweigh harms, notice to affected third parties, and weight given to concerns of fairness, equity, dignity and respect. The central issues for accountability are that there is a proper documenting of both the intervention and its planning, so that oversight can occur where necessary. It is also essential that such interventions are properly evaluated, so that the true benefits of coercive measures can be assessed and tested against the detriments.

In addition to these traditional issues of police accountability for use of power and force, other recent trends have extended the notion of what police should be held accountable for. The trends in new public management (discussed in Chapters 1 and 2) have required all government organizations to become more accountable for their effectiveness and efficiency (see generally, Considine, 2002). For police, this has translated into a need to be able to justify the use of resources in terms of outcomes, and new forms of managerial accountability for their administrative and functional processes (Reiner, 1993). Police now have to comply with the managerialist ethos dominating the public sector in most western nations. So police accountability is now three pronged: organizations need to be accountable for their use of powers, their efficiency in expending public resources and their effectiveness in achieving desired outcomes.

From the discussion above, police accountability can be conceptualized in two separate sections: the need to control uses of power, largely by individual officers or small groups of them; and the need to control police organizations and their managers, for their use of resources and effectiveness of their outcomes (Waddington, 1999). For much of the 1970s, 1980s and early 1990s, the focus of attention was on the first form of accountability, fuelled by scandals in the United States, Britain and Australia about inadequate organizational responses to excessive police force and other forms of corruption. The Scarman and McPherson inquiries in Britain, the Knapp, Christopher and Mollen Commissions in the United States, and the Fitzgerald and Wood Commissions in Australia, all exposed police corruption and misuse of force, and unwilling or inadequate organizational responses to those problems (Prenzler, 2002a). All of these inquiries and commissions proposed some form of reform or mechanism aimed at strengthening the accountability of individual police officers and the way they fulfilled their functions.

With the 1990s, the mood shifted. While concerns about accountability for use of force and individual policing occasionally recur, particularly with the call for independent external oversight of investigations against police (Prenzler, 2002a), the new public management has shifted attention onto organizational accountability as well (Reiner, 1993). Waddington (1999) calls this focus controlling police organizations, as opposed to the traditional accountability concern of controlling police officers.

Accountability of individual police

Accountability mechanisms designed to control police officers tend to be legal, such as statutorily delineated police powers; administrative, such as Commissioners' directions and orders, codes of conduct and rules; managerial, such as supervision and record-keeping; educational and training, such as ethics courses; and cultural, such as perceptions of what constitutes appropriate behaviour in a particular police service or unit. Enforcement follows similar patterns – in response to complaints an internal or external investigation will be held, and if the complaint is proven, a penalty will be imposed, either legal (prosecution, dismissal, fine), managerial (increased supervision, transfer, notation on record) or educational (training). The nature of the enforcement process varies among jurisdictions according to the extent of civilian involvement and availability of external review of complaints processes (Prenzler, 2002b), but the problems are relatively common, including low substantiation rates, excessive legalism, dissatisfaction by complainants, adverse impacts on cleared officers, and problematic legitimacy especially among marginalized communities (Reiner, 1993).

A major problem in some agencies is a culture where a degree of certain types of misconduct is tolerated, by individual officers and by the organization – whether it be racist policing (as in the Los Angeles Police Department response to the Rodney King beating, or the London Metropolitan Police response to the Stephen Lawrence case), or police involvement in drug dealing (for example, in New South Wales – see the Wood Royal Commission report). Dixon (1997) argues that far from controlling police malpractice, courts in Britain and Australia have tolerated and even encouraged them. Even in the United States, with its constitutional protection of due process, there are suggestions that the Supreme Court has weakened these protections through decisions downgrading the exclusion of illegally obtained evidence (Waddington, 1999).

One of the responses to controlling police behaviour and particularly discretionary police power has been to legislate clearly defined limits to those powers. Thus, in Queensland, a *Police Powers and Responsibilities Act* 2000 attempts to stipulate when and how police may exercise powers of arrest, search and the use of force, and to impose accountability for those powers, in a similar way to Britain's *Police and Criminal Evidence Act* 1984. The problem with these legislated methods of control is first that they only affect a limited part of police functions, that concerned with criminal investigations and arrest but not reaching into the patrolling, preventive nature that constitutes most police work. And second, legislated schemes find it difficult to penetrate police cultures, so that the problems of enforcement mentioned above, such as low substantiation and evidentiary difficulties, become amplified.

What then are the accountability mechanisms affecting police officers involved in third party policing, and how effective are they likely to be? The answers to these questions depend to some extent on variables – is the third party policing action managerially sanctioned, does it take place under a legislative or other legal framework, are police powers and discretions within the partnership clearly defined and subject to controls and limits? Police officers will continue to be accountable for any breaches of the law, such as committing assaults. Similarly, they will be responsible for any breaches of departmental policy, such as on the use of force, or engaging in unauthorized activities. These types of activities would be subject to the accountability and enforcement processes described above.

Other situations will be more problematic: for example, an officer who encourages a landlord to evict a problem tenant in breach of tenancy laws probably commits no criminal or disciplinary offence. Nevertheless, the officer's intervention has resulted in the tenant's rights being adversely affected. What recourse does the tenant have? He or she could complain in the normal way, but if no offence has been committed, there is unlikely to be any penalty imposed. Private litigation might be possible, alleging the officer was party to a trespass or some type of conspiracy, but apart from the tenuous nature of the claim, the tenant against whom such action is taken is likely to be least able to afford or even contemplate private legal action. For similar reasons the tenant is not likely to seek governmental or political intervention to censure the officer or police department. The same difficulties could arise if police partner with regulatory authorities who exceed their authority. A sanitation inspector may only have authority to enter premises on the basis of due cause or reasonable suspicion. A police officer who regularly tips off the official asks him or her to enter and inspect a suspected drug house, to bring pressure on the owner of the premises to evict the tenants. The official may be answerable for exceeding authority, any action taken may be unlawful, but what can happen to the police officer? The hidden and private nature of most third party policing partnerships, coupled with the lack of any supervision or guidelines make it difficult for any sort of accountability to be exacted, at least at the level of individual officers. The next section examines whether organizational accountability is any more likely.

Accountability of police organizations

The accountability of police organizations has always been marked by a central tension between independence and control. On the one hand, governments fund and are electorally responsible for the policing services they provide, so they need some ability to shape, focus and prioritize the services they establish. On the other hand, the tradition in Britain and Australia at least, has been for a relative degree of political independence of police services, with a public unwillingness for political control to intervene in operational issues. This tension has frequently been problematic, with police commissioners asserting their right to make decisions free of political control, and governments intent on exerting the same sort of managerial control over police as they would over other agencies for which they bear ministerial responsibility (see for example Fleming, 2004).

While the constitutional position has traditionally been stated as involving some degree of police and constabulary independence (Walker, 2000), this situation has been changing ever since the beginnings of Peel's *New Police* and of modern police management structures. Statutory frameworks now make clear the power of governments to dictate not just policy and managerial issues, but to intervene by imposing operational requirements and objectives (community policing, targets, crime prevention objective).

The imposition of these policies and objectives requires police organizations to be accountable for their achievements, and the means for
them doing so are diffuse, and bear some jurisdictional differences. In
Britain, with the centralization of authority over policing in the Home
Office, that department now exerts overwhelming authority over police
organizations. It sets objectives, imposes reporting requirements, and even
sets the contract period for Chief Constables (Loveday, 2000; Waddington,
1999).

In Australia, with seven separate state based police services and a federal police, such centralization is not possible. Political control is achieved
through each state government and its minister responsible for police, and
the federal minister for justice. Much of the control is now budgetary, so that
police services must account for their efficiency and effectiveness each year
as part of establishing their claim to a renewed budget. Australian governments increasingly impose targets, such as the numbers of police required
to be in operational rather than administrative functions. Policy directions
may also be imposed, such as crackdowns on certain offences (prostitution, drugs), or non-prosecution of certain offences (cannabis possession).
Australian policing now also has a federal overlay, with regular meetings of
police ministers and national organizations aimed at achieving consistency.
Fleming (2004) refers to this as a network approach, meaning there is no single infallible accountability system, but rather a regulatory web (Braithwaite
and Drahos, 2000) overlaying police-government relations promoting strategies to further the public interest.

How accountable, then, are police organizations for the third party policing activities they adopt? As with individual accountability, there is likely to
be considerable variation in the level of accountability required. In Britain,
police agencies must report regularly on their partnership activities under
the *Crime and Disorder Act.* At the very least, this imposes a level of transparency on what types of activities are being undertaken, and with whom.
Similarly, Fleming (2004) argues that the crucial aspect of accountability and
also the maintenance of public confidence is achieved by keeping decision-
making and its regulation in the public eye, saying "all debates must be public, transparent, contested and contestable – they must not become a species
of private government" (p. 13). One method of achieving this openness without raising operational concerns would be by requiring police agencies to
include in their annual report a summary of their policies and protocols
for involving third parties in crime control initiatives, and any guidelines.
Police could also report basic annual statistics, including the numbers of
interventions of various types, and give an overview of outcomes.

The ethical and accountability concerns

Problems will occur with accountability first, when existing mechanisms do not extend to the new situations arising under third party policing, for example if there are no established protocols or rules for the situation. Second, problems may arise because of the plurality of policing agents, including the possession by numerous agencies of coercive, intrusive, legal powers over citizens' lives, and the impact of the "quiet force" of these agencies, in terms of their impact on usage of public space, patterns of action and inaction, surveillance decisions and decisions about how, when and over whom to use their powers (Loader, 2000). Other problems will arise if there is conflict between the ethical and accountability regimes of police and the third party organization, whether it is a state regulator, housing authority, or business-owner. Finally, there is the need for accountability and ethical considerations to be taken into account in choosing when and where to deploy third party policing – to consider whether that decision means potential crime victims elsewhere or at other times are being abandoned to their fate.

How can these hurdles be overcome? One response is to suggest a need for new legal frameworks as well as managerial, training and administrative responses, both within police services and likely proximate targets. This may be seen in training programs for state agency regulators, but also for housing associations and individual property owners.

Another response is to call for new institutional forms of accountability stretching across the borders of existing agencies. Thus Loader (2000) suggests a new accountability commission for public and private police, taking into account the shared nature of much of their work. Could this model be extended to also include regulatory agencies and officials, many of which currently lack strongly developed accountability mechanisms?

A less institutional, more managerial model would require much more transparency of third party policing, perhaps through some form of register of cooperative relationships. This would enable the conduct of individual officers to be known and monitored, and the agency could also be called to account and report on the effectiveness of its activities on a regular basis.

Conclusion

In this chapter we have argued that there are many potential intended and unintended, positive and adverse side effects and accountability issues arising from third party policing strategies. Many of these issues are similar to those arising from standard problem-oriented policing, and relate to the choice of targets and strategies, distribution of policing services, and accountability for use of coercion and force. But there are also some special issues raised in the third party context, to do with the coercion of regulators and other third parties, the impact of the intervention on them, and the distortion of the legal lever used as the basis of the operation.

There are no uniform or simple answers to the question of how to maximize positive outcomes and minimize negative ones. There are too many potential situations, third parties and levers to allow this. The recommendations we have made in this chapter cluster in three main areas – the need for careful planning and consideration of all possible aspects of any proposed intervention, the need for detailed protocols and guidelines to be developed about how and when third party policing can be used, and the need for open reporting and assessment of those guidelines and completed programs. Police agencies need to be able to explain and defend their use of third party policing, and to change protocols when problems do occur. The final area we see as needing considerable work is the development of pyramids of sanctions, so that police can approach third parties first with cooperative and consultative strategies, before progressing on to those that are more coercive. And unlike in regulatory systems, in criminal justice there is a shortage of positive incentives that can be used to facilitate and encourage that cooperation.

CHAPTER 8

Directions for the future

Third party policing represents a major shift in crime control. It is a trend in policing that mirrors wider societal transformations in regulatory practices concomitant with the emergence of the "risk society." In third party policing, responsibility for crime control no longer rests with state agencies, but is shared with a wide range of regulatory nodes (both formal and informal) including regulatory agencies, local councils, businesses and individuals. Police partner with property owners, local residents, business owners, parents, health and fire regulators and local councils to control and prevent crime. Third party policing is thus defined in our book as police efforts to persuade or coerce organizations or non-offending persons, such as public housing agencies, property owners, parents, health and building inspectors, and business owners to take some responsibility for preventing crime or reducing crime problems (Buerger and Mazerolle, 1998: 301). In third party policing, the police *create* or *enhance* crime control guardians in locations or situations where crime control guardianship was previously absent or non-effective.

Our book had four main goals: first, to define and describe third party policing. What does third party policing look like in practice? How is third party policing implemented at the coalface of policing? What are the key dimensions of third party policing? What types of legal levers are used in third party policing and why? Our second goal was to link up third party policing with what we understand to be two broad trends: first, the move towards the "new regulatory state" and second, shifts in legal practice, notably the blurring of the criminal and civil laws. We describe global transformations in regulation as moving away from traditional, command and control towards contemporary approaches that tend to use what we have described as "responsive regulation" or the regulation of activities through coercion and consent. We also analyze some legal trends where criminal law is increasingly using civil processes and remedies, while in both regulatory and private law serious misbehaviours are criminalized. The third goal of our book was to systematically review the evaluation literature to scope out the range of third party policing practices and to determine the types of legal levers and third parties that are most effective in controlling a variety of crime problems. Finally, our book sought to raise a number of issues and dilemmas for further thought and research. In Chapter 7 we examined the side effects and unintended consequences of third party policing. Integrating what we know from original research and theory, we identified a number of practical issues and discussed the ethical implications of the third party policing approach. In this, our final chapter, we revisit the major themes from the earlier chapters and we examine a range of theoretical propositions that map out a broad research agenda in the area of third party policing.

The intent of this chapter is to reiterate what we consider to be the major challenges in further developing the theory and practice of third party policing. We identify four broad topics for future research and critical thinking. These topics include: building a more comprehensive understanding of the effectiveness of third party policing approaches, coming up with creative approaches to dealing with some of the unintended side effects and consequences of third party policing, developing an understanding of the costs and benefits of third party policing approaches, and developing a program of research to better understand societal, organizational and individual relationships to third party policing. We examine each of these broad topics for future research in turn.

Building an evidence base

In Chapters 5 and 6, we presented a comprehensive review of the third party policing evaluation literature as it currently stands. Our review of the evaluation literature, however, revealed a number of major shortcomings. First, third party policing is not part of the common lexicon in policing circles. As such, research is not indexed to identify interventions that clearly fit within the realm of third party policing. This caused all types of difficulties in our efforts to build a comprehensive database of third party policing interventions. It required a very broad range of keywords to search on. Many times, the items located in the search fell outside the scope of what we defined as third party policing. Our search also turned up a number of interesting "thought pieces" about tactics that clearly fit within our definition of third party policing, but they failed to provide any type of evaluation evidence. We note that these "thought pieces," whilst not helpful in our efforts to build a comprehensive database of third party policing interventions, were exceptionally helpful in scoping out legal dilemmas, unintended side effects and ethical challenges raised by third party policing. Our hope is that this book will raise the profile of third party policing and begin the process of stimulating the use of the term in policing research and evaluation.

Second, many police efforts to control crime involve multiple tactics: crackdowns, third party policing, arrests, street patrols, and a variety of responses following the SARA approach in problem-oriented policing. This is not a bad thing from a practical perspective. However, most research suffers from poor evaluation design and fails to create opportunities to disentangle and isolate the impact of the various interventions. The evaluations that we identified using third party policing tactics suffered severely from this general deficit in policing research. As such, many of the evaluations reviewed in Chapters 5 and 6 provided insufficient information on which to base a sound judgment as to whether the success of the intervention was due to the third party policing tactic or any one of the other tactics that were part of the overall intervention program. Our general plea to future researchers is to create evaluation designs that disentangle the unique contributions of the various intervention tactics. Our specific plea is to design evaluations that can strategically isolate the independent effects of third party policing tactics from other intervention approaches.

A third issue that emerged from our review of third party policing evaluations was the dearth of high quality evaluations and the failure of many of the evaluations to provide sufficient statistical data on which to calculate an effect size. Indeed, just twelve of the seventy-seven studies (15.6 percent) itemized in Chapters 5 and 6 provided enough information for us to calculate an effect size. For those studies that had provided sufficient data to calculate an effect size, the diversity of outcome measures utilized in third party policing research precluded us from conducting a meta-analysis. The lack of reporting integrity in evaluation studies is an oft-cited issue by many meta-analysts (e.g. David Farrington, Brandon Welsh, Anthony Petrosino, Mark Lipsey and David Wilson). Indeed, Farrington (2003: 66) reports that "It is important to develop methodological quality standards for evaluation research that can be used by systematic reviewers, scholars, policy makers, the mass media, and the general public in assessing the validity of conclusions about the effectiveness of interventions in reducing crime." We concur with this sentiment and similarly ask that evaluators provide the basic data (such as sample and sub-sample sizes, complete descriptive statistics, detailed description of statistical methods used, effect sizes) that form the building blocks for meta-analysis.

Minimizing the side effects of third party policing

The quiet proliferation of third party policing has obscured, at least to some extent, discussion of the range of ethical dilemmas that accompany the strategy (for exceptions see Chapter 7 of this book; Cheh, 1998; Mazerolle and Prenzler, 2004; Meares, forthcoming). In some ways, the "success" of problem-oriented policing and the inability of much of the problem-oriented policing literature to isolate the effects of one response over another (when multiple response options have been implemented together and at the same time) has contributed to the lack of discourse surrounding the dilemmas raised in third party policing. That is, ethical issues are relegated to the backseat when third party policing tactics are used as just one of many POP responses that together solve an ongoing crime problem.

The fact that third party policing is not institutionalized as part of the policing lexicon also obscures the tactic from comment and critique. Nonetheless, given the probability that the rate of third party policing is likely to escalate in the future as regulatory practices are further diffused in contemporary democratic societies and, given the evidence (to date) suggesting that third party policing is a tactic that reduces crime and disorder problems (see Chapters 5 and 6), it is our view that a number of creative approaches should be considered to minimizing the future side effects of third party policing. We discuss four broad issues with some ideas for the future.

Improving consultation between police and potential third parties is, in our view, the first matter that the police need to work on to ensure fairness in the use of third party policing. Advocating the importance of consultation with community members in general and community meetings in particular is an oft discussed and well-worn issue in the community policing literature (Bayley, 1994). Bayley suggests that community meetings serve four functions: they create a forum for community members to advise police about local problems and needs; they help police educate people about crime and disorder and enlist the cooperation of the public in dealing with these problems; they allow people to ventilate grievances against the police face to face, unimpeded by bureaucracy; and finally, they provide feedback to the police about the success (or failure) of their efforts (1994: 105–106).

The importance of community consultation is a matter that has special significance in third party policing. One of the necessary conditions of third party policing is the threat or use of some type of legal lever to insure compliance. The presence of a legal lever (whether explicit or implicit) alters the dynamic between police and potential third parties and perhaps changes the form of police-community interactions from being "consultative" to being "coercive." We argue that the primary concerns with the "consultative process" in third party policing are the degree to which the legal lever is used in a coercive manner and whether or not police have used a graduated scale of cooperation and consultation before resorting to the legal lever to insure compliance. It is an argument akin to the debates articulated in the use of force literature. As Terrill (2001) explains

> The [force] continuum provides an analytic tool for measuring and examining police use of force relative to citizen resistance. The benefit of examining police force through use of a force continuum is that it allows for the identification of instances when officers fail to escalate or de-escalate force in small increments in relation to resistant behavior. Concerns over the proper use of force is most pronounced when it appears the level of police force is not congruent with the level of resistance that preceded it. [. . .] Such an approach speaks directly to the transactional nature of the police citizen encounter . . .   (2001: 227)

Similarly, we argue that police need to use a graduated "continuum" of coercive practice to enlist third parties in controlling or preventing crime. There are many methods for obtaining cooperation and compliance from potential third party partners and that utilizing a legal lever should not be the first point of call. We would even go so far as to suggest that the policing literature is entirely underdeveloped in understanding the micro nature of police-community interactions (for exceptions see Reiss, 1971; Mastrofski et al., 1998). We know quite a bit about the police use of force in arrest situations, but we know very little about the conversations that police have with non-offending community members and the methods, words and tone of voice that they use to insure cooperation and compliance. From a research perspective, we suggest that much more needs to be learned about these micro-level processes such that we can better understand the continuum of police-community "cooperation." From a policy perspective, we need to use this research to create guidelines, policies and procedures that better direct police activities when they engage with the community to control and prevent crime.

Mazerolle and Prenzler (2004) identified some general principles that we suggest should guide police practice and the "consultative process" in using third party policing. Mazerolle and Prenzler (2004) suggest that the police should: first, insure that the planning process is inclusive of all groups who may have a stake in the crime problem or may be affected by interventions; second, insure that negotiation and persuasion is prioritized over threats and use of force; third, consider the impacts of the initiatives; fourth, insure mechanisms are in place for assessing the full range of possible impacts of interventions, including displacement of crime; fifth, insure all the impacts of the proposed remedy are proportionate to the harm it is supposed to be stopping; sixth, give recognition to the fact that offenders have numerous needs and may themselves be victims of abuse; seventh, insure that any third parties who might be affected are afforded notice and an opportunity to explain or propose alternative responses; eighth, insure that basic principles of fairness and equal access have been considered; ninth, insure that all groups, including young people, are treated with dignity and respect; tenth, police officers engaged in a third party policing initiative who are presented with ethical challenges should consult with police internal affairs or the civilian oversight agency for advice; and eleventh, insure that the development phase of a third party policing program has not involved any other challenges to the police professional code such as requests for confidential information, offers of gratuities or bribes, or requests for preferential treatment that might risk the integrity and impartiality of the police service.

We argue that these general principles should not only shape police-citizen interactions in a general context, but particularly in the third party policing context when police are actively recruiting the services of a third party to work with them to solve crime and disorder problems. Process matters and, in our view, the process for engaging third parties has been largely absent of examination, critique and discourse.

Understanding how the police and other regulatory nodes work together in third party policing is the second issue that we believe requires a better understanding. In Chapter 7, we identified some potential problems with the way the police co-opt regulatory resources to assist them in their crime control and prevention activities. One of the biggest problems is the de-facto redirection of regulatory resources away from perhaps core business activities into crime control and prevention activities. In some cases, the crime control goals may be in conflict with the goals of the regulatory agencies. One would like to think that the missions and goals of police and other regulatory agencies are consistent with one another. But this is unlikely to be the case. Indeed, we argue that as regulatory activities have become more diffused in recent years, the matrix of public agency missions, goals and policies has become increasingly complex and less cohesive. Thus it is likely that the missions, goals and policies of one agency will clash with the missions, goals and policies of another.

The growing complexity of regulation creates both barriers and opportunities for third party policing. In Oakland, California, for example, the police worked very creatively with a variety of government agencies including fire, health and safety, rodent control, sidewalks and sewers (Green, 1996). None of these regulatory agencies sanctioned the police co-option of regulatory resources. Indeed, the individual agents used their discretion in their choice to cooperate (or not) with the police in their third party policing efforts to control drug problems. Policies and procedures did not govern when or where regulatory resources would be directed towards places with crime and disorder problems. In contrast to the Oakland experience, it is likely that when the police attempt to work with highly centralized, rule-bound regulatory agencies (non-police), the opportunities for third party policing are likely to be more restrictive. In these types of agencies, the priorities and processes for the utilization of regulatory resources are likely to be more rigid than in agencies that are more decentralized. Thus, we argue that decentralized regulatory agencies are likely to be more responsive to calls from the police for help in their crime control and prevention activities. We elaborate on this idea below, but for now we suggest that it is important that mutually agreed upon dyad policies are determined between police and the array of regulatory agencies to guide the circumstances that should (and should not) invoke the utilization of regulatory resources for crime control and prevention purposes. The value of these policies are both to mobilize agencies to cooperate more fully with the police where a deficit in cooperation has occurred in the past (and thus increase the use of third party policing in some circumstances) and, conversely, restrain the over-arching use of regulatory resources where the police may be exploiting weaknesses in the policies of some regulatory agencies.

The third side-effect that we believe has the potential to undermine the effectiveness of third party policing involves the processes used to motivate and mobilize third parties. In most of the literature we have covered, we have identified tactics and procedures used to coerce third parties to comply with the wishes of the police. We have highlighted the legal levers used to gain this compliance. We believe, however that the "stick" approach has some serious side-effects that we have outlined in Chapter 7. In short, the side-effects of a punitive approach to third party policing include exposing third parties to reprisal by offenders, exacerbating family conflict, and evictions of disadvantaged persons who become homeless.

In other domains of regulation, incentive-based systems to obtain compliance are standard practice (Friedrichs, 2004). For example, taxation departments may agree to waive fines and penalties where taxpayers come forward and comply with tax laws within a stipulated period. Based on the strength of their good compliance record, corporations with a strong internal audit system may be subject to less intrusive external audits. In crime control, by contrast, incentives systems to dissuade people from crime and disorderly behavior are somewhat an anomaly. The only example that we came across in our systematic review of evaluation studies (covered in Chapters 5 and 6) was the Secured Car Park (SCP) Award established in the UK in 1992. This scheme was designed to encourage car park operators to improve security as a means of reducing criminal activity and fear of crime. Car parks that achieved high standards were given an award, which lasted for one year. Award recipients were able to publicize the fact their car parks provided high levels of security.

It is our view that incentive-based systems to encourage law-abiding behavior is particularly under-utilized in the control and prevention of street crimes. As such, we believe that a priority for policing in the future is to develop systems that create incentives to people to comply with the law. Project U-Turn, a federally funded program for young offenders in Australia, gets close to the type of incentive system we are imagining. In this project, young car thieves are given the opportunity to participate in a course that offers motor mechanic, panel beating and spray-painting tuition. We would take this type of program one step further and link the cost of the motor mechanic course to a pledge from the young offender to abstain from car theft for one year. We also believe that the police are well positioned to work creatively and include incentive based systems to encourage third parties to work with the police with the goal of reducing crime and disorder problems.

The final area of concern that was raised in Chapter 7 is the issue of police accountability. Third party policing, like other police practices, can be a double-edged sword. On the one hand, the evidence to date suggests that third party policing is an effective intervention that has the potential to grow and develop over the years. On the other hand, the hidden, coercive nature of third party policing has the potential to undermine ethical conduct in police practice, particularly in departments where patrol officers are under pressure to perform (e.g. COMPSTAT) and where ends are emphasized over the means. In Chapter 7 we suggested that most accountability problems occur when first, existing mechanisms do not extend to the new situations arising under third party policing. For example if there are no established protocols or rules for police use of legal levers. Second, accountability problems may arise because of the plurality of policing agents, including the possession by numerous agencies of coercive, intrusive, legal powers over citizens' lives, and the impact of the "quiet force" of these agencies, in terms of their impact on usage of public space, patterns of action and inaction, surveillance decisions and decisions about how, when and over whom to use their powers (Loader, 2000). Other problems will arise if there is conflict between the ethical and accountability regimes of police and the third party organization, whether it is a state regulator, housing authority, or business-owner. Finally, there is the need for accountability and ethical considerations to be taken into account in choosing when and where to deploy third party policing.

We conclude that accountability in third party policing can be achieved with careful implementation of two initiatives: first, there is a need for careful planning and consideration of all possible side effects of any proposed intervention. This points to the need for detailed protocols and guidelines to be developed about how and when third party policing can be used, and the need for open reporting and assessment of those guidelines and completed programs. Second, the use of third party policing requires a development of pyramids of sanctions, so that police can approach third parties first with cooperative and consultative strategies, before progressing on to those that are more coercive.

The costs and benefits of third party policing

Cost benefit analysis and similar techniques, such as cost effectiveness analysis, were developed by economists during the 1930s (Mishan, 1971) and designed as a tool for assessing the financial costs and benefits of competing alternative programs. Cost benefit analysis involves estimating the monetary value of program resources (costs) and the outcomes (benefits). Cost effectiveness analysis, by contrast, involves estimating the monetary value of program costs but it does not include the extra step involved in cost benefit analysis of estimating the *monetary* value of program outcomes (Welsh and Farrington, 1999; 2000). The "efficiency" of a program intervention is expressed as the relationship between the cost of a program and its effectiveness. (e.g. the cost of the third party policing intervention per unit of crime that is reduced; the cost of interdiction per unit of drug sales reduced; the cost of treatment programs per unit of crimes reduced).

Estimating the monetary value of all costs and benefits is an extensive task that, like any social science research, involves placing parameters around what will or will not be measured and then justifying these decisions (Welsh and Farrington, 1999, 2000). Estimating costs of running the program are important for determining which program is best. A program that has a small effect size but is relatively cheap to run may be a more cost effective intervention than something that is very expensive and very effective.

While an emerging literature exists on the cost-effectiveness of many types of crime control programs (especially drug control strategies like drug treatment, drug courts, mandatory minimum sentences etc), Caulkins (1998) laments the dearth of available data and lack of attempts to estimate the cost effectiveness or cost benefits of civil remedy programs like third party policing. Indeed, in our review of the literature on third party policing (including a review of civil remedy programs more broadly defined), Caulkins (1998) provided the one and only attempt to conceptualize an approach to estimate the costs and benefits of third party policing initiatives. Caulkins (1998) lays out a detailed approach for assessing the cost effectiveness of drug control programs using third party tactics and identifies the complexities of undertaking such an activity. Overall, Caulkins (1998) provides important insights for future research that seeks to assess the costs and benefits of third party policing.

We suggest three key areas for future research that should help policy makers determine whether or not third party policing is the type of crime control approach that governments should overtly facilitate and encourage. The key areas for future research include: first, classifying and categorizing third party policing approaches and then conducting cost-benefit analysis on homogeneous groups of third party policing interventions rather than attempting to assess the costs and benefits of a heterogeneous class of interventions. For example, the classification systems might distinguish between third party policing interventions by crime type (e.g. drugs, property crime, violent crime etc), by the third parties involved (i.e. categories of burden bearers such as property owners, parents, business owners), or by the types of laws leveraged (e.g. statute, subordinate legislation, contract, tort).

Second, we suggest that the most fruitful area of research for disentangling the costs and benefits of third party policing is to assess the impact on specific crime problems (e.g. drug problem places) rather than attempting to assess the individual benefits that might accrue as a result of third party policing interventions (e.g. reduction in drug use). This issue is similar to the challenges identified in meta-analytic research that involves isolating the various outcomes of an intervention. More often than not the units of analysis vary in third party policing evaluations (e.g. places, individuals) and the outcomes used are highly varied as well (self reported drug use, observations, official crime data). Our assessment of the third party policing literature suggests that a cost benefit analysis using the crime-place impacts is probably the most useful place to start. But the assumptions underlying a crime-place cost benefit analysis are fundamentally different to the assumptions that might dictate the costs and benefits when an individual person becomes the focus of the analysis.

Third, we believe that cost benefit analysis would be well suited to research that seeks to disentangle the disjuncture between the initiator (e.g. the police) and the third party (e.g. the burden bearer). How far apart are the interests of these two groups? Do property owners and police share common interests? If they do, then is the lever more or less coercive? Or more or less costly?

In short, there is an enormous amount of work that needs to be undertaken to fully understand the costs and benefits of third party policing. What we suggest is a prioritization of the work that reflects the dominant patterns of third party policing implementation.

Mapping out a research agenda

We note, from the outset, that theories of policing are rare. Most literature and research in policing is oriented towards understanding the normative aspects of police work (Crank, 2003). That is, police research is typically focused on evaluating programs, tactics and strategies, assessing the impact of law enforcement interventions on crime outcomes, and understanding what works and under what conditions (Crank, 2003; Sherman, Farrington, Welsh and MacKenzie, 2002). This "effectiveness" body of research is important and provides vital evidence for improving police practice (see Chapters 5 and 6).

However, scholars such as Bob Langworthy, John Crank, George Kelling, Ed Maguire and Steve Mastrofski have oft lamented the limitations of the normative perspective and have made many attempts throughout their careers to contextualize the institutional and societal environments that shape police practice (see also Read and Tilley, 2000). Langworthy (1986) for example argues that the search for effectiveness structures or "best practices" fail to account for the mediating effects of context. Crank and Langworthy (1992) advocate careful analysis of the institutional environment that shapes police organizations and how these environments constrain or enable reform. In short, police theorists lament the failure of much police research to contextualize police practice and propose that policing and police practice is best understood at three levels of analysis: the individual behavior of police personnel, the behavior of police organizations and the characteristics of the justice system in political, economic and social context (see Crank, 2003).

Our articulation of a research agenda in the area of third party policing begins with an examination of a dozen factors that we think shape third party policing across these three levels of analysis. At the societal level of analysis we focus on the global context of regulation and discuss how the shift towards a risk-based society is increasingly creating opportunities for police agencies to adopt third party policing tactics. At the organizational level of analysis we examine the key features of police organizations and identify the characteristics that are likely to shape adoption of third party policing practices. At the individual level of analysis we examine the types of supervisory and patrol officer traits and characteristics that are most likely to lead officers to use third party policing tactics.

Societal context of third party policing

A number of trends and characteristics of late twentieth and early twenty-first century society influence police practice and are driving the push towards third party policing. In the preceding chapters we have examined the global trends in regulation and policing. We noted the shrinkage of state activities that was coupled with a growing global recognition of the value of a plurality of regulatory methods. This dual trend in society provides fertile ground for governments to depart from reliance on command and control as the preferred way for securing compliance to what is generally known as responsive regulation that includes persuasion, self-regulation, professional discipline, and the like (see Ayres and Braithwaite, 1992).

In this section we refer back to our earlier chapters and identify three basic, societal conditions that we believe will continue to shape the proliferation of third party policing. These include first, the emergence and nature of de-regulated, democratic systems of law and government; second, spatial patterns in the distribution of crime; and third, the community context of social control. Below we discuss each of these societal conditions and how we propose they influence the adoption of third party policing.

1. Systems of regulation

In our opening chapter we explored the broader societal trends and forces that have influenced police practice and driven the push to third party policing. Prime among these is the transformation of governance in western democracies that has seen a movement from state sovereignty and control to networks of power, with the state providing only one node in the network, even though that may often be a central or authorizing node. This transformation has occurred within the context of political, economic and moral neo-liberalism, replacing previous notions of Keynesian state control. The shift in underlying ideology has been from welfarism, state dominance and concern with social apparatus, to the economic and moral responsibility of autonomous agents (individuals, families, communities, schools, firms), who are then made accountable for their own choices. The main mechanism for this transformation has been the development of the notion of risk – economic, social and political activities are no longer to be subject to central control, but to be monitored for risks that need to be managed. The key technology in managing risk is the use of statistical and other data that are analyzed to reveal risky groups, activities and individuals, who then become the focus of policies and strategies designed to limit or control the risks they pose.

The impact of these trends on crime control and policing has been to change the focus from state responsibility for preventing and correcting criminal behavior to a system where crime control and prevention networks are responsible for identifying and managing risks. Public police form one node of these networks, with private police, regulatory agencies, communities, business owners, schools and parents as other nodes. These networks may exist within legislated frameworks, but are often episodic and ad hoc. The prime concern of police and the criminal justice system is no longer with the detection and rehabilitation of individual offenders, but with identifying and corralling risky groups – repeat offenders, sex offenders, drug users, or mentally ill people. The new technologies involve profiling to identify the target groups, and then incapacitation, by longer or mandatory sentences, new forms of surveillance, or preventive detention.

These changes in societal context have far-reaching implications for police and the organization of police work. Police no longer (if they ever did) have a monopoly over responding to and preventing crime, but are expected to work in partnership with a range of other institutions, agencies and individuals. There is no clear framework for these types of partnership, but rather a set of expectations that police will work cooperatively with their partners in identifying and responding to crime, in ways that are likely to vary from community to community and problem to problem. Police have become, as Ericson and Heggarty (1997) described, the brokers for these partnerships – coordinating, providing information and resources, responding to the risks. Risks are identified through the analysis of statistical data and technologies like COMPSTAT, for which police are responsible.

While neo-liberalism and risk have transformed the role and nature of policing, regulation and the role of regulators have also been fundamentally affected. The overarching regulatory systems developed to accompany

Keynesian economic and political theory have had to adapt to the neo-liberal emphasis on individual autonomy and pluralism. The practical effect has been a shift in regulatory model, from state control to market models, from hierarchical systems of command and control to responsive regulation. There are many parallels between the transformation of police and regulators. Both are expected to work in partnership with their relevant communities, and to do so as cooperatively as possible. Risk is central to both, with regulators now focused on identifying risks to market stability or the public good, rather than on generalized rule-making. Many of the barriers between regulators and police that, as discussed, only developed with the onset of industrialization, are now dissolving again. For example, many regulators preside over systems applying criminal sanctions, using sophisticated methods of investigation of wrongdoing, and operating in adversarial, rights-based environments. But at the same time as regulators have become more like police, police have also shifted back along the continuum, developing pyramids of sanctions and rewards, attempting to persuade or coerce cooperation both from potential offenders (e.g. through situational prevention), and third parties, through third party policing.

The transformation of governance we have described has therefore been the key societal force driving the development of third party policing. It has been responsible for the shift away from central control and towards networks, for the new dominance of risk and its technologies of statistics and information, and the creation of systems of responsive regulation that are increasingly similar in style and application to new policing forms such as community policing. As such, we argue that a broader context for third party policing exists when there is an emphasis on:

- networks rather than centralized police responsibility for crime and social order;
- individual communities and sub-communities and their problems, rather than generalized crime scares;
- identification and management of risks, rather than a traditional focus on reacting to individual offenders;
- co-existing changes in regulatory practice, so that regulatory and policing goals and strategies tend to converge.

We propose that the emergence of third party policing parallels the democratization of societies and the de-regulation of existing democracies. As new democracies emerge, we would expect them to develop nodes of regulation, creating incentive systems for compliance, where the police become, in Ericson and Heggarty's (1997) terms, "brokers" of these crime control partnerships. We identify several other societal characteristics that we expect to be associated with the proliferation of third party policing. We expect that where there is a greater plurality of regulatory methods in a country, there will be greater opportunities for third party policing. We also anticipate that the more that regulation is market based and the more that regulation is pushed down to social institutions and local communities, there will be greater opportunities for third party policing. We also contend that opportunities for third party policing will expand as regulation becomes more diffused in a society. Table 8.1 below depicts these anticipated relationships.

2. Spatial crime patterns

In thinking about the societal context of third party policing, one cannot look past the spatial clustering of crime problems and think about how these spatial (and perhaps temporal) crime patterns create (or inhibit) opportunities (or barriers) for third party policing. Attempts to understand the spatial distribution of crime problems are not new. Place-oriented theories of criminal activity have a long history dating back to some of the early analysis of differential crime rates between provinces in France during the nineteenth century (e.g. see Guerry, 1833; Quetelet, 1842). In the United States, the tradition of "ecological theories" of crime emerged with the Chicago School-area analyses of delinquent behavior pioneered by Park, Burgess and McKenzie (1925), later made popular by Shaw and McKay (1942). These studies sought to understand social structural influences on the behavior of people living in high-crime areas and aimed to determine the array of ecological factors that contributed to delinquent behavior. Shaw and McKay (1942), for example, examined the reasons why some communities experienced high levels of delinquency over successive generations and why some demographic changes had little impact on the rate of offending. They concluded that disparity in community social values and levels of social organization led to differences across communities in their rates of delinquency. In these "disorganized" neighborhoods, Shaw and McKay (1942) suggested that local communities often failed to realize the common values of their residents or were unable to solve commonly experienced problems (e.g. see Bursik, 1988; Kornhauser, 1978; Thomas and Znaniecki, 1920).

The pioneering works of these Chicago School sociologists spawned a tremendous amount of research examining the relationship between places and criminal activity. A recent development in place-based research of criminal activity is the gradual movement away from the neighborhood or community as the geographic unit of analysis. Much recent research now centers on more specific, micro-units of analysis which focus on hotspots of crime or the high-crime address or place (see Eck and Weisburd, 1995; Pierce, Spaar and Briggs, 1986; Sherman et al., 1989; Sherman and Weisburd, 1995; Taylor, 1998; Weisburd and Green, 1994, 1995).

Recent hotspots of crime and place-specific analyses suggest that even within so-called deviant neighborhoods there are relatively large geographic areas that are free of criminal behavior (Weisburd and Green, 1994; Weisburd, Maher and Sherman, 1993). This finding challenges the spatial context of "bad areas" by suggesting that crime may be concentrated in places or locations that are only a few blocks in size, as opposed to entire areas or neighborhoods (Weisburd et al., 1993). The relative concentration of some categories of crime identified in hotspots research tends to refute the universalist concept of "dangerous neighborhoods" (Maher, 1990; Sherman et al., 1989).

The implications of this research suggest that there is likely to be a great deal of spatial variation in the use of third party policing tactics. Recent research, however, suggests that the spatial relationship between third party policing and crime is unlikely to be linear. That is, we expect that the perhaps obvious relationship of where there is more crime, there is more third party policing will not withstand empirical scrutiny. Indeed, recent research by Mazerolle and her colleagues (2003) finds that in some of the worst drug market places, the police resorted to traditional policing strategies (surveillance, arrests, street "pops" or "pat-downs"). Conversely, in some of the least serious drug market places, very little third party policing efforts were identified. By contrast, it appears that some constellation of middle ground places including commercial and residential locations with moderate crime problems are most likely to be the locations where third party policing proliferates.

We suggest that the hyperbolic shape of the relationship between drug market places and third party policing (see Mazerolle et al., 2003) is likely to hold for other categories of crime, most likely street-level violent and property crimes. We suspect that third party policing occupies some type of middle ground in police practice for several reasons: first, most of third party policing is ad hoc and episodic. As such, it is unlikely that the police would use third party policing in places where problems can be averted with simple measures. At the other end of the spectrum, traditional police tactics seem likely to dominate in places with more serious, intractable problems. While police policy makers, researchers and police leaders would like to imagine innovative practices being utilized in the most problematic places, it appears that, at least in targeting drug market problems, when the going gets tough, the police revert to familiar ground of traditional policing approaches (e.g. arrests).

A second area of spatial difference in the proliferation of third party policing is likely to be between rural/regional and urban areas. Given the coercion spectrum of third party policing (see Chapter 3) we expect that more legalistic third party policing practices are more likely in highly urbanized places where residents are less known to the police. In rural/regional and suburban locales, where the police are more integrated and known within the community, we would expect less reliance on third party policing and the legal levers used to coerce compliance. In those communities, where the police and community members (including business owners) have a more intimate relationship, we would expect the police to be less likely to use legal levers to elicit support to control or prevent crime.

3. Community context

The spatial distribution of third party policing is of great interest to us and we have described above some of the relationships that we would expect to prevail. We recognize, however, that the spatial distribution of third party policing will be greatly contextualized by community characteristics. We expect tremendous variation in the issues that confront the police in their efforts to motivate and mobilize third parties. At the more benign end of the spectrum, the police can approach third parties and politely ask them to cooperate. The police might consult with members of the community as well as local property owners and ask them about ways that they see fit to control an existing crime problem or help them to alter underlying conditions that the police believe might lead to future crime problems. At this low-key, benign end of the spectrum, the ultimate sanctions that might be used generally go unnoticed. The police may, themselves, consciously utilize their persuasive powers, yet be discreet about the alternative methods of coercion that they may resort to if the third party target proves to be an unwilling participant.

At the more potent end of the spectrum the police coerce third parties to participate in their crime control activities by threatening or actually initiating actions that compel the third party to cooperate. Threats may include inspectorial or regulatory intervention, or communication about the adverse consequences for the third party for not following police advice, often the threat of civil litigation.

We propose that the key community feature that differentiates the manner in which police mobilize third parties has more to do with the degree of collective efficacy in a community (see Sampson et al., 1997) than some of the typical structural characteristics of a community that co-vary with street crime outcomes (e.g. poverty, low social capital, single-headed households etc). Collective efficacy is a *process* for mobilizing social capital to tackle specific neighborhood problems. It is a *task-specific* construct that describes community-based mechanisms that facilitate social control without necessarily requiring strong ties or associations amongst community members. Research in Chicago (Sampson et al., 1997), Stockholm (Wikstrom and Sampson, 2002) and several smaller US cities (see Gibson, Zhao, Lovrich and Gaffney, 2002) shows that collective efficacy helps to explain the relationship between neighborhood social composition and crime levels.

Sampson's research in Chicago has found that traditional ecological constructs such as social disorganization, social structure and even social capital (see Coleman, 1988, 1990; Putnam, 2000) fail to explain contemporary spatial variations in crime across the Chicago landscape. Alternatively Sampson and his colleagues identified that collective efficacy better fit the data on the spatial patterns of crime. Collective efficacy assumes that the degree of and mechanisms for informal control are not the same in all neighborhoods. Sampson and Raudenbush (2001: 2) say that:

> . . . where there is cohesion and mutual trust among neighbors, the likelihood is greater that they will share a willingness to intervene for the common good. This link of cohesion and trust with shared expectations for intervening in support of neighborhood social control has been termed "Collective Efficacy," a key social process proposed . . . as an inhibitor of both crime and disorder.

Third party policing appears, at least on the surface, to be a practical manifestation of how the police might work in communities to mobilize the cohesion and mutual trust among neighbors, local businesses, school associations and the like to deal with highly specific, localized crime problems. An interesting pattern is likely to emerge around the ideas of collective efficacy and third party policing. In communities that score high in collective efficacy, the police are likely to use third party policing tactics to control crime problems, but are less likely to unleash legal levers to elicit support to be task specific to solve a recurring crime problem. In these communities, the police are more likely to use more benign, coercive tactics to elicit support. By contrast, in communities that score low in collective efficacy, we would expect the police to have more success in mobilizing third parties by using the full array of legal levers and coercive practices. The corollary of formalized third party policing in communities with low collective efficacy is that the very process of third party policing action is likely to create a collective efficacious capacity within a community that was previously latent at best and non-existent at worst. This proposition can be tested by measuring the degree of third party policing activity and collective efficacy that exist in a community before a program of third party policing is implemented and then measuring the amount of collective efficacy in a community post third party policing implementation. We would expect communities to score higher on the collective efficacy scale after the police implemented third party policing than they did before a program of third party policing was implemented.

The community context of third party policing has several other facets. We would expect that visibility of crime will also influence the distribution of third party policing. That is, in Chapter 3, we discussed several reasons why third party policing occurs often to control street level crimes (including street violence, crimes committed by young people). There are two primary reasons for this pattern. First, disadvantaged people are less likely to mount a challenge against the administration of laws that might be unequally distributed (see Chapter 7) and second, higher level crimes are more likely to be the subject of third party policing efforts that are initiated by regulators other than the police. Given these reasons, we would expect that communities that endure more visible categories of crime (vandalism, street fights and the like) are probably the communities that attract more third party policing.

Organizational context of third party policing

In the late 1960s and early 1970s police departments in democratic societies were heavily committed to the professional or "reform model" of policing (see Kelling and Moore, 1988). The police drew their legitimacy and authority through the law and by "professionalizing" their management practices, they emphasized crime control as the central function of police, they centralized their organizational structures and emphasized crime investigative, rapid response and preventive patrolling activities.

By the early 1980s it was clear that the reform model of policing was in crisis. George Kelling and Catherine Coles in their book *Fixing Broken Windows* provide an excellent summary of the context in which the reform model of policing was collapsing (Kelling and Coles, 1996, Chapter 3). Police Chiefs in key city police agencies and scholars alike pointed at the overloaded emergency call system (911 in the United States) as being symptomatic of a much larger crisis in policing. At least two widely read books – *The New Blue Line* (Skolnick and Bayley, 1986) and *Beyond 911* (Sparrow, Moore and Kennedy,

1990) – captured the frustrations felt at the coalface and were influential in identifying the crisis in policing and paved the way for reform.

The nail in the coffin for the reform model of policing came by the early 1990s when it appeared that every major police strategy to prevent or control crime had been "unmasked" by scientific research (see Bayley, 1994; Weisburd and Eck, 2004). For example, in a major evaluation of preventive patrol in Kansas City, Missouri, the Police Foundation concluded that increasing or decreasing the intensity of preventive patrol did not affect either crime, service delivery to citizens or citizen feelings of security (Kelling, Pate, Dieckman and Brown, 1974). Similarly, in another large-scale study that assessed the effectiveness of rapid response, Spelman and Brown (1984) concluded that improvement in police response times had no appreciable impact on the apprehension or arrest of offenders (see also Bieck and Kessler, 1977; Tien, Simon and Larson, 1978).

Weisburd and Eck (2004) observe that these and other studies in the 1970s and 1980s led scholars to challenge the fundamental premise of whether the police could have a significant impact on crime (see also Greenwood, Chaiken and Petersilia, 1977; Levine, 1975). They suggest that while the police had long considered their function as effective "crime fighters" as central to police identity, the scientific evidence seemed to suggest otherwise (Weisburd and Eck, 2004; see also Bayley, 1994; Klockars, 1988). Michael Gottfredson and Travis Hirschi highlighted the general sentiments of police scholars, policy makers and community members when they stated:

> No evidence exists that augmentation of patrol forces or equipment, differential patrol strategies, or differential intensities of surveillance have an effect on crime rates. (Gottfredson and Hirschi, 1990: 270)

Similarly, David Bayley, in his 1994 book *Police for the Future* begins with the following statements:

> The police do not prevent crime. This is one of the best-kept secrets of modern life. Experts know it, the police know it, but the public does not know it. Yet the police pretend that they are society's best defense against crime and continually argue that if they are given more resources, especially personnel, they will be able to protect communities against crime. This is a myth. What is the evidence for this heretical and disturbing assertion? First, repeated analysis has consistently failed to find any connection between the number of police officers and crime rates. Second, the primary strategies adopted by modern police have been shown to have little or no effect on crime. (1994: 3)

These are indeed, strong words. Reading David Bayley's (1994) introductory chapter makes one wonder how the police in the United States managed to lobby for more personnel well into the 1990s. But then, perhaps the myth still prevails in Australia. As recently as 2002, the police union in Queensland mounted an intensive campaign to increase the number of sworn personnel (*Courier Mail*, 2002a).

Despite perhaps the reluctance of some police to admit that they were largely ineffective during the 1970s and 1980s in reducing crime, it is clear that police organizations have undergone significant change in the last decade of the twentieth century. George Kelling and Mark Moore (1988) identify seven major characteristics of what they call the "community era in policing." First, in the community era of policing the source of authority stems from community support; second, the primary function of community era police agencies is balanced between crime control, crime prevention and problem solving; third, the organizational design is decentralized, task-oriented and utilizing matrix structures to prevent and respond to crime problems; fourth, the relationship to environment is consultative where the police defend values of law and professionalism, but listen to community concerns; fifth, demand for police service is channeled through analysis of underlying problems rather than via emergency calls; sixth, foot patrol and problem solving predominate as the preferred tactics and technology; and seventh, organizational performance is measured by outcomes of quality of life and citizen satisfaction, not by the number of arrests or other indicators of crime control.

Some evidence exists of this paradigm shift in policing. Many police departments have changed their emphasis from almost exclusive focus on crime control to more fully embrace crime prevention and problem-solving as central to their mission (but see Goldstein, 2003). This transformation process has led the police to become more consultative with community members and stakeholders, adopting a variety of new approaches to policing under the auspices of the community era (e.g. see Skogan and Hartnet, 1997). There is also a growing body of scientific evidence to suggest that the police can be effective at reducing crime problems when they take a focused, partnership approach (see Sherman et al., 2002; Weisburd and Eck, 2004). Evidence of successful police practices summarized by Weisburd and Eck include foot patrol (Trojanowicz, 1986); directed patrols in crime hot spots (Koper, 1995; Sherman and Weisburd, 1995); specific deterrence for some categories of offenders (e.g. employed domestic batterers) (Sherman and Berk, 1984); proactive arrests particularly for traffic and disorderly conduct (Weiss and McGarrell, 1996; Katz, Webb and Schaefer, 2001), drug market crackdowns (Kleiman, 1988; Sherman and Rogan, 1995; Weisburd and Green, 1995; Zimmer, 1990); drunk driving road blitzes (Homel, 1993) and problem-oriented policing (Braga et al., 1999; Kennedy et al., 1996; Sherman et al., 2002). Additionally, some elements of community policing activities such as door-to-door visits (Laycock, 1991; Skogan, 1990) are clearly effective.

In short, we recognize that the police have undergone significant changes over the last ten years or so. They have re-organized and changed many of their operational practices. At the same time external influences such as the proliferation of private security, technological innovation and global reforms in regulation have pressured the public police to be more effective within existing resource levels. With these changes in the background, we adhere to the view that policing over the last ten years has undergone a significant paradigm shift. It is now becoming clear that Bayley's view from 1994 that the "police do not prevent crime . . . [and] that the primary strategies adopted by modern police have been shown to have little or no effect on crime" (1994: 3) is no longer entirely true. It is from this frame of reference that we examine the organizational context of the adoption of third party policing.

Police scholars typically identify a number of organizational characteristics that define and distinguish the reform era of policing from the community era of policing (see Bayley, 1994; Kelling and Moore, 1988; Maguire, 1997; 2003; Reiss, 1992; Skolnick and Bayley, 1986). Some of the dominant themes in the police organizational literature include the amount of centralized decision-making, the level of work specialization in a police organization, the hierarchy of authority, the degree of formalization of rules and regulations, the nature of accountability structures, the nature of external partnerships, and the diffusion of technology. These organizational characteristics all have relevance to the prevalence of third party across police agencies. We discuss each of these characteristics in turn.

4. Centralization

Decision-making authority and power resided at the top of the organizational hierarchy in the reform era of policing (Kelling and Moore, 1988). Top executives in these highly centralized organizations were responsible for coordinating organizational activities, policy development, goal setting and major financial decisions (Kuykendall and Roberg, 1982). By contrast, one of the key defining features of community era police organizations is the decentralization of decision-making (see Kelling and Moore, 1988; Maguire, 1997; Moore, 1992; Reiss, 1992). Decentralized organizations assume that the location of knowledge can reside anywhere within an organization, not necessarily the top level (Kuykendall and Roberg, 1982). This locus of knowledge becomes an ad hoc center of control, authority and communication. Therefore when knowledge centers at lower levels of the organization, there is more opportunity for street level bureaucrats to be more creative in their problem-solving efforts. This is the case for both the police as well as for other government agencies and their accompanying regulatory units. As such, we expect that third party policing is more likely to be initiated in police agencies that have more de-centralized structures. Likewise, regulatory partners in third party policing are more likely to stem from agencies with more decentralized structures than from agencies and regulatory functions that are part of agencies that are more centralized.

5. Levels of work specialization

The structure of police work in traditional, reform era police agencies tended to be largely specialized with many ways of dividing labor responsibilities. Task specialization can be seen when police agencies have clearly defined, narrow job assignments, such as that of a traffic patrol officer, arson detective, or child safety officer. Classical management theorists (e.g. see Burns and Stalker, 1961; Kuykendall and Roberg, 1982) argue that task specialization is a means to concentrate expertise in one area. With a strong division of labor, workers primarily are concerned with their own work objectives and are less concerned with overall organizational objectives. Advocates of work specialization argue that these types of organizations foster officers who tend to focus more clearly on their unit objectives rather than broader organizational ends. It is further argued that specialization tends to make unit goals and objectives paramount by enabling workers to narrowly concentrate on specific unit tasks to the exclusion of broader goals (Kuyendall and Roberg, 1982).

In contrast to the traditional era of policing, the goals of the community era are to de-emphasize specialized assignments and tasks, focusing on directing specialized knowledge and experience toward the common task of the organization (Kelling and Moore, 1988; see also Maguire, 1997, 2003). In community policing, for example, officers take on a broad array of responsibilities to solve community problems. The community era also advocates task force approaches to crime problems that combine various specialties and emphasizes a more generalist perspective.

Third party policing offers some interesting insight into the issue of task specialization in police agencies. We would expect that police agencies that have made efforts to reduce the task specialization of officers are *less* likely to take on third party policing than those agencies that maintain task specialization roles. This proposition may seem counter-intuitive, but our logic is as follows: one of the fundamental notions that we have argued in this book is that third party policing is differentiated from problem-oriented policing by the process used to initiate third party policing interventions. We argue (see Chapter 4) that legal provisions and parameters dictate the process of third party policing and that third party policing is generally devoid of problem scanning and analysis. Indeed, we have argued elsewhere in this book that third party policing is used as a one-size-fits-all response to similar categories of crime problems. If this is the case, then officers in highly specialized units or performing specialized tasks (e.g. traffic, child safety, fraud, arson, robbery) are likely to forge synergies and partnerships with regulators and other nodes in the regulatory network they come in contact with most often and use legal levers they are most familiar with in their crime control and prevention efforts. If this one-size-fits-all approach is correct, we would expect to see a positive relationship between the degree of task specialization and the uptake of third party policing.

6.   Hierarchy of authority

Highly bureaucratic, reform era police agencies favor tall hierarchies, with numerous layers of authority in place to oversee and make decisions. This hierarchy of authority establishes the levels of subordinate-superior relationships that tend to be dominated by top-down decisions from superiors to subordinates. In police settings, the rank structure signifies the importance placed in the hierarchy of authority as a crucial decision-making instrument.

The task structure of more contemporary, community era police organizations are typically less hierarchical and more fluid (Bayley, 1994; Kelling and Moore, 1988). Rather than having distinct tasks reconciled by supervisors into an aggregate of unit work (such as a traffic division), community era agencies continually redefine and adjust individual tasks through collaboration with others. Kuykendall and Roberg (1982) term this as a collegial structure that incorporates horizontal as well as vertical interactions. In these models, police officers are encouraged to discuss information with peers, using a network structure of control, authority and communication. The emphasis on collegial decision making in contemporary organizations renders "tall" hierarchies obsolete.

The collegial nature of decision making is crucial for the adoption of third party policing. We know that third party policing is a diffuse, amorphous approach to solving problems with a large range of potential legal levers (see Chapter 4). As such, third party policing is dependent on the exchange of knowledge and the breakdown of vertical hierarchies of authority. As such, we would expect third party policing to flourish in departments that have flatter organizational structures and collegial decision-making practices.

7. Formalization

The reform era of policing was also characterized by a high degree of formalization of rules and regulations in which organizational norms and rules are explicit (Hage and Aiken, 1969). These types of organizations are rule-oriented, placing high reliance on written rules, policies and procedures to govern behavior (Reiss, 1992; Weber, 1947). Police departments that score high on the scale of formalization place heavy reliance on standard operating procedures as a means of guiding behavior of street-level officers (Maguire, 1997; Moore and Stephens, 1991).

By contrast, community era police agencies aim to be less rule-oriented, where individual assignments are less structured, officers rely less upon strict methods and procedures, there is less effort to codify all work processes within the organization and there is more emphasis placed upon accomplishing goals (see Bayley, 1994; Kuykendall and Roberg, 1982). Third party policing clearly is more likely to occur in agencies that are less rule oriented and provide opportunities for police to go outside of the box and seek the help of external partners in controlling crime.

8. Accountability systems

Unlike many other front-line workers in numerous other occupations, police face many opportunities for misconduct and corruption (Cohen and Feldberg, 1991; Kleinig, 1996). On a daily basis, ethical dilemmas arise for police where they must make decisions on the fly from competing choices about where to prioritize resources and how to maximize efficiency (Mazerolle and Prenzler, 2004). One of the interesting features of the reform era of policing was the emphasis on accountability structures (Kelling and Moore, 1988). Indeed, one of the major factors driving the shift from the political era to the reform era was the degree of corruption and the lack of accountability that characterized police agencies that were beholden to political influences (for an excellent example, see Queensland Commission of Inquiry into Possible Illegal Activities and Associated Police Misconduct, 1989).

In contrast to the political era, police agencies reflecting the reform era of policing tended to foster broad standardization of work processes and other organizational activities as a means to increase the degree of accountability. But the shift in accountability structures with the emergence of the community era of policing has challenged many to question the degree to which the community era exposes police to increased opportunity for corruption (Bracey, 1992; Nelligan and Taylor, 1994).

The emergence of third party policing is intrinsically linked with many facets of the community era in policing and raises similar concerns regarding the potential for corruption and misconduct. Indeed, the diffused nature more generally of regulation, creates many unclear structures of accountability.

9.   External partnerships

The role of external partnerships (or what we term "third party") is central to the notion of third party policing. Throughout this book we have talked about who these partners are, the coercion/co-option of these third parties, the ethics and processes for recruiting these partners and the role these partners (and their legal levers) play in reducing crime problems. But we know that the quality, quantity and nature of these external "third" parties vary from one agency to another, one partner to the next and from one jurisdiction to another. But why? One of the first factors that we suggest dictates the quantity of third parties is the number of opportunities that operational organizational units within a police agency have to forge external partnerships. Some organizational units are more integrated with external partners than others (e.g. child safety units). These types of units are, logically, more likely to adopt more third party policing tactics than those units that have fewer operational external partners and opportunities. Hence, from a pure quantity perspective, the more external partners a police department fosters in general, the greater the adoption of third party policing. Moreover, we would expect that jurisdictions with regulatory agencies with consistent policies and synergies are more likely to repeatedly exploit existing partnerships that use third party policing tactics than in those jurisdictions where regulatory entities are in conflict or lack coordination and cooperation.

Related to this notion of a coordinated approach to the uptake of third party policing is the idea that the more that external partners in a community are sympathetic to crime control goals, the greater the adoption of third party policing. That is to say that in communities where the missions and objectives of a range of regulatory nodes coalesce are likely to be those communities that experience more third party policing interventions.

We would also argue that more opportunities for episodic third party policing exist in communities that house chaotic external partner organizations. Earlier, we talked about the exploitation by the police of regulatory nodes that lack cohesiveness in their policies. We pick up on this point here and thus argue that episodic use of third party policing is likely in these organizations where the police form personal synergies with individual regulators and where the priorities and directives for these individual regulators are less rigid and pre-determined.

10.   Technology

Ed Maguire (2003) defines "organizational technology" as the activities, mechanisms and systems used in achieving organizational goals (2003: 81). Police agencies that experiment and use new, innovative technologies (e.g. crime mapping, digital communications systems, enhanced-emergency call systems, non-emergency call systems) are often less bureaucratic, flexible organizations that are able to adjust to the changing technological landscape (see Moore, Thacher, Hartmann, Coles and Sheingold, 1999). By contrast, traditional organizations that tend to foster broad standardization of work processes such as answering certain police calls, investigating crimes and documenting police actions (Sparrow, Moore and Kennedy, 1990) are less likely to adapt to new technologies. We argue that third party policing is more likely to be adopted in police agencies that respond to new technologies and adapt their processes and procedures to accommodate these new technological opportunities. New technologies (e.g. non-emergency call systems implemented alongside of organizational reforms) are likely to reduce the amount of time officers spend responding to calls for service and create opportunities for police to explore alternative crime control and prevention approaches. The uptake of third party policing is thus more likely in those departments using technological innovation (particularly information technology) to support organizational reform.

Third party policing at the individual level

Our goal in this section is to suggest that certain types of supervisory and patrol officer characteristics are likely to be associated with creating opportunities for third party policing. In third party policing, we are interested in a very specific category of proactive police activities; those police activities where the police use a variety of civil, criminal or administrative laws to proactively engage a third party in order to control or prevent a crime problem. We are particularly interested in the way that the police are mobilized to engage these third parties. Are they directed to use third party practices by their superior officers? Do they self-initiate the action? Do they arrive at a third party policing action after careful analysis of the crime problem and a comprehensive search of "best practice" responses? Are police simply using third party policing as a means to "off-load" their crime prevention or crime control responsibilities? Is third party policing one of the first or is it one of the last tactics used by the police in their effort to solve the problem? Are external forces (e.g. government policy) pushing individual officers to use third party policing tactics where they might have otherwise used another tactic? Are other regulatory entities driving/encouraging/enticing individual police officers to use third party policing?

11. Supervisory characteristics

A recent study by Famega, Frank and Mazerolle (forthcoming) indicates that front line supervisors are falling far short of what we would want or expect. Supervisors provide few directives to patrol officers, and they are not specific in nature. This finding may not be surprising as Skogan et al. (2004: 155) noted, "every police department has trouble making problem-solving work." Research suggests that at least a good part of the "problem" is ineffective supervisors (Famega et al., forthcoming; see also DeJong et al., 2001). As supervisors are not providing directives, officers are *choosing* to remain in their cars, randomly patrolling and waiting for calls for service.

We have contemplated the role of supervisors in fostering or restraining the use of third party policing. In our view, we expect that supervisors who provide detailed directives to subordinates will likely generate more third party policing than those supervisors who provide less direction to subordinates. We expect, however, that different supervisors will foster different types of third party interventions. Consistent with our notion that the process of third party policing is intrinsically linked to legal processes and that officers will be more likely to match legal levers to problems (than vice versa), it would be conceivable that certain supervisors will stress the use of particular legal levers over others from a pure familiarity perspective.

12. Officer characteristics

The level of discretion in policing is a major determinant of the way that officers will vary in their decision to implement third party policing initiatives or not, as well as the type of third party policing initiatives that they choose to use. While it is mere speculation as to the nature of the relationship between third party policing and the individual officer characteristics, we would expect a number of relationships to be found under empirical scrutiny. For example, we would expect higher educated officers to be more drawn to third party policing than less educated officers. We also suspect that officers with coercive personalities are more likely to adopt third party policing than those with less coercive personalities.

In earlier discussions we talked about the prevalence of third party polic-ing activities and how they would "map" to the specialized roles of individual officers. Hence, we would expect that officers in specialized roles, seeing similar types of cases on a regular basis are more likely to use third party policing tactics (and the same tactics over and over again) than their gen-eralist counterparts. Similarly, we would expect that officers who feel under more pressure to solve commonly recurring problems (pressure from the community as well as supervisors) will be more likely to use third party policing practices than those who do not feel as much pressure.

Third party policing propositions

Our discussions above have led us to present a series of propositions that we believe capture the essence of third party policing. We propose three levels of inquiry to guide the direction for future research: exploring the societal, organizational and individual factors that shape and constrain the proliferation of third party policing. Within these three levels of inquiry, we present twelve broad areas of exploration under which we identify forty-two propositions. These propositions are displayed in Table 8.1. We stress that this list of propositions is not exhaustive. Indeed, there are likely to be many other dimensions of the police environment that shape the adoption (or not) of third party policing practice. Suffice to say, that this list merely begins the process for researchers, policy makers and police to better under-stand third party policing in theory and practice.

Final word

Our exploration of third party policing has defined the concept, placed it in societal context and shown it to be an effective approach to reducing a range of crime problems. But our analysis has also raised many problems, dilemmas and issues with the policing approach. Our central interest in third party policing is that it is an approach to crime control that shares intrinsic links with a wide range of theoretical and practical developments. It is an intimate part of global trends in regulation, it is a strategy that has emerged at the same time that legal practice has blurred the lines between criminal and civil laws, it appears to be a practical application for increasing what Sampson and his colleagues have termed "collective efficacy" in a com-munity struggling with crime problems, and it is a police tactic that shares some common ground with Routine Activities Theory, Problem-Oriented Policing and Situational Crime Prevention. Our book goes a long way to

Table 8.1 *Third party policing propositions*

Level of analysis	Area	Propositions
1. Societal	1. Systems of regulation	• Democratic systems of government are likely to experience more third party policing than non-democratic systems of government
		• The greater the plurality of regulatory methods in a society, the greater the opportunities for third party policing
		• Adversarial legal systems are likely to support more third party policing practices than inquisitorial legal systems
		• Systems where power is not centralized in the state, but operated through networks, are more likely to give rise to third party policing
		• Systems that see crime control and prevention in terms of risk identification and management, rather than responses to individual offenders, are more likely to give rise to third party policing
		• Systems where regulation has moved away from command and control style rule enforcement, to responsive regulation, are more likely to provide opportunities for regulators to network with police
		• Systems where regulators are more free to develop their own system of sanctions and strategies, rather than following those prescribed in law, will facilitate third party policing
		• Systems where achieving compliance is the key objective, will give more opportunity for third party policing rather than stakeholder satisfaction as the key objective, will give more opportunity for third party policing
		• Systems that operate in a cooperative, rather than adversarial legal and social context, will be more likely to encourage regulator involvement in third party policing
		• Systems that provide some legal framework for policing partnerships, usually by legislation or regulation, will encourage systemized rather than ad hoc third party policing
		• Systems where both policing and regulatory functions have become pluralized and community based, will provide the greatest opportunity for third party policing

1. Societal	2. Spatial crime patterns	• The relationship between crime and third party policing is non-linear; and most likely hyperbolic. That is, places with the most and least amount of crime are likely to have the least amount of third party policing. Third party policing occupies the middle-ground of police interventions
• The adoption of third party policing varies across urban and rural areas. Coercive third party policing is more likely to prevail in rural areas whereas legal action within a third party policing context is more likely to prevail in urban areas
1. Societal	3. Community context	• The more collective efficacy in a neighborhood, the greater the likelihood that third party policing is at the more benign end of the scale. Conversely, the less collective efficacy in a neighborhood, the more third party policing will be coercive in nature and utilize legal provisions to obtain cooperation from third parties
• Communities with more visible crime problems (e.g. street crimes) are more likely to be places with third party policing than in communities with little or less visible crime problems
2. Organizational	4. Centralization	• Police agencies where decision-making is more de-centralized are likely to be departments that experiment more with third party policing initiatives
• Government agencies that are more decentralized are more likely to forge third party partnerships with the police than government agencies that are more centralized
2. Organizational	5. Levels of specialization	• The greater the level of task specialization within a police organization, the more likely that a police organization will adopt third party policing
• The greater the division of labor within a police organization, the more likely third party policing will be adopted in an episodic manner, as opposed to a programmatic manner
2. Organizational	6. Hierarchy of authority	• Third party policing is more likely to flourish in departments that have flatter organizational structures than "tall" organizational structures
• Third party policing is more likely to exist in departments that practice collegial decision-making practices than in departments with top-down authority structures

(*cont.*)

Table 8.1 (*Cont.*)

Level of analysis	Area	Propositions
2. Organizational	7. Formalization	• The degree to which organizational norms and rules are explicit, the more likely the adoption of third party policing programs rather than episodic instances of third party policing • The more that problem-oriented policing is institutionalized, the greater the likelihood of third party policing being implemented
2. Organizational	8. Accountability systems	• The greater a department's accountability structures, the more likely third party policing will flourish as a program rather than as an episodic approach to crime control • The greater the adoption of COMPSTAT (or COMPSTAT-like programs), the greater the likelihood that the organization will adopt third party policing • The more evidenced-based (or evidence-oriented) a police department, the more likely the adoption of third party policing • The more conscious a police department is of programmatic costs and benefits, the more likely the adoption of third party policing
2. Organizational	9. External partnerships	• Operational organizational units that have more opportunities to forge external partnerships are more likely to adopt third party policing than those units that have fewer operational external partners • The more external partners a police department fosters in general, the greater the adoption of third party policing • The more that external partners in a community are sympathetic to crime control goals, the greater the adoption of third party policing • Chaotic external partner organizations are more likely to create opportunities for episodic third party policing than more organized external partners

2. Organizational	10. Technology	• The greater the diffusion of technological innovation within a department, the greater the adoption of third party policing
		• The greater the adoption of information based technologies within units across an organization, the greater the adoption of third party policing
		• The greater the historical use of innovative methods, the more likely the police organization will adopt third party policing practices
		• Over time, the use of third party policing tactics will become more routinized
3. Individual	11. Supervisor characteristics	• Supervisors who are more willing to provide direction to subordinates will be more supportive of third party policing than those who provide less direction to subordinates
		• Different supervisors will emphasize different legal levers, dependent on their familiarity
3. Individual	12. Patrol officer characteristics	• Higher educated officers will be more drawn to third party policing than less educated officers
		• Officers with coercive personalities are more likely to adopt third party policing than those with less coercive personalities
		• Officers serving in more specialist roles (e.g. child safety) are more likely to adopt third party policing than their generalist counterparts
		• Officers who feel under more pressure to solve commonly recurring problems (pressure from the community as well as supervisors) will be more likely to use third party policing practices than those who do not feel as much pressure

building a comprehensive understanding of the third party approach to crime control. Where we have been able to point to ways that third party policing can be implemented in fair and equitable ways, we hope that police agencies will take up the challenge. But as with most early analysis of emerging trends, it is our hope that the many unanswered questions become the focus for future research.

Notes

5 CONTROLLING DRUG PROBLEMS

1. For example, Section 11570 of the California Health and Safety Code states: "Every building or place used for the purpose of unlawfully selling, serving, storing, keeping, manufacturing, or giving away any controlled substance, precursor or analog specified in this division, and every building or place wherein or upon which those acts take place, is a nuisance which shall be enjoined, abated and prevented, and for which damages may be recovered, whether it is a public or a private nuisance."

   In addition, Section 11366.5 (a) stipulates that persons managing or controlling a building who allow the unlawful manufacturing, storing, or distributing of any controlled substance can be imprisoned for up to one year.

   Some of the local municipal codes that are enforced include obstructions (6-1.09), building constituting a menace to public safety (2-4.09), unnecessary noises (3-1.01), unsecured buildings (2-4.09), and dumping garbage (4-5.12).

2. There are two basic advantages of using a block randomized design: first, computations with randomized block designs are simpler than those with covariance analysis, and second, randomized block designs are essentially free of assumptions about the nature of the relationship between the blocking variable and the dependent variable, while covariance analysis assumes a definite form of relationship. A drawback of randomized block designs is that somewhat fewer degrees of freedom are available for experimental error than with covariance analysis for a completely randomized design (Neter, Wasserman and Kutner, 1990).

3. Courier Mail (2003). Rock band defies authority in bid to stage suicide at concert. 1 October, p. 24. See also the *New York Times* (2003). Florida: Band promises suicide concert. 30 September, late edition, p. 24.

4. There were twenty-one drug crime studies identified and described in this chapter. Of these, just eight studies were used in our quantitative review. We calculated effects sizes for eighteen outcome measures across these eight studies. Two outcomes were from Eck and Wartell (1998) using a standardized mean difference, the remaining sixteen effect size outcomes were calculated using odds-ratios.

References

Aboriginal and Torres Strait Islander Women's Task Force on Violence (2000). Brisbane: Queensland Government, Department of Aboriginal and Torres Strait Islander Policy Development.

Abru, E. (2001) Car theft, *N.S.W. Police News*, 81 (5): 31–33.

Adams, J. (1995) *Risk*, London, UCL Press.

Alexandria Police Department (1995) Alexandria Alcohol Interdiction Program, *Submission for the Herman Goldstein Award for Excellence in Problem-Oriented Policing*, [Online] available at: http://www.popcenter.org/library-goldstein.htm

Arlington Police Department (1998) Cowboys: a problem solving initiative, *Submission for the Herman Goldstein Award for Excellence in Problem-Oriented Policing*, [Online] available at: http://www.popcenter.org/library-goldstein.htm

Ayres, I. and Braithwaite, J. (1992) *Responsive Regulation: Transcending the Deregulation Debate*, New York, Oxford University Press.

Bagaric, M. (2001) *Punishment and Sentencing*, London, Cavendish Publishing.

Baker, I. (2004) Assault reduction strategy, paper presented at 3rd International Conference on *Nightlife, Substance Use and Related Health Issues*, Club Health 2004, Melbourne, 18–20 April.

Baker, T. E. and Wolfer, L. (2003) The crime triangle: alcohol, drug use, and vandalism, *Police Practice and Research*, 4 (1): 47–61.

Baldwin, R. (2004) The new punitive regulation, *The Modern Law Review*, 67 (3): 351–383.

Baldwin, R. and Cave, M. (1999) *Understanding Regulation-theory, strategy and practice*, Oxford, Oxford University Press.

Baldwin, R., Scott, C. and Hood, C. (1998a) *A Reader on Regulation*, Oxford, Oxford University Press.

Baldwin, R., Scott, C. and Hood, C. (1998b) *A Reader on Regulation*, Oxford, Oxford University Press.

Baltimore Police Department (2000) Canton middle school truancy abatement program, *Submission for the Herman Goldstein Award for Excellence in Problem-Oriented Policing*, [Online] available at: http://www.popcenter.org/library-goldstein.htm

Barton, A. and James, Z. (2003) "Run to the sun": policing contested perceptions of risk, *Policing and Society*, 13 (3): 259–270.

Bayley, D. (1994) *Police for the Future*, New York, Oxford University Press.

Bayley, D. and Shearing, C. (1996) The future of policing, *Law and Society Review*, 30 (3): 585–606.

Beck, U. (1992) *Risk Society*, New York, Sage.

Beckman, K., Lum, C., Wyckoff, L. and Larsen-Vander Wall, K. (2003) Trends in police research: a cross-sectional analysis of the 2000 literature, *Police Practice and Research*, 4 (1): 79–96.

Bellamy, L. (1996) Situational crime prevention and convenience store robbery, *Security Journal*, 7: 41–52.

Bevir, M., Rhodes, R. A. W. and Weller, P. (2003) Comparative governance: prospects and lessons, *Public Administration*, 81 (1): 191–210.

Biek, W. and Kessler, D. A. (1977) *Response Time Analysis*, Kansas City, Board of Police Commissioners.

Bittner, E. (1970) *The Functions of Police in Modern Societies*, Washington, National Institute of Mental Health.

Björ, J., Knutsson, J. and Kühlhorn, E. (1992) The celebration of Midsummer Eve in Sweden: a study in the art of preventing collective disorder, *Security Journal*, 3 (3): 169–174.

Blanchard, L. and Lui, L. (2000) *The Impact of Aboriginal Night Patrols as a Juvenile Crime Prevention Strategy: An Evaluation of the Four Pilot Programmes in New South Wales*, Sydney, Centre for Peace and Conflict Studies and Koori Centre.

Bottomley, S. and Parker, S. (1997) *Law in Context*, Sydney, Federation Press.

Bourdieu, P. (1984) *Distinction*, London, Routledge.

Boyne, R. (2000) Post-Panopticism, *Economy and Society*, 29 (2): 285–307.

Braga, A. (2001) The effects of hot spots policing on crime, *The Annals of the American Academy of Political and Social Sciences*, 578: 104–125.

Braga, A., Kennedy, D., Waring, E. and Piehl A. M. (2001) Problem-oriented policing, deterrence, and youth violence: An evaluation of Boston's Operation Ceasefire, *Journal of Research in Crime and Delinquency*, 38 (3): 195–225.

Braga, A., Weisburd, D., Waring, E., Mazerolle, L., Spelman, W. and Gajewski, F. (1999) Problem-oriented policing in violent crime places: a randomized controlled experiment, *Criminology*, 37 (3): 541–580.

Bracey, D. (1992) Police corruption and community relations: community policing, *Police Studies*, 15 (4): 179–183.

Braithwaite, J. (1999) Accountability and governance under the new regulatory state, *Australian Journal of Public Administration*, 58 (1): 90–97.

Braithwaite, J. (2000) The new regulatory state and the transformation of criminology, *British Journal of Criminology*, 40: 222–238.

Braithwaite, J. (2003) What's wrong with the sociology of punishment, *Theoretical Criminology*, 7(1): 5–28.

Braithwaite, J. and Braithwaite, V. (1995) The politics of legalism: rules versus standards in nursing-home regulation, *Social and Legal Studies*, 4: 307–341.

Braithwaite, J., Clarke, M., Slapper, G. and Tweedale, G. (2002) Understanding regulation?, *Social & Legal Studies*, 11 (1): 113–133.

Braithwaite, J. and Drahos, P. (2000) *Global Business Regulation*, Melbourne, Cambridge University Press.

Breyer, S. (1998) Typical justifications for regulation, in Baldwin, R., Scott, C. and Hood C. (eds.) *A Reader on Regulation* (pp. 59–92), Oxford, Oxford University Press.

Brokenshire, R. (2001) S.A. hydroponic shop licencing review, press release, 13 November.

Budz, D. (1998) *Beenleigh Calls for Service Project: Evaluation Report*, Brisbane, Criminal Justice Commission.

Buerger, M. E. (1994a) A tale of two targets: limitations of community anticrime actions, *Crime and Delinquency*, 40 (3): 411–436.

Buerger, M. E. (1994b) The problems of problem-solving: resistance, interdependencies, and conflicting interests, *American Journal of Police*, 13 (3): 1–36.

Buerger, M. E. (1998) The politics of third party policing, in L. Green Mazerolle and J. Roehl (eds.) *Civil Remedies and Crime Prevention*, Crime Prevention Studies, vol. 9 (pp. 89–116), Monsey, Criminal Justice Press.

Buerger, M. E. and Mazerolle, L. (1998) Third party policing: a theoretical analysis of an emerging trend, *Justice Quarterly*, 15 (2): 301–328.

Buerger, M. E., Petrosino, A. J. and Petrosino, C. (1999) Extending the police role: implications of police mediation as a problem-solving tool, *Police Quarterly*, 2 (2): 125–149.

Bullock, K. and Jones, B. (2004) *Acceptable Behaviour Contracts: Addressing Antisocial Behaviour in the London Borough of Islington*, Home Office Online Report 02/04, London, Home Office.

Burchell, G. (1996), Liberal government and techniques of the self, in A. Barry, T. Osborne and N. Rose (eds.) *Foucault and Political Reason* (pp. 19–36), Chicago, Chicago University Press.

Burns, T. and Stalker, G. M. (1961) *The Management of Innovation*, London, Tavistock.

Bursik, R. (1988) Social disorganization theories of crime and delinquency: problems and prospects, *Criminology*, 26: 519–552.

Butler, S. (1998) *Access Denied: The Exclusion of People in Need from Social Housing*, London: Shelter 6.

Canberra Times (2001) Terrorists' assets frozen, 8 September: 6.

Caulkins, J. P. (1998) The cost-effectiveness of civil remedies: the case of drug control interventions, in L. Green Mazerolle and J. Roehl (eds.) *Civil Remedies and Crime Prevention*, Crime Prevention Studies, vol. 9 (pp. 219–237), Monsey, Criminal Justice Press.

Challinger, D. (1996) Refund fraud in retail stores, *Security Journal*, 7: 27–35.

Chan, W. and Rigakos, G. (2002) Risk, crime and gender, *British Journal of Criminology*, 42: 743–761.

Charlotte-Mecklengurg Police Department (2000) Homeless men's shelter, *Submission for the Herman Goldstein Award for Excellence in Problem-Oriented Policing*, [Online] available at: http://www.popcenter.org/library-goldstein.htm

Cheh, M. (1991) Constitutional limits on using civil remedies to achieve criminal law objectives: understanding and transcending the criminal-civil law distinction, *Hastings Law Journal*, 42: 1325–1413.

Cheh, M. (1998) Civil remedies to control crime: legal issues and constitutional challenges in L. Green Mazerolle and J. Roehl (eds.) *Civil Remedies and Crime*

Prevention, Crime Prevention Studies, vol. 9 (pp. 45–66), Monsey, Criminal Justice Press.

Chenery, S., Holt, J. and Pease, K. (1997) *Biting Back II: Reducing Repeat Victimisation in Huddersfield*, Crime Detection and Prevention Series Paper 82, London, Police Research Group, [Online] available at: http://www.homeoffice.gov.uk/prgpubs/fcdps82.pdf

Chevy, L. (1996) *A License to Steal: The Forfeiture of Property*, Chapel Hill, University of North Carolina Press.

Clarke, M. (2000) *Regulation: The Social Control of Business between Law and Politics*, New York, St Martin's Press.

Clarke, R. V. (1992) *Situational Crime Prevention: Successful Case Studies*, New York, Harrow and Heston.

Clarke, R. V. (1995) Situational crime prevention, in M. Tonry and D. P. Farrington (eds.), *Building a Safer Society: Strategic Approaches to Crime Prevention*, Crime and Justice, vol. 19 (pp. 91–150), Chicago, University of Chicago Press.

Clarke, R. V. (ed.) (1997) *Situational Crime Prevention: Successful Case Studies* (2nd ed.), New York, Harrow & Heston.

Clarke, R. V. and Bichler-Robertson, G. (1998) Place managers, slumlords and crime in low rent apartment buildings, *Security Journal*, 11: 11–19.

Clarke, R. and Goldstein, H. (2002) Reducing thefts at construction sites: lessons from a problem-oriented project, in N. Tilley (ed.) *Analysis for crime prevention*, Crime Prevention Studies, vol. 13 (pp. 89–130), Monsey, Criminal Justice Press.

Clarke, R. V. and Weisburd, D. (1994) Diffusion of crime control benefits: observation on the reverse of displacement, *Crime Prevention Studies*, vol. 2 (pp. 165–184), Monsey, Criminal Justice Press.

CNN (2001) Rodney King reluctant symbol of police brutality, *CNN.com Law Center*, 3 March, [Online] available at: http://www.cnn.com/2001/LAW/03/02/beating.anniversary.king.02

Cohen, D. (1995) *The Misfortunes of Prosperity: An Introduction to Modern Political Economy*, translated J. Lindenfeld, Cambridge, MIT Press.

Cohen, H. and Feldberg, M. (1991) *Power and Restraint: The Moral Dimension of Police Work*, Westport, Praeger.

Cohen, L. E. and Felson, M. (1979) Social change and crime rate trends: a routine activity approach, *American Sociological Review*, 44: 588–605.

Cohen, N. (2004) Turning right to wrong, *The Observer*, 1 August, accessed at: http://observer.guardian.co.uk/comment/story/0,,1273776,00.htm

Coldren, J. R. and Higgins, D. (2003) Evaluating nuisance abatement at gang and drug houses in Chicago in D. Decker (ed.) *Policing Gangs and Youth Violence* (pp. 131–166), Belmont, Wadsworth.

Coleman, J. C. (1988) Social capital in the creation of human capital, *American Journal of Sociology*, 94: 95–120.

Coleman, J. C. (1990) *Foundations of Social Theory*, Cambridge, Harvard University Press.

Commonwealth of Australia (2004) *Protecting Australia Against Terrorism*, [Online] http://www.pmc.gov.au/publications/protecting_australia/

Considine, M. (2002) The end of the line? Accountable governance in the age of networks, partnerships, and joined-up services, *Governance: An International Journal of Policy, Administration, and Institutions*, 15 (1): 21–40.

Cook, T. D. and Campbell, D. T. (1979) *Quasi-Experimentation: Design and Analysis Issues for Field Settings*, Boston, Houghton Mifflin.

Cordner, G. (1998) Problem-oriented policing vs. zero tolerance, in T. O'Connor Shelley and A. Grant (eds.) *Problem-Oriented Policing: Crime-Specific Problems, Critical Issues and Making POP Work*, Washington, Police Executive Research Forum.

Cornish, D. (1994) The procedural analysis of offending and its relevance for situational prevention, in R. Clarke (ed.) *Crime Prevention Studies*, vol. 3 (pp. 151–196), Monsey, Criminal Justice Press.

Cornish, D. and Clarke, R. V. (eds.) (1986) *The Reasoning Criminal: Rational Choice Perspectives on Offending*, New York, Springer-Verlag.

Cornish, D. and Clarke, R. V. (1987) Understanding crime displacement: an application of rational choice theory, *Criminology*, 25: 933–947.

Cornish, D. and Clarke, R. (2003) Opportunities, precipitators and criminal decisions: a reply to Wortley's critique of situational crime prevention, in M. Smith and D. Cornish (eds.) *Theory for Practice in Situational Crime Prevention*, Crime Prevention Studies, vol. 16 (pp. 41–96), Monsey, Criminal Justice Press.

Cotterrell, R. (1992) *The Sociology of Law: An Introduction* (2nd ed.), London, Butterworths.

Courier Mail (2002a) Police do more for less cash, says union, 20 June: 6.

Courier Mail (2002b) Parents charged over truants, 7 November: 1.

Crank, J. P. (2003) Institutional theory of police: a review of the state of the art, *Policing: An International Journal of Police Strategies and Management*, 26 (2): 186–207.

Crank, J. P. and Langworthy, R. (1992) An institutional perspective on policing, *Journal of Criminal Law and Criminology*, 83: 338–363.

Curtis, P. (2002) Truancy sweeps reap rewards, *The Guardian*, 18 June, accessed at www.EducationGuardian.co.uk

Curtis, R. and Wendel, T. (2000) Lockin' niggas up like it's goin' out of style: the differing consequences of police interventions in three Brooklyn, New York, drug markets, Paper presented at the National Institute of Justice Conference Drug Markets and Law Enforcement Strategies, Arlington.

Curtis, S. (2002) Proactive crime prevention in schools: a Queensland perspective, Paper presented at the *Role of Schools in Crime Prevention Conference*, AIC, Melbourne, 30 September–01 October.

Daily Telegraph (2004) Street drink ban for Bondi Junction, 22 January: 21.

Davis, R. and Lurigio, A. (1998) Civil abatement as a tool for controlling drug dealing in rental properties, *Security Journal*, 11: 45–50.

Davis, G. and Rhodes, R. A. (2000) From hierarchy to contracts and back again: reforming the Australian public service in M. Keating, J. Wanna and P. Weller (eds.) *Institutions on the Edge? Capacity for Governance* (pp. 74–98), Sydney, Allen and Unwin.

DeJong, C., Mastrofski, S. D. and Parks, R. B. (2001) Patrol officers and problem solving: an application of expectancy theory, *Justice Quarterly*, 18: 31–60.

de Lint, W. (2000) Regulation and the police beat, *Social and Legal Studies*, 9 (1): 55–83.

Delta Police Department (1997) The Elite arcade: taming a crime generator, *Submission for the Herman Goldstein Award for Excellence in Problem-Oriented Policing*, [Online] available at: http://www.popcenter.org/library-goldstein.htm

DeYoung, K. and Eggen, D. (2001) $100 million in terrorists' assets frozen, U.S. says; money from foreign and domestic bank accounts not directly tied to Bin Laden or al Qaeda', *The Washington Post*, 3 October.

Dickson, C. (1988) Drug stings in Miami, *FBI Law Enforcement Bulletin*, 57 (1): 1–6.

Ditton, J. and Nair, G. (1994) Throwing light on crime: a case study of the relationship between street lighting and crime prevention, *Security Journal*, 5 (3): 125–132.

Dixon, D. (1997) *Law in Policing: Legal Regulation and Police Practices*, Oxford, Clarendon Press.

Douglas, M. (1998) Restriction of the hours of sale of alcohol in a small community: a beneficial impact, *Australian and New Zealand Journal of Public Health*, 22 (6): 714–719.

Dullroy, J. (2004) Schools step up discipline, *Courier Mail*, 25 February: 1.

Dupont, B., Grabosky, P. N. and Shearing, C. (2003) The governance of security in weak and failing states, *Criminal Justice*, 3 (4): 331–349.

Eck, J. (1994) Drug places: drug dealer choice and the spatial structure of illicit drug markets, PhD thesis, University of Maryland.

Eck, J. E. (2002) Learning from experience in problem-oriented policing and situational prevention: the positive functions of weak evaluations and the negative functions of strong ones in N. Tilley (ed.) *Evaluation for Crime Prevention*, Crime Prevention Studies, vol. 14 (pp. 93–118), Monsey, Criminal Justice Press.

Eck, J. E. and Spelman, W. (1987) *Problem Solving: Problem-Oriented Policing in Newport News*, Washington, Police Executive Research Forum and National Institute of Justice.

Eck, J. E. and Wardell, J. (1998) Improving the management of rental properties with drug problems: a randomised experiment, in L. Green Mazerolle and J. Roehl (eds.) *Civil Remedies and Crime Prevention* (pp. 161–186), Crime Prevention Studies, vol. 9, Monsey, Criminal Justice Press.

Eck, J. E. and Weisburd, D. (eds.) (1995), *Crime and Place*, Crime Prevention Studies, vol. 4, Monsey, Criminal Justice Press and Police Executive Research Forum.

Ericson, R. V., Barry, D. and Doyle, A. (2000) The moral hazards of neo-liberalism, *Economy and Society*, 29 (4): 532–558.

Ericson, R. V. and Haggerty, K. D. (1997) *Policing in the Risk Society*, Toronto, University of Toronto Press.

Famega, C., Frank, J. and Mazerolle, L. (forthcoming) Managing police patrol time: the role of supervisor directives, *Justice Quarterly*.

Farrington, D. P. (2003) Methodological quality standards for evaluation research, *Annals of the American Academy of Political and Social Sciences*, 587: 49–68.

Farrington, D. P. and Petrosino, A. (2000) Systematic reviews of criminological interventions: the Campbell Collaboration Crime and Justice Group, *International Annals of Criminology*, 37: 1–2.

Farrington, D. P. and Welsh, B. (2002) *Effects of Improved Street Lighting on Crime: A Systematic Review*, Home Office Research Study 251, London, Home Office.

Feeley, M. (2003) Crime, social order and the rise of neo-Conservative politics, *Theoretical Criminology*, 7 (1): 111–130.

Feeley, M. and Simon, J. (1992) The new penology: notes on the emerging strategy of corrections and its implications, *Criminology*, 30 (4): 449–470.

Feeley, M. and Simon, J. (1994) Actuarial justice: the emerging new criminal law, in D. Nelken (ed.) *The Futures of Criminology* (pp. 173–201), London, Sage.

Felson, M. (1994) *Crime and Everyday Life: Insights and Implications for Society*, Thousand Oaks, Pine Forge Press.

Felson, M. (1995) Those who discourage crime, in J. E. Eck and D. Weisburd (eds.) *Crime and Place*, Crime Prevention Studies, vol. 4 (pp. 53–66), Washington, Criminal Justice Press and Police Executive Research Forum.

Felson, M., Berends, R., Richardson, B. and Veno, A. (1997) Reducing pub hopping and related crime, in R. Homel (ed.) *Policing for Prevention: Reducing Crime, Public Intoxication and Injury*, Crime Prevention Studies, vol. 7 (pp. 115–132), Monsey, Criminal Justice Press.

Felson, M. and Clarke, R. V. (eds.) (1997) *Business and Crime Prevention*, Monsey, Criminal Justice Press.

Ferguson, H. and Fitzsimons, P. S. (1990) Drug abatements: an effective tool in the war on narcotics, *The Police Chief*, 57: 46–49.

Fleming, J. (2004) Les liaisons dangereuses: relations between police commissioners and their political masters, *Australian Journal of Public Administration*, 63 (3): 1–15.

Finn, P. and Hylton, M. O. (1994) *Using Civil Remedies for Criminal Behavior: Rationale, Case Studies, and Constitutional Issues*, Washington, National Institute of Justice, US Department of Justice.

Fitzgibbons, A. (1995) *Adam Smith's System of Liberty, Wealth and Virtue: The Moral and Political Foundations of the Wealth of Nations*, Oxford, Clarendon Press.

Fontana Police Department (1998) "Ten-4": the transient enrichment program, *Submission for the Herman Goldstein Award for Excellence in Problem-Oriented Policing*, [Online] available at: http://www.popcenter.org/library-goldstein.htm

Forbes, G. (2000) Immobilising the fleet, paper presented at the Australian Institute of Criminology and National Motor Vehicle Theft Reduction Council conference *Reducing Car Theft: How Low Can We Go?* Adelaide, 30 November–1 December.

Foucault, M. (1979) *Discipline and Punish: The Birth of the Prison*, translated by A. Sheridan, New York, Vintage Books.

Foucault, M. (1991) Governmentality, in G. Burchell, C. Gordon and P. Miller (eds) *The Foucault Effect: Studies in Governmentality* (pp. 88–105), Chicago, University of Chicago Press.

Fried, J. P. and Harden, B. (1999) Officer is guilty in torture of Louima, *The New York Times*, 9 June: 1.

Friedrichs, D. O. (2004) *Trusted Criminals: White Collar Crime in Contemporary Society* (2nd ed.), Belmont, Wadsworth/Thomson.

Fukuyama, F. (1995) *Trust: The Social Virtues and the Creation of Prosperity*, New York, Free Press.

Gabor, T. (1978) Crime displacement: the literature and strategies for its investigation, *Crime and Justice*, 6: 100–107.

Gabor, T. (1981) The crime displacement hypothesis: an empirical examination, *Crime and Delinquency*, 27: 390–404.

Gabor, T. (1990) Crime displacement and situational prevention: toward the development of some principles, *Canadian Journal of Criminology*, 32: 41–74.

Gant, F. and Grabosky, P. (2000) Preventing motor vehicle theft in NSW, in *The Promise of Crime Prevention* (2nd ed.), AIC Research and Public Policy Series (pp. 50–51), Canberra, Australian Institute of Criminology.

Garland, D. (1996) The limits of the sovereign state, *British Journal of Criminology*, 36: 445–471.

Garland, D. (1997) Governmentality and the problem of crime: Foucault, criminology, sociology, *Theoretical Criminology*, 1 (2): 173–214.

Garland, D. (2001) *The Culture of Control: Crime and Social Order in Contemporary Society*, Oxford, Oxford University Press.

Gibson, C., Zhao, J., Lovrich, N. and Gaffney, M. (2002) Social integration, perceptions of collective efficacy, and fear of crime in three cities, *Justice Quarterly*, 19 (3): 537–564.

Giddens, A. (1990) *The Consequences of Modernity*, Stanford, Stanford University Press.

Gill, P. (2002) Policing and regulation, *Social and Legal Studies*, 11 (4): 523–546.

Gimenez-Salinas, A. (2004) New approaches regarding private/public security, *Policing and Society*, 14 (2): 158–174.

Glendale Police Department (1997), Day labor project, *Submission for the Herman Goldstein Award for Excellence in Problem-Oriented Policing*, [Online] available at: http://www.popcenter.org/library-goldstein.htm

Goldfinch, S. and Hart, P. (2003) Leadership and institutional reform: engineering macroeconomic policy change in Australia, *Governance: An International Journal of Policy, Administration, and Institutions*, 16 (2): 235–270.

Goldstein, H. (1990) *Problem-Oriented Policing*, New York, McGrawHill.

Goldstein, H. (2003) On further developing problem-oriented policing: the most critical need, the major impediments and a proposal, in J. Knutsson (ed.) *Mainstreaming Problem-Oriented Policing*, Crime Prevention Studies, vol. 15 (pp. 13–48), Monsey, Criminal Justice Press.

Gostzyla, E. and George, S. (2003) Our kids matter – Paint sniffing: the Charters Towers story, Paper presented at the *Inhalant Use and Disorder Conference*, Australian Institute of Criminology, Townsville, 7–8 July.

Gottfredson, M. and Hirschi, T. (1990) *A General Theory of Crime*, Stanford, Stanford University Press.

Gow, D. (1997) Business and government as regulation in H. K. Colebatch, S. Prasser & J. R. Nethercote (eds.) *Business-Government Relations: Concepts and Issues* (pp. 101–123), South Melbourne, Nelson.

Grabosky, P. (1993) Rewards and incentives as regulatory instruments, *Administration, Compliance, and Governability Program Working Paper 13*, Canberra, Research School of Social Sciences, Australian National University.

Grabosky, P. (1995) Regulation by reward: on the use of incentives as regulatory instruments, *Law and Policy*, 17 (3): 257–282.

Grabosky, P. (1996) The future of crime control, *Trends and Issues in Criminal Justice*, vol. 63, Canberra, Australian Institute of Criminology.

Grabosky, P. (2004) Toward a theory of public/private interaction in policing, in J. McCord (ed.) *Beyond Empiricism* (pp. 69–82), New Brunswick, Transaction Publishers.

Grabosky, P. and Braithwaite, J. (1986) *Of Manners Gentle: Enforcement Strategies of Australian Business Regulatory Agencies*, Melbourne, Oxford University Press.

Grabosky, P. N. (1995a) Rewards and incentives as regulatory instruments, *Law and Policy*, 17 (3): 256–281.

Grabosky, P. N. (1995b) Using non-governmental resources to foster regulatory compliance, *Governance: An International Journal of Policy, Administration, and Institutions*, 8 (4): 527–550.

Grabosky, P. N. (1996) Unintended consequences of crime prevention, in R. Homel and R. Clarke (eds.), *The Politics and Practice of Situational Crime Prevention*, Crime Prevention Studies, vol. 5 (pp. 25–56), Honsey, Criminal Justice Press.

Grabosky, P. N. (2004) Toward a theory of public/private interaction in policing, in J. McCord (ed.), *Beyond Empiricism: Institutions and Intentions in the Study of Crime*, Advances in Criminological Theory, vol. 13 (pp. 69–82), Picataway, NJ, Transaction Books.

Graham, K., Osgood, D. W., Zibrowski, E., Purcell, J., Gliksman, L., Leonard, K., Pernanen, K., Laltz, R. F. and Toomey, T. (2003) The effect of the Safer Bar Program on physical aggression in bars: result of a randomized control trial, paper presented at *Preventing Substance Use, Risky Use and Harm: What is Evidence-Based Policy*, Perth, February 24–27.

Gray, D., Saggers, S., Atkinson, D., Sputore, B. and Bourbon, D. (2000) Beating the grog: an evaluation of the Tennant Creek liquor licensing restrictions, *Australian and New Zealand Journal of Public Health*, 24 (1): 39–44.

Green Bay Police Department (2000) Street sweeping, Broadway style, *Winning submission for the Herman Goldstein Award for Excellence in Problem-Oriented Policing*, [Online] available at: http://www.popcenter.org/library-goldstein.htm

Green, L. (1996) *Policing Places with Drug Problems*, Thousand Oaks, Sage.

Greenwood, P., Chaiken, J. and Petersilia, J. (1977) *The Criminal Investigation Process*, Lexington, Heath.

Gregory, J. (2003) Parents of truants placed on probation, *Courier Mail*, 30 August: 5.

Griffiths, Mr. (2001) WA announces new policy to clamp down on violence, press release, 9 November.

Griffin, Mr. (2001) New way to deal with shop thieves (SA), press release, 12 November.

Grogger, J. (2002) The effect of civil gang injunctions on reported violent crime: evidence from Los Angeles County, *Journal of Law and Economics*, 45 (1): 69–90.

Guerry, A-M. (1833) *Essay on the Moral Statistics of France*, translated (2002) by H. P. Whitt and V. W. Reinking, Lewiston, Edwin Mellen Press.

Hage, J. and Aiken, M. (1969) Routine technology, social structure and organization goals, *Administrative Science Quarterly*, 14: 366–376.

Haggerty, K. D. (2004) Displaced expertise: three constraints on the policy-relevance of criminological thought, *Theoretical Criminology*, 8 (2): 211–231.

Haines, F. (1997) *Corporate Regulation: Beyond "punish or persuade,"* New York, Oxford University Press.

Hakala, L. A. (1997) Opposing forfeiture, *The Yale Law Journal*, 106 (4): 1319–1324.

Halton Regional Police Service (2002) Let's Dance: a community collaborative response to the problems created by an all ages nightclub, *Submission for the Herman Goldstein Award for Excellence in Problem-Oriented Policing*, [Online] available at: http://www.popcenter.org/library-goldstein.htm

Harrell, A. and Smith, B. (1996) Effects of restraining orders on domestic violence victims, in E. Buzawa and C. G. Buzawa (eds.) *Do Arrest and Restraining Orders Work?* (pp. 214–244), Thousand Oaks, Sage.

Hauritz, M., Homel, R., McIlwain, G., Burrows, T. and Townsley, M. (1998) Reducing violence in licensed venues: community safety actions projects, *Trends and Issues in Crime and Criminal Justice*, vol. 101, Canberra, Australian Institute of Criminology.

Hawkins, K. (1984) The enforcement process in regulatory bureaucracies in K. Hawkins and J. M. Thomas (eds.) *Enforcing Regulations* (pp. 3–22), Boston, Kluwer-Nijhoff.

Hawdins, K. and Thomas, M. (eds.) (1984) *Enforcing Regulations*, Boston, Kluwer-Nijhoff.

Hawks, D., Rydon, R., Stockwell, T., White, M., Chikritzhs, T. and Heale, R. (1999) *The Evaluation of the Fremantle Police-Licensee Accord: Impact on Serving Practices, Harm and the Wider Community*, Perth, National Drug Research Institute, Curtin University of Technology.

Hayek, F. A. (1949) *Individualism and Economic Order*, London, Routledge.

Hayes, L., Shipway, C. and Taperell, J. (1999) The Children (Protection and Parental Responsibility) Act 1997 – Implementation issues, Paper presented at the *Australian Institute of Criminology Conference, Children and Crime: Victims and Offenders*, Brisbane, 17–18 June.

Herlihy, J. (1995) Julalikari night patrol in P. Grabosky and M. James (eds.) *The Promise of Crime Prevention: Leading Crime Prevention Programs* (pp. 6–7), Canberra, Australian Institute of Criminology.

Higgins, D. F. and Coldren, J. R. (2000) *Evaluating Gang and Drug House Abatement in Chicago*, Chicago, Illinois Criminal Justice Authority.

Hindess, B. (1998) Neo-liberalism and the national economy, in M. Dean and B. Hindess (eds.) *Governing Australia: Studies in Contemporary Rationalities of Government*, Melbourne, Cambridge.

Hinds, L. (2002) Law and order: the politics of get tough crime control, PhD thesis, Brisbane, Griffith University.

Holder, H. D., Gruenewald, P. J., Ponicki, W. R., Treno, A. J., Grube, J. W., Saltz, R. F., Voas, R. B., Reynolds, R., Davis, J., Sanchez, L., Gaumont, G. and Roeper, P. (2000) Effect of community-based interventions on high-risk drinking and alcohol-related injuries, *Journal of the American Medical Association (JAMA)*, 284: 2341–2347.

Home Office (2003a) *Together, Tackling Anti-Social Behaviour*, London, Home Office, [Online] available at http://www.together.gov.uk/

Home Office (2003b) *Respect and Responsibility: Taking a Stand Against Anti-Social Behaviour*, London, Home Office, [Online] available at www.official-documents.co.uk/ document/cm57/5778/5778.pdf

Halligan-Davis, G. and Spicer, K. (2004) *Piloting 'on the Spot Penalties' for Disorder: Final Results from a One-Year Pilot*, Findings 257, London, Home Office, Research, Development and Statistics Directorate.

Homel, R. (1993) Random breath testing in Australia: getting it to work according to specifications, *Addiction*, 88 (Supplement): 27–33.

Homel, R. and Clark, J. (1994) The prediction and prevention of violence in pubs and clubs, in *Crime Prevention Studies*, vol. 3, ed. R. Clarke, pp. 1–46, Monsey, Criminal Justice Press.

Homel, R., Hauritz, M., Wortley, R., McIlwain, G. and Carvolth, R. (1997) Preventing alcohol-related crime through community action: the Surfers Paradise Safety Action Project in R. Homel (ed.) *Policing for Prevention: Reducing Crime, Public Intoxication and Injury*, Crime Prevention Studies, vol. 7 (35–90), Monsey, Criminal Justice Press.

Hope, T. (1994) Problem-oriented policing and drug market locations: three case studies in R. Clarke (ed.) *Crime Prevention Studies*, vol. 2 (pp. 5–31), Monsey, Criminal Justice Press.

Hill, P. (1998) *Preventing Car Theft in Australia: "Golden Opportunity" for Partnerships*, Trends and Issues in Crime and Criminal Justice, no. 86, Canberra, Australian Institute of Criminology.

Hughes, G. and Ryle, G. (1997) Bribe offered by police to "spot drug", *The Age*, 28 October: 1.

Independent (2004) Keep off the grass, 16 August, [Online] available at http://news.independent.co.uk/uk/legal/story.jsp?story=552023

Indiana State Police Department (1997) Methcathinone "cat" laboratories, *Submission for the Herman Goldstein Award for Excellence in Problem-Oriented Policing*, [Online] available at: http://www.popcenter.org/library-goldstein.htm

Ireland, S. (1995) Alcohol and its contribution to violence: new directions for policing alcohol-related violence, crime and anti-social behaviour in New South Wales, in D. Chappell and S. J. Egger (eds.) *Australian Violence: Contemporary Perspectives vol. II* (pp. 155–180), Canberra, Australian Institute of Criminology.

Jacobs, K. and Arthurson, K. (2003) *Developing Effective Housing Management Policies to Address Problems of Anti-Social Behaviour*, Melbourne, Australian Housing and Urban Research Institute.

Jason-Lloyd, L. (2003) *Quasi-Policing*, London, Cavendish Publishing.

Jensen, E. L. and Gerber, J. (1996) The civil forfeiture of assets and the war on drugs: expanding criminal sanctions while reducing due process protections, *Crime and Delinquency*, 42 (3): 421–434.

Johnston, L. (2003) From "pluralisation" to "the police extended family": discources on the governance of community policing in Britain, *International Journal of the Sociology of Law*, 31: 185–204.

Joliet Police Department (2000) Repairing neighborhood with partnerships, *Excellence in Problem-Oriented Policing: the 2000 Herman Goldstein Award Winners*, National Institute of Justice, Office of Justice Programs, US Department of Justice, [Online] available at: http://www.popcenter.org/library-goldstein.htm

Jones, T. and Newburn, T. (2002) The transformation of policing? Understanding current trends in policing systems, *British Journal of Criminology*, 42: 129–146.

Kagan, R. (1984) On regulatory inspectorates and police in K. Hawkins and J. M. Thomas (eds.) *Enforcing Regulations*, (pp. 37–64), Boston, Kluwer-Nijhoff.

Kagan, R. (1994) Regulatory enforcement in Rosenbloom, D. H. and Schwarts R. D. (eds.) *Handbook of Regulation and Administrative Law* (pp. 423–463), New York, Marcel Dekker.

Katz, C. M., Webb, V. J. and Schaefer, D. R. (2001) An assessment of the impact of quality-of-life policing on crime and disorder, *Justice Quarterly*, 18 (4): 825–864.

Kelling, G. L. and Coles, C. M. (1996) *Fixing Broken Windows: Restoring Order and Reducing Crime in Our Communities*, New York, Martin Kessler Books.

Kelling, G. and Moore, M. (1988) From political to reform to community: the evolving strategy of police, in J. R. Greene and S. Mastrofski (eds.) *Community Policing Rhetoric or Reality*, New York, Praeger.

Kelling, G., Pate, A., Dieckman, D. and Brown, C. E. (1974) *The Kansas City Preventive Patrol Experiment: A Summary Report*, Washington, Police Foundation.

Kempa, M., Stenning, P. and Wood, J. (2004) Policing communal spaces: a reconfiguration of the "mass private property" hypothesis, *British Journal of Criminology*, 44 (4): 562–581.

Kemshall, H. (2003) *Understanding risk in criminal justice*, Berkshire, Open University Press.

Kennedy, D. M., Piehl, A. M. and Braga, A. (1996) Youth violence in Boston: gun markets, serious youth offenders, and a use-reduction strategy, *Law and Contemporary Problems*, 59: 147–196.

Kleiman, M. (1988) Crackdowns: the effects of intensive enforcement on retail heroin dealing, in M. Chaiken (ed.) *Street-level drug enforcement: Examining the issues*, Washington, National Institute of Justice, US Department of Justice.

Klein, A. R. (1996) Re-abuse in a population of court-restrained male batterers: why restraining orders don't work, in E. Buzawa and C. G. Buzawa (eds.) *Do Arrest and Restraining Orders Work* (pp. 192–213), Thousand Oaks, Sage.

Kleinig, J. (1996) *The Ethics of Policing*, New York, Cambridge University Press.

Klockars, K. (1988) The rhetoric of community policing, in J. R. Greene and S. Mastrofski (eds.) *Community Policing: Rhetoric or Reality* (pp. 239–258), New York, Praeger.

Koper, C. (1995) Just enough police presence: reducing crime and disorderly behavior by optimizing patrol time in crime hot spots, *Justice Quarterly* 12: 649–671.

Kornhauser, R. R. (1978) *Social Sources of Delinquency: An Appraisal of Analytic Models*, Chicago, University of Chicago.

Kuykendall, J. and Roberg, R. R. (1982) Mapping police organizational change, *Criminology*, 20: 241–256.

Laycock, G. (1991) Operation Identification, or the power of publicity?, *Security Journal*, 2: 67–72.

Langworthy, R. (1986) *The Structure of Police Organizations*, New York, Praeger Publishers.

Law Commission of Canada (2002) *In Search of Security: The Roles of Public Police and Private Agencies*, Ottawa, Law Commission of Canada.

Levine, J. P. (1975) The ineffectiveness of adding police to prevent crime, *Public Policy*, 23: 523–545.

Lipsey, M. (1990) *Design Sensitivity: Statistical Power for Experimental Research*, California, Sage.

Loader, I. (2000) Plural policing and democratic governance, *Social and Legal Studies*, 9 (3): 323–345.

Loughlin, J. (2004) The "transformation" of governance: new directions in policy and politics, *Australian Journal of Politics and History*, 50 (1): 8–22.

Loveday, B. (1996) New directions in accountability, in F. Leishman, B. Loveday and S. P. Savage (eds.) *Core Issues in Policing* (2nd ed.) (pp. 213–231), London, Pearson and Longman.

Loveday, B. (2000) New directions in accountability, in F. Leishman, G. Loveday and S. Savage (eds.) *Core Issues in Policing* (2nd ed.) (pp. 213–231), London, Longman.

Lurigio, A., Davis, R., Regulus, T., Gwiasda, V., Popkin, S, Dantzker, M., Smith, B. and Ovellet, L. (1998) More effective place management: an evaluation of Cook County's Narcotics Nuisance Abatement Unit, in L. Green Mazerolle and J. Roehl (eds.) *Civil Remedies and Crime Prevention*, Crime Prevention Studies, vol. 9 (pp. 187–218), Monsey, Criminal Justice Press.

Maguire, M., Nettleton, H., Rix, A. and Raybould, S. (2003) *Reducing alcohol-related violence and disorder: An evaluation of 'TASC' project*, Home Office Research Study 265, London, Home Office.

Maher, L. (1990) Politics, policy and space: Spatial polemics in contemporary criminology, Unpublished Masters thesis, Rutgers University.

Maher, L. and Dixon, D. (1999) Policing and public health: law enforcement and harm minimization in a street-level drug market, *British Journal of Criminology*, 39 (4): 488–512.

Makkai, T. and Braithwaite, J. (1993) Praise, pride and corporate compliance, *International Journal of the Sociology of Law*, 21: 73–91.

Males, M. and Macallair, D. (1999) An analysis of curfew enforcement and juvenile crime in California, *Western Criminology Review*, [Online] available at: http://www.wcr.sonoma.edu/v1n2/males.html

Marks, K. (2003) Curfew that targets teenage Aborigines is criticised as racist, *The Independent*, 8 September, [Online], available at http://news.independent.co.uk/world/australasia/story.jsp?story=441253

Mastrofski, S., Parks, R. B., Reiss, A. J. Jr., Worden, R., DeJong, C., Snipes, J. B. and Terrill, W. (1998) *Systematic Observation of Public Police: Applying Field Research Methods to Policy Issues*, Washington, National Institute of Justice.

Maxson, C., Hennigan, K. and Sloane, D.C. (2003) For the sake of the neighborhood? Civil gang injunctions as a gang intervention tool in Southern California in S. Decker (ed.) *Policing gangs and youth violence* (pp. 239–266), Belmont, Wadsworth.

Mazerolle, L., Kadleck, C. and Roehl, J. (1998) Controlling drug and disorder problems: the role of place managers, *Criminology*, 36: 371–404.

Mazerolle, L., Kadleck, C. and Roehl, J. (2004) Differential police control at drug-dealing places, *Security Journal*, 17 (1): 61–69.

Mazerolle, L. and Prenzler, T. (2004) Third party policing: considering the ethical challenges, in J. R. Greene, A. R. Piquero and M. M. Hickman (eds.) *Supporting Police Integrity*, Belmont, Wadsworth.

Mazerolle, L., Price, J. and Roehl, J. (2000) Civil remedies and drug control, *Evaluation Review*, 24: 212–241.

Mazerolle, Green L. and Roehl, J. (1998) Civil remedies and crime prevention: an introduction, in L. Green Mazerolle and J. Roehl (eds.) *Civil Remedies and Crime Prevention*, Crime Prevention Studies, vol. 9 (pp. 1–20), Monsey, Criminal Justice Press.

Mazerolle, Green L., Roehl, J. and Kadleck, C. (1998) Controlling social disorder using civil remedies: results from a randomized field experiment in Oakland,

California in L. Green Mazerolle and J. Roehl (eds.) *Civil Remedies and Crime Prevention*, Crime Prevention Studies, vol. 9 (pp 141–160), Monsey, Criminal Justice Press.

McEwen, T. and Uchida, C. (n.d.) *An Evaluation of the COPS Office Methamphetamine Initiative*, Washington, Office of Community Oriented Policing, US Department of Justice, [Online] available at: http://www.usdoj.gov/cops

McNees, P., Kennon, M., Schnelle, J., Kirchner, R. and Thomas, M. (1980) An experimental analysis of a program to reduce retail theft, *American Journal of Community Psychology*, 8 (3): 379–385.

Meares, T. (1998) Social organization and drug law enforcement, *American Criminal Law Review*, 35: 191–227.

Meares, T. (forthcoming, 2005) in D. Weisburd and A. Braga (eds.) *Prospects and Problems in an Era of Police Innovation*, New York, Cambridge University Press.

Merseyside Police (2001) Operation Crystal/Crystal Clear: crime and disorder reduction, *Winner of the Tilley Award 2001*, London, Home Office, [Online] available at http://www.crimereduction.gov.uk/tilley2001win.pdf

Miller, M. J. and Selva, L. H. (1994) Drug enforcement's double-edged sword: an assessment of asset forfeiture programs, *Justice Quarterly*, 11 (2): 313–335.

Miller, N. (2004) *Reality meets law in push for police power*, West Australian, 31 January.

Miller, P. and Rose, N. (1990) Governing economic life, *Economy and Society*, 19: 1–31.

Millner, F. (2003) Operation Shuteye: youth curfew in South Australia, *Indigenous Law Bulletin*, 5 (26): 6–7.

Milmo, C. (2004) Westminster council finds a new enemy – screaming girls, *Independent*, 26 April: 20.

Mishan, E. J. (1971) *Cost-Benefit Analysis: An Informal Introduction*, London, Allen and Unwin.

Mitchell, K. (2001) Transnationalism, neo-liberalism, and the rise of the shadow state, *Economy and Society*, 30 (2): 165–189.

Molidor, M. C. (2003) Citywide nuisance abatement program, Los Angeles Community Policing, accessed at www.Lacp.org/2003-articles-Main/CNAProgram.html

Moore, M. H. (1992) Problem-solving and community policing in M. Tonry and N. Morris (eds.) *Modern Policing*, Crime and Justice – A Review of Research, vol. 15 (pp. 99–158), Chicago, University of Chicago Press.

Moore, M. H. and Stephens, D. W. (1991) *Beyond Command and Control: The Strategic Management of Police Departments*, Washington, Police Executive Research Forum.

Moore, M. H., Thacher, D., Hartmann, F. X., Coles, C. and Sheingold, P. (1999) Case studies of the transformation of police departments: a cross-site analysis, Working Paper # 99-05-16, Program in Criminal Justice Policy and Management, John F. Kennedy School of Government, Harvard University.

Moran, M. (2001) Property, business power and the constitution, *Public Administration*, 79 (2): 277–296.

Morenoff, J., Sampson, R. and Raudenbush, S. (2001) Neighborhood inequality, collective efficacy, and the spatial dynamics of urban violence, *Criminology*, 39: 517–560.

Morris, P. and Heal, K. (1981) *Crime Control and the Police: A Review of Research*, Home Office Research Study 67, London, Home Office.

Morris, S. (1998) A case for partnership: the local authority landlord and the local police, in L. Green Mazerolle and J. Roehl (eds.) *Civil Remedies and Crime Prevention*, Crime Prevention Studies, vol. 9 (pp. 329–346), Monsey, Criminal Justice Press.

Nassau County Police Department (1998) Crimes against senior citizens, *Submission for the Herman Goldstein Award for Excellence in Problem-Oriented Policing* [Online], available at http://www.popcenter.org/library-goldstein.htm

National Motor Vehicle Theft Reduction Council (NMVTRC) (1999) *Evaluation of the Impacts of the New South Wales Written-Off Vehicle Register on Professional Motor Vehicle Theft*, Melbourne, National Motor Vehicle Theft Reduction Council.

National Crime Prevention Council (1992) *Creating a Climate of Hope: Ten Neighborhoods Tackle the Drug Crisis*, Washington, National Crime Prevention Council.

National Crime Prevention Council (1996) *New Ways of Working with Local Laws to Reduce Crime*, Washington, National Crime Prevention Council.

National Drug Intelligence Center (2001) *Information Bulletin – Raves*, [Online] available at: http://www.usdoj.gov/ndic/pubs/656/656t.htm

Nelligan, P. and Taylor, R. (1994) Ethical issues in community policing, *Journal of Contemporary Criminal Justice*, 10 (1): 59–66.

Nelson, N., Mendoza, C., Silverstein, B. and Kaufman, J. (1997) Washington State's law night retail worker crime protection regulation: relationships with employer practices, *Journal of Occupational and Environmental Medicine*, 39: 1233–1239.

Neter, J., Wasserman, W. and Kutner, J. H. (1990) *Applied Linear Statistical Models: Regression, Analysis of Variance, and Experimental Designs* (3rd ed.), Homewood, Irwin.

Nozick, R. (1974) *Anarchy, State and Utopia*, Oxford, Blackwell.

NSW Ombudsman (2003) *Discussion paper: The Justice Legislation Amendment (Non-association and Place Restriction) Act 2002*, Sydney, NSW Government Publication.

Observer (2004b) I would rather be dead than live next to them, 4 July: 10.

Office of COPS (1998) *Problem-Solving Tips: A Guide to Reducing Crime and Disorder through Problem-Solving Partnerships: Case Study*, Redmond, US Department of Justice.

Ogus, A. (1994) *Regulation: Legal Form and Economic Theory*, Oxford, Clarendon Press.

O'Malley, P. (1992) Risk, power and crime prevention, *Economy and Society*, 21 (3): 252–275.

O'Malley, P. (1994) Neo-liberal crime control: political agendas and the future of crime prevention in Australia in D. Chappell and P. Watson (eds.) *The Australian Criminal Justice System: The Mid 1990s* (pp. 283–298), Sydney, Butterworths.

O'Malley, P. (1996) Risk and responsibility in A. Barry, T. Osborne and N. Rose (eds.) *Foucault and Political Rationality* (pp. 189–208), London, UCL Press.

O'Malley, P. (2000) Risk, crime and prudentialism revisited, in K. Stenson and R. Sullivan (eds.) *Risk, Crime and Justice: The Politics of Crime Control in Liberal Democracies* (pp. 89–103), London, Willan.

O'Malley, P. (2002) Globalizing risk? Distinguishing styles of "neo-liberal" criminal justice in Australia and the USA, *Criminal Justice*, 2 (2): 205–222.

O'Malley, P. and Palmer, D. (1996) Post-Keynesian policing, *Economy and Society*, 25 (2): 137–155.

Organisation for Economic Co-operation and Development (2000) About regulatory reform, *Regulatory Reform*, [Online] available at: http://www1.oecd.org/subject/regreform/about

Osborne, D. and Gaebler, T. (1992) *Reinventing Government,* New York, Addison-Wesley.

Osborne, D. and Gaebler, T. (1993) *Reinventing Government: How the Entrepreneurial Spirit is Transforming the Public Sector,* New York, Ringwood.

Park, R. E., Burgess, E. W. and McKenzie, E. (1925) *The City,* Chicago, University of Chicago Press.

Parker, C. (2002) *The Open Corporation: Effective Self-Regulation and Democracy,* London, Cambridge University Press.

Potter, G., Gaines, L. and Holbrook, B. (1990) Blowing smoke: an evaluation of marijuana eradication in Kentucky, *American Journal of Police,* 9 (1): 97–11.

Penrod, G. S. (2001) Operation CleanSWEEP: The school safety program that earned an A+, *FBI Law Enforcement Bulletin,* 70 (10): 20–23.

Petrosino, A., Boruch, R. F., Rounding, C., McDonald, S. and Chalmers, I. (1999) A social, psychological, educational, and criminological trials register (SPECTR) to facilitate the preparation and maintenance of systematic reviews of social and educational interventions, *Evidence-Based Policy and Indicators Conference,* University of Durham.

Pierce, G. L., S. Spaar and L. R. Briggs (1986) *The Character of Police Work: Strategic and Tactical Implications,* Boston, Center for Applied Social Research, Northeastern University.

Poyner, B. (1993) What works in crime prevention: an overview of evaluations, in R. Clarke (ed.) *Crime Prevention Studies,* vol. 1 (pp. 7–34), Monsey, Criminal Justice Press.

Prenzler, T. and King, M. (2002) *The Role of Private Investigators and Commercial Agents in Law Enforcement,* Trends and Issues in Crime and Justice, vol. 234, Canberra, Australian Institute of Criminology.

Pratt, J. (1999) Governmentality, dangerousness and neoliberalism, in R. Smandych (ed.) *Governable Places* (pp. 133–162), Dartmouth, Aldershot.

Pratt, J. (2002) *Punishment and Civilization: Penal Tolerance and Intolerance in Modern Society,* London, Sage.

Prostitution Task Force of Buffalo (1999) *Report: Workable solutions to the problem of street prostitution in Buffalo,* [Online] available at: http://members.tripod.com/ptfofbuffalo/reports.htm

Putnam, R. D. (1995) Bowling alone: America's declining social capital, *The Journal of Democracy,* 6 (1): 65–78.

Putnam, R. D. (2000) *Bowling Alone: The Collapse and Revival of American Community,* New York, Simon and Schuster.

Putnam, S., Rockett, I. and Campbell, M. (1993) Methodological issues in community-based alcohol-related injury prevention projects: attribution of program effects, in T. K. Greenfield and R. Zimmerman (eds.) *Experience with Community Action Projects: New Research in the Prevention of Alcohol and Other Drug Problems* (pp. 31–39), Rockville, Center for Substance Abuse Prevention.

Queensland Commission of Inquiry into Possible Illegal Activities and Associated Police Misconduct (1989) *Report of a Commission of Inquiry pursuant to orders in Council,* Brisbane, Government Printer.

Queensland Government (2004) *Meeting Challenges, Making Choices* (MCMC), [Online] http://www.mcmc.qld.gov.au

Quetelet, A. J. (1842) *A Treatise of Man,* Gainsville, Scholars' Facsimiles and Reprints.

Ramker, G. (1999) Kankakee MEG unit employs problem-solving approach to combat drug crime, *On Good Authority*, vol. 3, no. 4. Illinois Criminal Justice Information Authority.

Ramsay, M. (1991) A British experiment in curbing incivilities and fear of crime, *Security Journal*, 2 (2): 120–125.

Ratcliffe, J. H. and Makkai, T. (2004) *Diffusion of Benefits: Evaluating a Policing Operation*, Trends and Issues in Crime and Criminal Justice, no. 278, Canberra, Australian Institute of Criminology.

Read, T. and Tilley, N. (2000) *Not Rocket Science? Problem-Solving and Crime Reduction*, Crime Reduction Research Series Paper 6, London, Home Office [Online], available at: http://www.homeoffice.gov.uk/rds/prgpdf/crrs06.pdf

Ready, J., Mazerolle, L. and Revere, E. (1998) Civil remedies and crime prevention, in L. Green Mazerolle and J. Roehl (eds.) *Civil Remedies and Crime Prevention*, Crime Prevention Studies, vol. 9 (pp. 307–328), Monsey, Criminal Justice Press.

Reiner, R. (1992) Policing a postmodern society, *Modern Law Review*, 55 (6): 761–781.

Reiner, R. (1993) Police accountability: principles, patterns, and practices, in R. Reiner and S. Spencer (eds.) *Accountable Policing: Effectiveness, Empowerment, and Equity* (pp. 1–23), London, Institute for Public Policy Research.

Reiner, R. (1994) What should the police be doing?, *Policing*, 10 (3): 151–157.

Reiss, A. J., Jr. (1971) *The Police and the Public*, New Haven, Yale University Press.

Reiner, R. (1997) Policing and the police, in M. Maguire, R. Morgan and R. Reiner (eds.) *The Oxford Handbook of Criminology* (2nd ed.) (pp. 997–1047), Oxford, Clarendon Press.

Reiss, A. J., Jr. (1984) Consequences of compliance and deterrence models of law enforcement for the exercise of police discretion, *Law and Contemporary Problems*, 47 (4): 83–122.

Reiss, A. J. Jr. (1992) Police organization in the twentieth century, in M. Tonry and N. Morris (eds.) *Modern Policing* (pp. 51–98), Chicago, University of Chicago Press.

Reppetto, T. A. (1976) Crime prevention and the displacement phenomenon, *Crime and delinquency*, 22: 166–177.

Reuter, P., MacCoun, R. and Murphy, P. (1990) *Money from Crime: A Study of the Economics of Drug Dealing in Washington, D.C.*, Santa Monica, RAND.

Reynolds, K. M., Seydlitz, R. and Jenkins, P. (2000) Do juvenile curfew laws work? A time-series analysis of the New Orleans law, *Justice Quarterly*, 17 (1): 205–230.

Rhodes, R. A. (1997) Understanding governance: policy networks, governance, reflexivity and accountability, *Public Administration*, 76: 408–410.

Roach Anleu, S. (1998) The role of civil sanctions in crime control: a socio-legal examination, in L. Green Mazerolle and J. Roehl (eds.) *Civil Remedies and Crime Prevention*, Crime Prevention Studies, vol. 9 (pp. 21–44), Monsey, Criminal Justice Press.

Roach Anleu, S., Mazerolle, L. and Presser, L. (2000) Crime prevention and social regulation: an analysis of insurance as a form of third party policing, *Law and Policy*, 22 (1): 67–87.

Rose, N. (1996) Sovereign advanced liberal democracies, in A. Barry, T. Osborne and N. Rose (eds.) *Foucault and Political Reason* (pp. 37–64), Chicago, Chicago University Press.

Rose, N. (2000) Government and control in D. Garland and R. Sparks (eds.) *Criminology and Social Theory* (pp. 183–208), New York, Oxford University Press.

Rose, N. and Miller, P. (1992) Political power beyond the state: problematics of government, *British Journal of Sociology*, 43: 173–205.

Ruefle, W. and Reynolds, K. M. (1996) Keep them at home: juvenile curfew ordinances in 200 American cities, *American Journal of Police*, 15 (1): 63–84.

Sampson, R. and Raudenbush, S. (2001) *Disorder in Urban Neighbourhoods – Does it Lead to Crime?* Research Brief, February, Washington, US Department of Justice, National Institute of Justice.

Sampson, R. J., Raudenbush, S. W. and Earls, F. (1997) Neighborhoods and violent crime: a multilevel study of collective efficacy, *Science*, 277 (15): 918–924.

San Bernardino Police Department (1999) Prostitution restraining order program, *Submission for the Herman Goldstein Award for Excellence in Problem-Oriented Policing*, [Online] available at: http://www.popcenter.org/library-goldstein.htm

San Diego Police Department (1994) Glitter Track, *Submission for the Herman Goldstein Award for Excellence in Problem-Oriented Policing*, [Online] available at: http://www.popcenter.org/library-goldstein.htm

San Diego Police Department (1998) Operation Hot Pipe, Smokey Haze, and Rehab., *Submission for the Herman Goldstein Award for Excellence in Problem-Oriented Policing*, [Online] available at: http://www.popcenter.org/library-goldstein.htm

San Diego Police Department (2000) The question of independent living, *Excellence in Problem-Oriented Policing: the 2000 Herman Goldstein Award* Winners, [Online] available at: http://www.popcenter.org/library-goldstein.htm

Scott, M. (2000) *Problem-Oriented Policing: Reflections on the First 20 Years*, Washington, Office of Community Oriented Policing Services, US Department of Justice.

Seidenstat, P. (2004) Terrorism, airport security, and the private sector, *The Review of Policy Research*, 21 (3): 275–291.

Shadish, W. R., Cook, T. D. and Campbell, D. T. (2002) *Experimental and Quasi-Experimental Designs for Generalized Causal Inference*, Boston, Houghton-Mifflin.

Shaw, C. and McKay, H. (1942) *Juvenile Delinquency in Urban Areas*, Chicago, University of Chicago Press.

Shearing, C. (1996) Reinventing policing: policing as governance, in O. Marenin (ed.) *Policing Change, Changing Police: International Perspectives* (pp. 285–308), New York, Garland.

Shearing, C. and Stenning, P. (1987) *Private Policing*, Thousand Oaks, Sage.

Sherman, L. (1990) Police crackdowns: initial and residual deterrence, in M. Tonry and N. Morris (eds.) *Crime and Justice: A Review of Research*, vol. 12 (pp. 1–48), Chicago, University of Chicago Press.

Sherman, L. (1998) *Evidence-Based Policing*, Washington, Police Foundation.

Sherman, L. W. and Berk, R. A. (1984) The specific deterrent effects of arrest for domestic assault, *American Sociological Review*, 49: 261–272.

Sherman, L., Gartin, P. and Buerger, M. (1989), Hot spots of predatory crime: routine activities and the criminology of place, *Criminology*, 27 (1): 27–55.

Sherman, L., Farrington, D., Welsh, B. and MacKenzie, D. L. (eds.) (2002) *Evidence-Based Crime Prevention*, London, Routledge and Kegan Paul.

Sherman, L. W., Gottfredson, G., MacKenzie, D., Eck, J., Reuter, P. and Bushway, S. (1997) *Preventing Crime: What Works, What Doesn't, What's Promising: A Report to the United State Congress*, College Park, Department of Criminology and Criminal Justice, University of Maryland.

Sherman, L. W. and Rogan, D. (1995) Deterrent effects of police raids on crack houses: a randomized, controlled experiment, *Justice Quarterly*, 12 (4): 755–781.

Sherman, L. W. and Weisburd, D. (1995) General deterrent effects of police patrol in crime 'hot spots': a randomized, controlled trial, *Justice Quarterly*, 12 (4): 625–648.

Simon, J. (1988) The ideological effects of actuarial practices, *Law and Society Review*, 22: 771–800.

Simon, J. (1995) They died with their boots on: the boot camp and the limits of modern penalty, *Social Justice*, 22: 25–48.

Simpson, M. (1999) Landlords evict 4 with new ordinance, *The Orange County Register*, 13 May.

Skiba, R., Simmons, A., Staudinger, L., Rausch, M., Dow, G. and Feggins, R. (2003) Consistent removal: contributions of school discipline to the school-prison pipeline, Paper presented at the *School to Prison Pipeline Conference: Harvard Civil Rights Project*, Cambridge, May 16–17.

Skogan, W. (1990) *Disorder and Decline*, New York, Free Press.

Skogan, W. and Hartnett, S. (1997) *Community Policing, Chicago Style*, New York, Oxford University Press.

Skogan, W., Steiner, L., Benitez, C., Bennis, J., Borchers, S., DuBois, J., Gondocs, R., Hartnett, S., Kim, S. Y. and Rosenbaum, S. (2004) *Community Policing in Chicago, Year 10: An Evaluation of Chicago's Alternative Policing Strategy*, Chicago, Illinois Criminal Justice Information Authority.

Skolnick, J. and Bayley, D. (1986) *The New Blue Line*, New York, Free Press.

Smith, A. (1978) *Lectures on Jurisprudence*, R. L. Meek, D. D. Raphael and P. G. Stein (eds.), Oxford, Clarendon Press.

Smith, D. G., Gregson, M. and Morgan, J. (2003) *Between the Lines: An Evaluation of the Secured Car Park Award Scheme*, Home Office Research Study 266, London, Home Office, Development and Statistics Directorate, [Online] available at: http://www.homeoffice.gov.uk/prgpubs/

Smith, M. (1996) Assessing vandalism cues in an experimental setting: a factorial design involving state of repair, presence of graffiti, target vulnerability, and target suitability, PhD thesis, Rutgers – The State University of New Jersey.

Smith, M. (1998) Regulating opportunities: multiple roles for civil remedies in situational crime prevention, in L. Green Mazerolle and J. Roehl (eds.) *Civil Remedies and Crime Prevention*, Crime Prevention Studies, vol. 9 (pp. 67–88), Monsey, Criminal Justice Press.

South Wales Evening Post (2003) Fears over child curbs, 19 November: 15.

Sparrow, M. (1994) *Imposing Duties: Government's Changing Approach to Compliance*, Westport, Praeger.

Sparrow, M. (2000) *The Regulatory Craft: Controlling Risks, Solving Problems, and Managing Compliance*, Washington, Brookings Press.

Sparrow, M., Moore, M. and Kennedy, D. (1990) *Beyond 911: A New Area for Policing*, New York, Basic Books.

Spelman, W. (1993) Abandoned buildings: magnets for crime?, *Journal of Criminal Justice*, 21: 441–495.

Spelman, W. and Brown, D. K. (1984) *Calling the Police: Citizen Reporting of Serious Crime*, Washington, National Institute of Justice.

Stenson, K. and Edwards, A. (2001) Rethinking crime control in advanced liberal government: the "third" way and the return of the local, in K. Stenson and R. Sullivan (eds.) *Crime Risk and Justice: The Politics of Crime Control in Liberal Democracies* (pp. 68–86), Cullompton, Willan Publishing.

Stockwell, T. (1997) Regulation of the licensed drinking environment: a major opportunity for crime prevention, in R. Homel (ed.), *Policing for Prevention: Reducing Crime, Public Intoxication and Injury*, Crime Prevention Studies, vol. 7 (pp. 7–36), Monsey, Criminal Justice Press.

Stockwell, T. (2001) Responsible alcohol service: lessons from evaluations of serving training and policing initiatives, *Drug and Alcohol Review*, 20: 257–265.

Stokes, R. (2002) Place management in commercial areas: customer service representatives in Philadelphia's central district business, *Security Journal*, 15 (2): 7–19.

Taylor, R. B. (1998) Crime and small-scale places: what we know, what we can prevent, and what else we need to know, in *Crime and Place: Plenary Papers of the 1997 Conference on Criminal Justice Research and Evaluation*, Washington, US Department of Justice.

Terrill, W. (2001) *Police Coercion: Application of the Force Continuum*, New York, LFB Scholarly Publishing LLC.

Thomas, W. and Znaniecki, F. (1920) *The Polish Peasant in Europe and America*, Boston, Gorham.

Tien, J., Simon, J. and Larson, R. (1978) *An Alternative Approach in Police Patrol: The Willmington Split-Force Experiment*, Washington, Government Printing Office.

Trojanowicz, R. (1986) Evaluating a neighborhood foot patrol program: the Flint, Michigan project, in D. Rosenbaum (ed.) *Community Crime Prevention: Does It Work?* (pp. 157–178), Beverly Hills, Sage.

Vancouver Police Department (2000) Excellence in problem-oriented policing: The 2000 Herman Goldstein Award Winners, *National Institute of Justice, Office of Justice Programs, US Department of Justice*, [Online] available at: http://www.popcenter.org/library-goldstein.htm

Van den Berg, E. (1995) Crime prevention on industrial sites: security through public-private partnerships, *Security Journal*, 6: 27–35.

Waddington, P. A. J. (1999) *Policing Citizens: Authority and Rights*, London, UCL Press.

Walker, N. (2000) *Policing in a Changing Constitutional Order*, London, Sweet and Maxwell.

Walters, R. (1996) The "dream" of multi-agency crime prevention: pitfalls in policy and practice, in R. Homel (ed.) *The Politics and Practice of Situational Crime Prevention*, Crime Prevention Studies, vol. 5 (pp. 75–96), Monsey, Criminal Justice Press.

Warburton, A., and Shepherd, J. (2000) Effectiveness of toughened glassware in terms of reducing injury in bars: a randomised controlled trial, *Injury Prevention*, 6: 36–40.

Warchol, G. and Johnson, B. (1996) Ensuring the future of asset forfeiture programs, *The Police Chief*, 63 (3): 49–51.

Ward, B. (1987) Drug abuse and trafficking: NYPCD meets the challenge, *The Police Chief*, 54 (10): 81–85.

Webb, B. (1994) Steering column locks and motor vehicle theft: evaluation from three countries, in R. Clarke (ed.) *Crime Prevention Studies*, vol. 2 (pp. 71–90), Monsey, Willow Tree Press.

Webb, B. (1996) Preventing plastic card fraud in the UK, *Security Journal*, 7: 23–25.

Weber, M. (1947) *The Theory of Economic and Social Organization*, New York, Oxford University Press.

Welsh, B. and Farrington, D. (1999) Value for money? A review of the costs and benefits of situational crime prevention, *British Journal of Criminology*, 39: 345–368.

Welsh, B. and Farrington, D. (2000) Monetary costs and benefits of crime prevention programs, in M. Tonry (ed.) *Crime and Justice: A review of Research, vol. 27* (pp. 305–362), Chicago, University of Chicago Press.

Weisburd, D. (1993) Design sensitivity in criminal justice experiments, *Crime and Justice*, 17: 337–379.

Weisburd, D. and Eck, J. (2004) What can police do to reduce crime, disorder, and fear? *Annals of the American Academy of Political and Social Sciences*, 593: 42–65.

Weisburd, D. and Green, L. (1994) Defining the street-level drug market, in D. L. MacKenzie and C. D. Uchida (eds.) *Drugs and Crime: Evaluating Public Policy Initiatives* (pp. 61–76), Thousand Oaks, Sage.

Weisburd, D. and Green, L. (1995) Assessing immediate spatial displacement: insights from the Minneapolis hot spots experiment, in J. Eck and D. Weisburd (eds.) *Crime and Place*, Crime Prevention Studies, vol. 4 (pp. 349–361), Monsey, Criminal Justice Press.

Weisburd, D., Maher, L. and Sherman, L. (1993) Contrasting crime general and crime specific theory: the case of hot spots of crime, in E. Adler and W. S. Laufer (eds.) *New Directions in Criminological Theory* (pp. 45–70), Advances in Criminological Theory vol. 4, New Brunswick, Transaction.

Weisburd, D. and Mazerolle, L. (1995) Policing drug hot spots: the Jersey City drug market analysis experiment, *Justice Quarterly*, 12 (4): 711–735.

Weisel, D. L. (1990) Playing the home field: a problem-oriented approach to drug control, *American Journal of Police*, 9 (1): 75–95.

Weiss, A. and Freels, S. (1996) Effects of aggressive policing: the Daytona traffic enforcement experiment, *American Journal of Police*, 15 (3): 395–416.

Whetstone, T. (2001) Measuring the impact of a domestic violence coordinated response team, *Policing: An International Journal of Police Strategies and Management*, 24 (3): 371–398.

White, M. D., Fyfe, J. J., Campbell, S. P. and Goldkamp, J. (2003) The police role in preventing homicide: considering the impact of problem-oriented policing on the prevalence of murder, *Journal of Research in Crime and Delinquency*, 40 (2): 194–225.

White, R. (1996) Ten arguments against youth curfew, *Youth Studies Australia*, 15 (4): 28–30.

White, R. (1998) Curtailing youth: a critique of coercive crime prevention, in L. Green Mazerolle and J. Roehl (eds.) *Civil Remedies and Crime Prevention*, Crime Prevention Studies, vol. 9 (pp. 117–140), Monsey, Criminal Justice Press.

Wikstrom, P. O. and Sampson, R. (2002) Social mechanisms of community influences on crime and pathways in criminality, in B. Lahey, T. Moffitt and A. Caspi (eds.) *The Causes of Conduct Disorder and Serious Juvenile Delinquency* (pp. 118–150), New York, Guilford Press.

Wilson, D. and Sutton, A. (2003) *Open-Street CCTV in Australia: A Comparative Study of Establishment and Operation*, Canberra, Australian Research Council.

Wortley, R. and Smallbone, S. (eds.) (in press) Situational perspectives on sexual offenses against children, Monsey, Criminal Justice Press.

Worrall, J. L. (2001) Addicted to the drug war: the role of civil asset forfeiture as a budgetary necessity in contemporary law enforcement, *Journal of Criminal Justice*, 29: 171–187.

Yeung, K. (1999), Quantifying regulatory penalties: Australian competition law penalties in perspective, *Melbourne University Law Review*, 23 (2): 440–461.

Zimmer, L. (1990) Proactive policing against street-level drug trafficking, *American Journal of Police*, 9 (1): 43–74.

Index